Education of Marginalised Community

By the same author

- Road Communication in North-East India and Beyond: Bridging Culture and People (Ed.)

About the Editor

Tarun Dutta, Assistant Professor in History (Assam University Diphu Campus) has completed his Post-Graduation in History from Dibrugarh University and Awarded Master of Philosophy (M.Phil.) and Doctor of Philosophy (Ph.D.) by Assam University, Silchar, Assam. He has been awarded numerous fellowships including the Indian Council of Historical Research-Junior Research Fellowship. He has authored and edited many books and publications.

Education of Marginalised Community

Issues, Policies and its Implementations in North-east India

Edited by
Tarun Dutta

CONCEPT PUBLISHING COMPANY PVT. LTD.
NEW DELHI-110059

ISBN-13: 978-93-86682-38-3

First Published 2018

Published and Printed by

Concept
Since 1974

Concept Publishing Company Pvt. Ltd.
A/15-16, Commercial Block, Mohan Garden,
New Delhi-110059 (India)
T : 91 11 25351460, 91 11 25351794
E : publishing@conceptpub.com, *W*: www.conceptpub.com

Cataloging in Publication Data--Courtesy: D.K. Agencies (P) Ltd. <docinfo@dkagencies.com>

Seminar on Education of Marginalised Community: Issues, Policy and its Implementation in North-Eastern Region of India (2016 : Diphu, India)

pages cm

"The papers included in this volume were presented at a Seminar on Education of Marginalised Community: Issues, Policy and its Implementation in North-Eastern Region of India, organised by Department of History, Assam University Diphu Campus, in 9th to 10th November, 2016"—Acknowledgements.

Includes bibliographical references and index.

ISBN 9789386682383

1. People with social disabilities—Education—India—Assam—Congresses. 2. People with social disabilities—Education—India, Northeastern—Congresses. 3. Education and state—India—Assam—Congresses. 4. Education and state—India, Northeastern—Congresses. 5. Right to education—India—Assam—Congresses. 6. Right to education—India, Northeastern—Congresses. I. Dutta, Tarun, editor. II. Assam University (Silchar, India). Diphu Campus. Department of History, organizer. III. Title.

LCC LC4097.I42A87 2016 DDC 371.826940954162 23

Acknowledgements

The papers included in this volume were presented at a Seminar on *Education of Marginalised Community: Issues, Policy and its Implementation in North-eastern Region of India,* organised by Department of History, Assam University Diphu Campus, in 9th to 10th November, 2016. The primary objective of the seminar was to bring academia, activist, civil society into one platform to discuss various issues related to the education of the marginalised people of North-east India in particular and other related issues on education in general. We are highly obliged to Prof. G. Hargopal, Visiting Professor, National Law School of Indian University, Bengaluru, who gave the keynote address at the Seminar with an exposition of the basic issues of the education of marginalised community of India as a whole and North-East India in particular.

We remain very thankful to UNICEF, Assam Field Office and Indian Council of Social Science Research, NERC, Vice Chancellor, Assam University and Pro-Vice Chancellor, AUDC for giving generous support to undertake this programme.

We wish to record our appreciation of the effort of Dr. Tushar Rane, Chief, UNICEF Field Office for Assam, Mrs. Chhaya Kunwar, Education Specialist, UNICEF Field Office for Assam, Dr. Deepa Das, former Head of Education, UNICEF, New Delhi, Dr. Dinesh Baishya, Retd. Principal, B. Barooah College, Guwahati, Prof. Sajal Nag, Assam University, Silchar, Mr. Mrinal Gohain, Regional Manager, ActionAid Association, Mr. Mukut Lochan Kalita, Guwahati—who gave their plenary/special lecture in the seminar.

We give our special thanks to all organising committee members and well wisher for their strong support and assistance towards the seminar.

To Mr. A.K. Mittal, Managing Director of Concept Publishing Co. Pvt. Ltd., New Delhi, we owe a debt of gratitude for agreeing to publish this volume expeditiously.

Tarun Dutta

Contents

Recommendations of the Seminar

The two-days UNICEF and ICSSR-NERC sponsored national seminar on "Education of Marginalised Community: Issues, Policy and its Implementation in North-eastern Region of India" was held in Department of History, Assam University Diphu Campus to discuss various issues related to education in North-Eastern Region of India as a whole and education of marginalised people in particular. Since the region is very deprived in terms of opportunity, access, and there are very few people who raise their voices for the education of marginalised community, the platform was very highly important one where more than 80 participants from various parts of India were present, and about 40 research papers on various themes of the seminar were discussed in the two days long activity.

In the end, the learned gathering comes into conclusion that the region has been facing multiple problems in education especially marginalised section from policy to implementation level and they forwarded a few recommendations to the policy-makers to address the issues. The outcome/recommendations of the seminar are as follows:

1. It is observed that in the present situation challenges faced by the marginalised groups provided quite significant insights. The major one being that there are different types of marginalisation or deprivation. If some communities have remained marginalised for ages, there are others who suddenly find themselves in such unenviable situation due to factors beyond their control—both natural and human-made. For example, among the population, there were not only historically marginalised groups such as Scheduled Tribes (ST), Scheduled Castes (SC), and

the minorities; but also groups which were once well to do peasants, artisans, and educated middle class etc., who found themselves suddenly pauperized due to sudden change either in the environment or the lifestyle.

2. It is observed that while the villages and remote habitations were getting exposed to many urbanising trends, the small towns were rapidly acquiring all the urban characteristics. At the same time, natural phenomena (paradoxically sometimes result of various man-made "developmental" projects or efforts) like flood, erosion, sand deposition, etc. too causes the immense change to the lives of those affected. And more alarmingly both the impact as well as the frequency of such "disasters" seem to have increased quite a lot in last two-three decades leading to large scale and acute marginalisation of people in the state. It is also observed that it was the historically marginalised communities like STs, SCs, and minorities, who are more vulnerable to the later types of phenomena quite often.

3. Major implications for those involved in the developmental sector—just as there are various types of disadvantageousness, they all require different handling. The whole developmental sector has to reinvent itself for the newer set of problems that the new circumstances brought. As such sudden changes affected everyone's life, including the skills and values related to one's livelihood and relationships. Obviously, the education sector needs to gear-up for such a rapidly changing society.

4. Very often it has been heard about the lack of transparency in the decision-making process. Many complained about the decision-making process becoming kind of a black box. There have been many changes in the delivery mechanism since the days of DPEP and early RTE in the recent times according to some who were involved in both the projects. There is much more multiplicity of agencies involved in the implementation now. The above situation leads to lack of accountability as no one is responsible. The various governmental agencies involved in the delivery of education have their rules, norms, and criteria leading to often situations where left hand did not know what the right was doing.

5. Too much of centralization has become a bane for the education system. The whole system is planned from the headquarters, and there is very little local participation in the planning process. Many teachers and CRCCs were quite

disillusioned and at times felt exploited by the senior decision-makers. Sometimes, they had to bear the brunt of becoming guinea pigs for various experiments designed from the top.

6. Various government policies such as providing free textbook under RTE Act, the addition of class V to primary section, no detention policy etc. has also lead to quite chaotic situations in many cases. For example, due to no detention policy students may practically enter the high school without really mastering the basic competencies in either language or mathematics, creating a frustrating situation for high school teachers.

7. The primary base of education is weakening day-by-day, now creating a very challenging situation for the secondary stage. The lack of specialist subject teacher at the elementary-level later creates difficulties as the new curriculum and textbooks require much more specialised knowledge on the part of the teachers. In such a scenario parents having to send their children either to private schools or provide private tuitions is becoming a necessity.

8. Changing courses and curricula are also affecting the education scenario. The curriculum and method of teaching are frequently changed. Interestingly, the textbooks have changed four times in last sixteen years. Adding of class V with the introduction of subjects like English, Hindi etc. is also creating problems in schools because most of the teachers find the additional subjects difficult for them. Same is the case with the mathematics of the class V level.

9. The introduction of free textbooks under RTE has too generated a tough situation. There also has been much confusion in the distribution—while in most of the cases they reached very late, in others they were less than required. There have also been allegations that in the name of free textbooks, the authorities suddenly introduced CBSE books which have been merely translated without any adaptation or localisation.

10. It is observed that all schemes of government have not been able to reach the most interior areas and most vulnerable groups even in terms of access, not to mention of retention and quality improvement. One felt that the schemes of education somehow reach usually those places which are reachable while the unreachable often remain still underdeveloped. It was unfortunate to find that there were still places where the system failed even in providing access to government schools for children of many

marginalised communities, even after ten years of the launching of SSA and shifting to RTE.

11. Lack of sufficient teachers is a major factor affecting the education sector in the whole state. The number of single teacher schools with high enrollment is quite alarming. In many cases, even the schools earlier having sufficient teachers have been rendered dysfunctional due to not filling-up the vacancies caused due to various reasons. What astonished us most was the fact that this has been the case for more than two decades while the authorities have done preciously little to remedy this basic problem. Though, it has been heard that further appointment of teachers remained banned by honourable High Court order since 2001, it was surprising to find the government not taking adequate steps to convince the honourable Judges about the absolute necessity of starting the recruitment process in the long ten years.

12. Mid-day Meal (MDM) though definitely acts as an incentive in poverty affected areas; another impression that it hampers the teaching-learning process as most of the children remain attracted towards cooking and having the meal. The scheme is not having its desired impact—rather, it has become counter-productive in many cases. There have been many allegations and counter-allegations of large-scale corruption that has affected this scheme.

13. There have been some other alarming trends affecting the educational scenario in recent past. First among them is the steep fall in enrollment in many Government schools—especially very acutely in some of the districts. Linked with this is the mushrooming of private schools, including in Assamese medium, even in rural areas. Many parents probably, rightly or wrongly, feel that the private schools equip their children better for the competitive market.

14. However, there were also many counter-examples to the popular myth that government schools in the urban setting are losing out to the private schools. There were a number of government schools in urban areas which were having very high enrollment and functioning well. Though there were also some schools in an urban setting where the enrollment is slowly dwindling in the last couple of years, the reason being that the child population of those localities is decreasing among certain communities, this whole phenomenon needs to be further studied before making any generalisations.

15. There were, however, quite a few positive achievements too. The civil works have been a strong component of SSA evidence of which could be seen in most of the districts. There were also schemes like Education Guarantee Scheme (EGS), bridge courses, Kasturba Gandhi Balika Vidyalaya (KGBV), community volunteer scheme etc. The EGS centres, especially, has been one of the very popular and successful interventions for the marginalised groups. However, there has been much bungling here regarding this by all the decision-makers who have led to a peculiar scenario where many who were closely involved now feel very frustrated. It has been felt that this may have very serious repercussions in the coming days.

16. Another issue is that those involved in the delivery mechanism at the various level they are quite overburdened and—at times exploited victims of a heartless system. The biggest weakness of the whole education system, it has been felt, is that it is very lazy—responses at every level always come very late, sometimes never and at times very inappropriate.

17. One major apprehension that encountered was that the standard of education is going down as the society is now putting emphasis on getting marks only. The moral education has taken back seat as very little is done to inculcate values through education. Many felt the present education system is developing human beings only as 'competitors', not as a human resource. One observed the equally significant trend that very few teachers and those involved in education system send their children to government schools.

List of Contributors

Achhiya Begam, Research Scholar, Department of Philosophy, Tripura University, Tripura.

Ameera Yasmin Mazumdar, Research Scholar, P.G. Department of Law, Gauhati University, Assam.

Prof. Archana Barua, Professor, Department of Humanities and Social Sciences, Indian Institute of Technology, Guwahati, Assam.

Dr. Bimal Chandra Pal, Assistant Professor, Department of Philosophy, Tripura University, Tripura.

Console Zamreinao Shimrei, Research Scholar, Department of History, Assam University, Diphu Campus, Assam, India.

Dr. Dibyajyoti Dutta, Assistant Professor, Department of Political Science, Dibrugarh, Assam University, Dibrugarh, Assam.

Gagan Nepal, Research Scholar, Department of Political Science, Assam University (Diphu Campus), Diphu Karbi Anglong-782462, Assam , India.
E-mail: *nepalgagan@gmail.com*

Girin Chetia, Director, NEADS, Dhekiakhowa, Jorhat, Assam.

Himangi Kalita, Research Scholar, Department of Anthropology, Assam University (Diphu Campus), Diphu Karbi Anglong, Assam.

Dr. Hiranya Saikia, Assistant Professor, Department of Education, Diphu Government College, Diphu, Assam.

Jharna Sharma, Research Scholar, Department of Peace and Conflict Studies and Management, Sikkim University, Sikkim.

Jyotismita Sharma, Research Scholar, Department of Anthropology, Assam University (Diphu Campus), Diphu Karbi Anglong-782462, Assam, India.
E-mail : *jyotisharmadpu@gmail.com*

K. Mema Singha, Research Scholar, Department of Manipuri, Assam University, Silchar, Assam.

K. Nirupama Singha, Research Scholar, Department of History, Assam University, Silchar, Assam.

Lanu Waneithang Aimol, Reach-M, Manipur.

Lipika Barman, Research Scholar, Department of Psychology, Gauhati University, Assam.

Luit Goswami, Director, Rural Volunteer Centre, Dhemaji, Assam.

Dr. M. Ningamba Singha, Assistant Professor, Department of History, Patharkandi College, Patharkandi, Assam.

M. Ninghaiba Singha, Research Scholar, Department of Manipuri, Assam University, Silchar, Assam.

Maheema Rai, Research Scholar, Department of Peace and Conflict Studies and Management, Sikkim University, Sikkim.

Nimkit Lepcha, Research Scholar, Department of Peace and Conflict Studies and Management, Sikkim University, Sikkim.

Dr. Nitish Mondal, Assistant Professor, Department of Anthropology, Assam University (Diphu Campus), Diphu Karbi Anglong, Assam.

Dr. Paul B. Chonzik, Associate Professor, Department of History, Assam University Diphu Campus, Karbi Anglong, Assam.

Pradip Kurmi, Research Scholar, Department of Economics, Assam University, Silchar, Assam.

Dr. Prafulla Kumar Nath, Assistant Professor, Centre for Tribal Studies, Assam University Diphu Campus, Karbi Anglong, Assam.

Pranay Deb, Guest Teacher, Department of Philosophy, Tripura University, Tripura.

Dr. Pranay Jyoti Goswami, Associate Professor, Assam University, Silchar, Assam.

Dr. Subit Dutta, Assistant Professor, Depatment of Commerce, Assam University Diphu Campus, Karbi Anglong, Assam.

Prof. Sumanash Dutta, Professor and Dean, Department of Economics, Assam University, Silchar, Assam.

Sumita Sinha, Research Scholar, Department of History, Assam University, Silchar, Assam.

Suneeta K. Ganguli, Research Scholar, Department of Psychology, Gauhati University, Assam.

Dr. Suryasikha Pathak, Associate Professor, Centre for Tribal Studies, Assam University, Diphu Campus, Karbi Anglong, Assam

Swgwmkhang Brahma, Research Scholar, Department of Peace and Conflict Studies and Management, Sikkim University, Sikkim.

Dr. Tarun Dutta, Assistant Professor, Department of History, Assam University Diphu Campus, Assam.

Dr. Thokchom Surjit Singh, National Executive Member, All India Forum for Right to Education; Project Director, Demonstrating an Alternative Vision of Education, SST, Shillong & Member, National Focus Group on Work and Education, NCERT, MHRD.

Tongpao Hoakip, Reach-M, Manipur.

Introduction

Last two and half decades saw much action in educational reforms in India—definitely in terms of formulation of quite a number of schemes, programmes, projects etc. In selective instances and at certain times it manifested as sincere efforts at field level leading to perceptible changes in classroom practices too. Post Jomtien and Dakar conferences, the country committing itself to the Millennium Development Goals, along with rest of the world, the universalization of Elementary Education became a major focus area for India. Apparently, there was strong political will on part of the ruling class to seriously address all the issues affecting Access, Retention and Quality Improvement especially in primary education.

If the 90s was the decade of various experimental projects like Lok Jhumbish, Andhra Pradesh Primary Education Project (APPEP), Bihar Education Project (BEP), Uttar Pradesh Basic Education Project (UPBEP), District Primary Education Project (DPEP) etc. which targeted districts/regions identified as having low female literacy, the next decade went for the massive all-encompassing effort—Sarva Shiksha Abhiyan (SSA). The goals were more or less the same—to provide quality primary education (up to class V in earlier cases, while in SSA it was up to class VIII) to all the children, especially those coming from various disadvantaged groups.

In Assam, too, SSA was launched in 2001 along with rest of the country and the state mission which was coordinating the DPEP in nine districts of the state took over the SSA Mission.

SSA has completed ten years of its project period and now SSA has taken the form of Right To Education (RTE) Act, 2009 and a new Rashtriya Madhyamik Shiksha Abhiyan (RMSA) focusing on secondary education and Rashtriya Ussotor Shikshya Abhiyan (RUSA) is being launched. It has been felt it is time for stocktaking as to how far SSA succeeded in achieving its goal in one whole decade in all the key areas of access, retention and quality improvement.

It has also been observed that the present situation and the challenges faced by the marginalised groups provided a quite significant insights. The major one being that there are different types of marginalisation or deprivation. If some communities have remained marginalised for ages, there are others who suddenly find themselves in such unenviable situation due to factors beyond their control—both natural and man-made. For example, among the population we studied, there were not only historically marginalised groups such as Scheduled Tribes (ST), Scheduled castes (ST) and the minorities; but also groups which were once well to do peasants, artisans, and educated middle class etc., who found themselves suddenly pauperised due to sudden change either in the environment or in the lifestyle. We also observed that while the villages and remote habitations were getting exposed to many urbanising trends, the small towns were rapidly acquiring all the urban characteristics. At the same time, natural phenomena (paradoxically sometimes result of various man-made "developmental" projects or efforts) like flood, erosion, sand deposition etc. too causes the immense change to the lives of those affected. And more alarmingly both the impact as well as the frequency of such "disasters" seem to have increased quite a lot in last two-three decades leading to large scale and acute marginalisation of community in the state. We also observed that it was the historically marginalised communities like STs, SCs and minorities, who are more vulnerable to the later types of phenomena quite often.

This has major implications for those involved in the developmental sector. Just as there are various types of disadvantageousness, they all require different handling. The whole developmental sector has to reinvent itself for the newer set of problems that the new circumstances brought. As such sudden changes affected everyone's life, including the skills and values related to one's livelihood and relationships. Obviously, the education sector too needs to gear-up for such a rapidly changing society.

Very often it has been heard about the lack of transparency in the decision-making process. Many complained about the decision-making process becoming kind of a black box. There have been many changes in the delivery mechanism since the days of DPEP and early RTE in the recent times according to some who were involved in both the projects. There is much more multiplicity of agencies involved in the implementation now. The above situation leads to lack of accountability as no one is responsible. The various governmental agencies involved in the delivery of education have their own rules, norms and criteria leading to often situations where left hand did not know what the right was doing.

Too much of centralization has become a bane for the education system. The whole system was planned from the headquarters and there is very little local participation in the planning process. Many teachers and CRCCs were, we found, quite disillusioned and at times felt exploited by the senior decision-makers. Sometimes, they had to bear the brunt of becoming guinea pigs of various experiments designed from the top.

Various government policies such as providing free textbook under RTE Act, the addition of class V to primary section, no detention policy etc. has also lead to quite chaotic situations in many cases. For example, due to no detention policy students may practically enter the high school without really mastering the basic competencies in either language or mathematics, creating a frustrating situation for high school teachers. The primary base of education is weakening day-by-day, now creating a very challenging situation for the secondary stage. The lack of specialist subject teacher at the elementary level later creates difficulties as the new curriculum and textbooks require much more specialised knowledge on part of the teachers. In such a scenario, parents having to send their children either to private schools or provide private tuitions is becoming a necessity.

Changing courses and curricula are also affecting the education scenario. The curriculum and method of teaching are frequently changed. Interestingly, we were told, the textbooks have changed four times in last sixteen years. Adding of class V with the introduction of subjects like English, Hindi etc. is also creating problems in schools, because most of the teachers find the additional subjects difficult for them. Same is the case with the mathematics of the class V level.

The introduction of free textbooks under RTE has too generated a tough situation. There also has been much confusion in the distribution—while in most of the cases they reached very late, in others they were less than required. There have been also allegations that in the name of free textbooks, the authorities suddenly introduced CBSE books which have been merely translated without any adaptation or localisation.

It has been felt that all schemes of government have not been able to reach the most interior areas and most vulnerable groups even in terms of access, not to mention of retention and quality improvement. One felt that the schemes of education somehow reach usually those places which are reachable while the unreachable remain often still underdeveloped. It was unfortunate to find that there were still places where the system failed even in providing access to government schools for children of many marginalised communities, even after ten years of the launching of SSA and shifting to RTE.

Lack of sufficient teachers is a major factor affecting the education sector in the whole state. The number of single teacher schools with high enrollment is quite alarming. In many cases, even the schools earlier having sufficient teachers have been rendered dysfunctional due to not filling-up the vacancies caused due to various reasons. What astonished us most was the fact that this has been the case for more than two decades while the authorities have done preciously little to remedy this basic problem. Though we heard that further appointment of teachers remained banned by honourable High Court order since 2001, it was really surprising to find the government not taking adequate steps to convince the honourable Judges about the absolute necessity of starting the recruitment process in the long ten years.

Mid-Day Meal (MDM) though definitely acts as an incentive in poverty affected areas; we also got an impression that it hampers the teaching—learning process as most of the children remain attracted towards cooking and having the meal. The scheme is not having its desired impact—rather, it has become counter-productive in many cases. There have been much allegations and counter-allegations of large-scale corruption that has affected this scheme.

There have been some other alarming trends affecting the educational scenario in recent past. First among them is the steep fall in enrollment in many government schools—especially very acutely in some of the districts. Linked with this is the mushrooming of private schools, including in Assamese medium, even in rural areas. Many parents probably, rightly or wrongly, feel that the private schools equip their children better for the competitive market.

However, there were also many counter examples to the popular myth that government schools in the urban setting are losing out to the private schools. There were a number of Government schools in urban areas which were having very high enrollment and functioning well. Though there were also some schools in an urban setting where the enrollment is slowly dwindling in the last couple of years, the reason being that the child population of those localities is decreasing among certain communities, this whole phenomenon needs to be further studied before making any generalisations.

There were, however, quite a few positive achievements too. The civil works have been a strong component of SSA evidence of which could be seen in most of the districts. There were also schemes like Education Guarantee Scheme (EGS), bridge courses, Kasturba Gandhi Balika Vidyalaya (KGBV), community volunteer scheme etc. The EGS centres, especially, has been one of the very popular and successful interventions for the marginalised groups. However, there has been much bungling here regarding this by all the decision-makers which have led to a peculiar scenario where many who were closely involved now feel very frustrated. It has been felt that this may have very serious repercussions in the coming days.

Another issue is that those involved in the delivery mechanism at the various level they are quite overburdened and—at times exploited victims of a heartless system. The biggest weakness of the whole education system, it has been felt, is that it is very lazy-responses at every level always come very late, sometimes never and at times very inappropriate.

One major apprehension that encountered was that the standard of education is going down as the society is now putting emphasis on getting marks only. The moral education has taken back seat as very little is done to inculcate values through education. Many felt the present education system is developing human beings only as 'competitors', not as a human resource. One observed the equally significant trend that very few teachers and those involved in education system send their own children to government schools.

In the light of above issues this book is trying to discuss various issues related to education from elementary to higher—especially among the marginalized people, Sixth Schedule—tribal areas (Hill districts of Assam and other Northeast states) and to make an assessment of achievements of various missions/ programmes in North-east Region specially for the most marginalised groups and in difficult areas. It also tries to understand the transition from the education sector is going presently.

Tarun Dutta
Department of History
Assam University Diphu Campus
Assam

SECTION-I

History, Politics and Development

1

Missionary Education and New Domesticities in Colonial North-east India

Suryasikha Pathak

The common belief about the introduction of Western education in India is that it is perceived as a gift of the British Raj to the indigenous people. New histories are questioning these very notions about the colonial past and attempting to rewrite the encounter between the colonized and colonizer. History of education is such an endeavour which looks into the pedagogical exercises of the colonial state, missionaries and nationalist from an ideological location. Within the large body of history of education, the question of women's education and also missionary efforts to educate form a very crucial and intersecting section. Debates raged around one or another and do so till date. The emancipatory politics of education has been assumed simplistically for a long time, without questioning the rationale behind such an effort. Education of women was seen as an important part of civilizing the society and building the character of a nation. But Christian norms espoused by missionaries went further still, while advocating emancipation of women from oppressive heathen customs and general backwardness, it nevertheless also pedalled notions of Western domesticity. Hence, despite having high number of women in schools the mission's educational agenda and pedagogical exercises were often limited by notions of morality and expectations regarding the role of women in society and church.

Missionaries of various denominations arrived in North-east India during the nineteenth century. One of the primary objectives was dissemination of education and civilizing the tribes along with spreading the message of Christ. The earliest missionary interest in the north-eastern part of India was shown by the Serampore Baptist Mission, which after 1837 was amalgamated again into the parent body of the Baptist Missionary Society (BMS). During the brief period of its independence from its parent body (1816-1837), the Serampore Mission started its work in Assam and Meghalaya. The work of the Mission was encouraged by David Scott, and they started with translation work of the Bible, one school in Guwahati though no before they could have a strong base the difficulties of the mission coupled with the amalgamation led to handing over the field to the American Baptists. The American Baptist also had official sanction to start its work. Commissioner Francis Jenkins invited the mission to work among the Khamtis and Singphos of the eastern most part of the Brahmaputra Valley. It has of course become a part of the lore of history of Christianity how the American Baptist Mission was not merely interested in evangelizing the "tribes of the frontier", but thought of it as a springboard to reach the Shan tribes of upper Myanmar and Southern China. Soon enough the futility of attempting to cross the eastern section of the Himalayas became apparent and the American Baptist Mission started focusing on the Brahmaputra Valley and its 'natives'. By 1845, the Baptist Church of Assam was established with three branches located at Guwahati, Nagaon and Sibsagar respectively, though the body was disbanded after few years, the individual mission centres functioned in lines of the mission structure. Soon schools were started in the Brahmaputra Valley among the caste Hindu Assamese people.

But despite relative success of the schools, the number of converts among these people were disappointing for the missionaries. This led to attempts to work with the non-caste Hindu population of the region, the 'tribes' of the hills and the plains. Though as a part of the earlier Shan Mission, the American Baptist Mission had attempted some mission work among the Nagas. In the 1850s, they started working among the Karbis, a 'tribe' living in the hills near Nagaon. By 1860s, starting work with the Garos, the American Baptist Mission encountered a field where the possibility of evangelization was vast. Initially, the Mission centre was the Goalpara, but with growing members in the church they relocated to Tura by 1877 and soon the Tura Station became one of the largest for the American Baptist Mission. After the failure to launch the Namsang Mission in 1841, the real mission among the Nagas was renewed when in 1871 Godhula and Assamese evangelist started from Sibsagar to work among the Ao Nagas. In 1876 E.W. Clark moved to the Naga Hills and started living in Molung and by 1880 another mission centre was established in Kohima among the Angami Nagas and in 1885 among the Lotha Nagas in Wokha the third centre was established. From Nagaland the mission's expansion to the neighbouring princely state of Manipur was by accident rather by design. William Pettigrew of the Arthington mission was allowed work among the Manipuris after the Political Agent of Manipur gave him permission to open a school in Imphal in 1894. British reluctance to jeopardize the political situation in Manipur and keeping in line with their policy of 'non-interference', the political agent asked Pettigrew to shift from Imphal to the adjoining hills which were under the direct control of the former. Pettigrew set-up the mission at Ukhrul among the Tangkhul Nagas and following this he resigned from the Arthington Mission and joined the American Baptist. By the end of the nineteenth century, the American Baptist Mission stations dotted the map of north-east India ranging from Garo hills, cutting across the Brahmaputra Valley and climbing the Naga and Manipur Hills. The mission official records document this successful journey of the Mission in celebratory terms referring usually to converting the "fierce headhunters" to good people of Christ. From these early days on the "civilizing mission" continued its forays with evangelization till the twentieth century transforming not merely through conversion, but also through education and influence. Gender relations, status of women in indigenous societies grabbed the attention of most protestant missions in India. As one of the official histories of the Baptist Mission in Assam states quite clearly: "The effort to lift womanhood to a higher social level among the people appealed to the Christian constituency in America, who supported the missionary enterprise."[1]

Transformed Domesticities: Missionary Schooling and Good Women

The rationale of the women's foreign missions societies were not merely to rescue their heathen sister and proselytize them but there were wide range of concerns "the need to provide Christian men with suitable wives, the desire to reduce resistance among women to social reform, and the wish to direct the energies of Indian wives and mothers towards reorganizing and reforming Indian homes."[2] Home became a site of re-ordering of the new cultural practices of the new indigenous Christians and also for the Missionary women. Victorian ideas about gender relations guided the formations of new domesticities with the women's role as the guardian and moral keeper of the domestic space. As Tim Allender writes, "For the government at least the mission compound was a stable repository for its trainee women because it could provide a cultured space where converts, oriented already to European sensibilities, offered more reliable outcomes in terms of morally sturdy teachers in the Raj. Mission education of girls occurred mostly in the central compound and dormitories were provided for the safety of the daughters of the rich who now mostly frequented these schools. Government increased its grant-in-aid funding to accommodate the new demand and school enrolments grew rapidly. Without providing additional staff this soon overburdened the European women who superintended them, most of whom had little experience of teaching beyond Sunday school, and certainly not of the nuances of female teacher training, even by the standards of the time."[3]

Hence while encouraging education for girls and women the mission did not want to step over boundaries set by Victorian morality and Indian social conditions. Providing Christian education to girls was the key to reordering indigenous societies. Bronson wrote in 1856, that the Nowgong Orphan school girls were educated to fill in as ideal wives of the male converts. Marrying non-Christians often led to reverting back to the heathen ways of life and also without a Christian wife, the practices of religion within the domestic space became increasingly challenged. Bronson wrote the need of containing the education of the girls were also needed, because "not elevating the girls of the schools above their future work and position in life, as wives of our Christian converts."[4] But even in the hills the rate of education for women progressed so slowly that women missionaries expressed their concerns and demanded that serious steps be taken to educate the girls. Pollie Keith rues: "For we have now 25 young men in the normal school learning the sciences, — of the books, — and of soap and water also. Where shall these go for their future companions in life? To their heathen countrywomen? How can they? We must think of these things."[5]

This attitude towards women's education did not radically alter till the twentieth century when need for indigenous educators and nurses made it imperative that women received secular education and prepared them for the public sphere as well. The problems encountered while education of the girls of the plains and the girls of the hills were manifold, the task of opening and successfully running schools for girls, both in the plains and in the hills seemed at times insurmountable. The Zenana mission of the plains often met with failure and resistance. Maria Bronson, daughter of one the first missionaries in Brahmaputra Valley, wrote about home about such challenges of encountering social resistance: "It is thought a shame to educate the girls; so they are left, if poor, to grow up in perfect ignorance, to do all the hard work in the burning sun... higher classes kept their girls and women shut up in small apartments... oh, what a life these creatures lead, and how unfit to train their little children! Even the educated... unwilling to send their wives to us."[6] The Nowgong Orphan school ran almost entirely on the orphaned children also met with social resistance peculiar to getting girl students due "the very strong prejudices of the natives against female education. A female who can read and write is, on that account, considered much less likely to make a good wife and mother."[7] Mrs. P. H. Moore writing about the presence, rather absence of girls in the Nowgong Mission school felt that "if it was not for religious predilections of the Vaishnava Gossains (priest) who raised objections to the secular and non-secular education conducted by the missionaries, more women would have come forward for educating themselves."[8] The internalization of these ideas by the Assamese women led to an apathy where "do not seek it themselves, or desire their daughters to obtain it" and they had few examples to follow emancipate themselves.[9] Even orphaned destitute girls were kept in the families, sometimes adopted by relatives, mostly to serve as menials, sometimes labouring in other families to pay back small debts.[10] Similar story is narrated by Elizabeth Vickland, where Nirupama, who loses her father, is left with her uncle and two brothers. Nirupama is sent away with a family to look after the babies of a rich Brahmin family. She was serving the family as a maid because her father asked the Brahmin of the family to conduct a *puja* for him and was not able to pay the costs of the ceremony.[11] Similar stories also echoed from the hills, some chiefs in Naga Hills objected to opening a school for the girls stating plaining—"You cannot teach our females, they are trained to bear burdens, to bring wood and water, and to make the salt by which we make our subsistence."[12] Though unlike the plains there issue was regarding the labour of the woman and her service to the family and village.

Orphans were not the first ones in the mission schools, bazaar girls were brought to the mission bungalow where they were instructed by the missionary wives. Missionary wives, like Jane Barker, gathered "wicked, dirty and idle girls" from the streets of Guwahati to educate them.[13] Throughout the nineteenth century, the curriculum for girls was limited and it was due to several defining concerns. The missionaries had to contend with social pressure as mentioned above which saw education for women as unproductive, moreover, there were several concerns whether girls who had stayed with the mission for too long would be able to adjust to indigenous life. Writing in the twentieth century, Linnie Holbrook notes that even among the Christian community in the nineteenth century no women considered life outside the domestic sphere. The earliest school girls from Tura in the nineteenth century were, "not highly educated, and they might work on rice and cotton fields, but they made Christian homes and what they had they gave."[14]

During the Jubilee Conference of the American Baptist Mission held in Nowgong, December 1886, Miriam Burdette presented a paper on "Work for Garo Women" and in response a Welsh Missionary attending the same reported "that while his mission was running many girls schools in the Khasi-Jaintia hills the education offered was only limited, and those women who had been enrolled in the normal school at Cherrapunji 'did not turn out well'." He further stressed that Khasi Christian families, otherwise devout, themselves resisted a mission proposal that a young woman be sent to Calcutta for medical studies.[15] The twentieth century witnessed transformations in terms of demands on the girls who reached middle level schools, and they were expecting to be trained as teachers and nurses and often left Tura for higher training. Linnie Holbrook writes about these changes as a positive aspect of continuous missionary endeavour to uplift women: "These new course of study opened a new vision of life for them and they responded heartily to the change. Now with both eyes upon their books and work they have little time to be on the outlook for a husband until their school days are over."[16]

Morality in the hills became an issue with the Mission as in the case of Kohima, where the Rivenburgs were stationed. It was a military station for the British troops in Naga hills and the officers were notorious for their "impure relations with native women."[17] The schools too kept strict watch on the morality of their young girl pupils and the control of the girls were often handed over to the missionary wives or single women missionaries. The Nowgong which was one of the first co-education institution later separated the girls' school from the boys. One of the annual report mirror this concern: "We believe that due attention has been paid to securing strict purity of morals in the Girls' Department. They are now entirely distinct from the Boys' Department, and under the immediate supervision and instruction of Mrs. Stoddard. Your committee are not aware that any instance of immorality had occurred under the present arrangement, nor do they apprehend that there is greater danger in this respect than there would be of the school was removed to any other station."[18] Control over pupils was forever an issue in case of men more difficult to impose as noted by Frederic Harding, missionary in Tura: "One of the problems in school work was that of disciplining the school boys and girls. The discipline was simple in the case of the girls. We turned it over to the Mem Sahibs and let them solve each case on its merits or demerits."[19] Likewise Anna Long notes that the girls are not angels and a lot of grief is caused by disobedient behaviour.[20]

Training to be Better Wives: Christian Women and their Domestic Roles

Towards the end of the nineteenth century, Garo Women's Christian Association wrote a letter to their American counterparts in America.

"To the Beloved Mothers in America, is this letter written.

> Before you, in love to us, sent us "lady missionaries", how much the Garo women spent their time in doing deeds of darkness that we cannot tell.
>
> According to our family laws the woman is master of the riches of the house; therefore, they magnified themselves, were proud, despised their husbands, were not in subjection to them, taught evil and to their daughters, and all went astray. But when, by the leading hand of God, you in love sent with the missionaries "lady teachers", viz., Miss Russell, Miss Mason, Miss Bond, and then Miss Rood, to show them what they were needing to learn, and thus starting the school for girls at Tura, gathering them together there, and with God's guidance zealously teaching them to read, to sew and to knit, because of this, the Garo women are now learning to read books, the Scriptures, to sew, and not these alone, for although they are not yet perfect they are better then (*sic*) before. They teach their children better, look after their houses and granaries better, love and honor their husbands more. Therefore, we thank God. We, the brothers, mothers, sisters of the churches of the Krima Association, seeing your loving help to us for the good of the Garo women, rejoice."[21]

The letter above is instructive in providing many insights into the transformation witnessed at the wake of Christianity. It critiques the traditions which are perceived as evil including matriliny which the Garo society was and is and also re-orients the domestic relationships in terms of respect and love due to husbands. The training ground for the "better wives", "better mothers", "better home makers" was the missionary initiative and the exemplary trainer were the women missionaries. Another example of how girls were educated is in the report of May Stevenson for the Impur station in 1921. She writes: "The girls are busy all day. They are up at 5.30, cook and eat their rice, get ready for school and are in school from 7.30 to 12 o'clock. In the afternoon they sew, weave or work in the garden, then they pound rice, bring wood and water, sweep their houses, clean lamps etc. We try to teach them to be better house-keepers than their mothers are."[22] Missionary accounts, reports, letters home are replete with such stories of domestic transformation.

The genteel influence of civilizing mission of Christian was soon noted in description of converts and their way of life in as studies in contrast with the 'heathens'. The cleanliness of homes, of bodies and spirit happened concurrently. As Anna Long hopes in her report on female education that though the girls were not perfect there was "steady growth in faith, patience, self-control and unselfishness" and saw "the spirit of God working in their hearts" and could possibly become "messengers of light to sisters in darkness."[23] She saw as most missionaries and social reformers in India did, women as agents of change, transforming society through the family, reaching the public through the private. References were made to changes in child rearing, grieving and dressing. Gradually, women who sew started making garments to cover their bodies, and some adopted the 'polite' dresses of the plains women. Mary M. Clark writes, "The Assamese costume of jacket and body cloth is now being adopted by many who have come under Christian influence, especially the pupils in the schools..." though the older coverts often choose to dress as before.[24] Women like Lucy who went to Naga hills led a sheltered life in the mission and was "naturally refined" and the Nagas were "dirty and repulsive" in contrast had to disseminate the genteel influence.[25] Tungbangla's daughter who grew up as a Christian girl is described as "a young miss, genteel in manner, with a quiet, pleasant face, clean and tidy."[26] Mary Clark compares them to flowers blooming, "growing in womenhood" becoming better wives and mothers, whereas girls in the valley would be married off by this age. These changes were celebrated in missionary reports, as Vickland write as a commentary: "Jesus Christ has been enlightening the manhood of India as to the treatment of women, and we find thousands of homes where the widow is sheltered and protected. Where daughters are being educated and the age of marriage pushed back, and where the girl has something to say about the choice of her mate. We find in such homes that the wife and husband are equals, the wife does not shrink into the background when her lord appears, but she joins in the conversation with him and the guest, a gracious, charming hostess."[27] But such idyllic picture of domesticity is contested by the restricted space of gentility, where not covering the upper body was critiqued, where drinking rice beer and smoking tobacco was prohibited, where loudly mourning was prohibited. The small world of the Christian converts was as it is very small and restrictive and the community closely observed violations and challenges to the newly established codes, hence making a closed space for women.

Notes

1. Victor Hugo Sword, 1992, *Baptist in Assam: A Century of Missionary Service, 1836 – 1936*, First published 1935, Indian reprint, Guwahati: Spectrum Publications, p. 136.
2. Eliza Kent, 2004, *Converting Women: Gender and Protestant Christianity in Colonial South India*, New York: OUP, p. 129.
3. Tim Allender, *Educational Futures: Creating a Female Education Space in Colonial India*, 1854-1934, p. 6.
4. Narola Imchen, 2003, *Remembering Our ForeMothers, Women studies series No. 2*, Eastern Theological College, Jorhat, p. 141.
5. Letter dated Gowalpara, January, 27, 1873, published in the Baptist Missionary Magazine, LIII.5, (May, 1873), p.143, quoted from Frederick S. Downs, *The Christian Impact on the Status of Women in North East India*, p. 57.
6. Narola Imchen, *op. cit.*, p. 147.
7. *Report of the Assam Orphan Institution at Nowgong*; at the close of the year 1851 (Sibsagor, Assam, printed at the American Baptist Mission Press, 1852), p. 14.
8. Suryasikha Pathak, *Missionary Wives in the Evangelical Project in Colonial Assam: Life and Times of Mrs. P.H. Moore*, ICHR lecture series, ICHR Publication 2008.
9. Report of Assam Orphan Institution, p. 14.
10. *Ibid.*
11. Elizabeth Vickland, *Daughter of Brahma*, in Liza Das ed.
12. Victor Hugo Sword, *op. cit.*, p. 62.
13. Aphuno Chase-Roy, *American Baptist Women Missionaries in North-east India* (1836-1950), Christian Literature Centre, Guwahati, 2011, p. 48.
14. Frederick S. Downs, *op. cit.*, p. 58.
15. *Ibid.*, pp. 43-44.
16. *Ibid.*
17. Narola Rivenburg, *op. cit.*, p. 70.
18. Report of the Nowgong Orphan Institution and the other schools in Asam, adopted February 1854 (Sibsagor, Assam, printed at the American Baptist Mission Press, 1854), p. 15.
19. Frederic Harding, 1974, *Christ and the Hillmen*, North Country Books, Lakemont, New York, p. 98.
20. Narola Imchen, *op. cit.*, p. 226.

21. Frederick S. Downs, *op. cit.*, pp. 79-80.
22. *Ibid.*, p. 57.
23. Narola Imchen, *op. cit.*, p. 226.
24. Mary Mead Clark, p. 54.
25. Elizabeth Vickland, "*On Pilgrimage*", pp. 112-113.
26. Mary Mead Clark, *op. cit.*, p. 87.
27. Elizabeth Vickland, "Boxes of Alabaster", p. 129.

2

Mainstreaming the Marginalised

Why to Revamp Education Policy for Inclusive Development in North-east India?

Dibyajyoti Dutta

Introduction

"An investment in knowledge pays the best interest."
—*Benjamin Franklin* (1706-1790)

Education is the key to inclusive development. The responsibility to advance education for all primarily rests with the State. This is arguably true that the State cannot backtrack from this primary responsibility. Considering the present strategies of the Government of India to revamp education under the new National Education Policy (NEP), 2016, this paper scrutinises the proposed *'inputs'* (the committee constituted for evolution of the NEP led by former Cabinet Secretary T.S.R. Subramanian were termed as inputs by the MHRD which was published in the MHRD website) and the *"Politics of guarded agenda"* (V. Gupta, 2016)[1] contextualising the aspirations of the people of the North-east to empower and mainstream the marginalised sections of the society. The term marginalised is used here to refer to the underprivileged groups of the region who are untouched by the developmental agendas of the State, regardless of their ethnic, caste and regional identities.

The New Education Policy, 1986 recommended spending of 6 per cent of the Gross Domestic Product (GDP) on education, which could not be attained as of today owing to the skewed and inadequate policies of the Government. The Subramanian

Committee noted that the actual expenditure on education has remained consistently below the recommended level and in recent years it has hovered around 3.5 per cent.[2] The total expenditure on education as percentage of GDP was highest (4.14 %) in 2000-01, but this level could not be sustained in the following year and comes down to 3.26 per cent in the year 2004-05. It again showed increasing trends, but at a very slow pace. If the percentages for centre and states were taken separately, it can be observed that centre's share show an increasing trend over the years and gone-up from 0.51 per cent in 2000-01 to 1.16 per cent in 2012-13, while state's share has declined from 3.63 per cent in the year 2000-01 to 3.13 per cent in 2012-13.[3] It is true that Government spending on education has increased over the period of time but, the widespread existence of malpractices and deep-rooted corruption in education sector as well as in allied areas have heavily impacted on the accessibility of education by all. Transparency International and Delhi-based Centre for Media Studies, a research firm, undertook to know the pattern of corruption in India in 2005 covering 14,405 respondents over 20 states and found that Indians pay around Rs. 21,068 crore as bribes while availing one of 11 public services.[4] The study revealed that 70 per cent respondents experienced corruption in education in some form or the other amounting to the all-India average of Rs. 4,137 crore per year (up to 12th standard).

The New Education Policy, 2016

The NEP, 2016 aims to address seven key areas of concern with respect to the Indian education sector. These are: access and participation, quality, equity, system efficiency, governance and management, research and development and financial commitment to education development. These areas are to be addressed through policy interventions broadly into preschool and adolescent education, curriculum development and examination reform, teacher and faculty training, lifelong literacy, higher education and long distance learning.[5] The New Education Policy, 2016 was drafted by an expert group headed by former Cabinet Secretary T.S.R. Subramanian. The Central Government modified the draft giving extensive emphasis on the need of re-aligning Indian educational system with the traditional values especially with the introduction of Sanskrit language and Yoga came under scathing attack even from the drafting committee. The T.S.R. Subramanian Committee had submitted 90 recommendations in their 200 page report to the Government, but the MHRD published only some key recommendations titled as "Some Inputs for Draft National Education Policy 2016". The key highlights of the proposed NEP, 2016 are:

1. The overall quality of education both in primary and higher stages is very bad and has further deteriorated in last 10-15 years although there is an increase in the number of educational institutions.
2. The discrimination against the weaker and marginalised children still persists in the Indian society and education system is not aloof from this aspect of education system. These children have equal rights as compared to other children as per RTE, but there is no significant improvement in their educational status so far.
3. The focus of educational institutions needs to be teacher oriented as they are the most important link between the institution and students. It has observed that teachers and their training are often neglected.
4. The Report has favoured for 6 per cent GDP for education, a well-structured public system of education and strengthening of Right to Education Act.
5. Universities and colleges are temples of learning. There is a need to restrict political and other distractions in these institutions.[6]

Prior to this, India had two previous National education policies. The first was introduced in 1968 during the Indira Gandhi regime and the other was in 1986 with revisions incorporated in 1992 under the Prime Ministership of Rajiv Gandhi and P.V. Narasimha Rao. In order to "meet the changing dynamics of the population's requirement with regards to quality education, innovation and research", the present dispensation is mulling over reforming the Indian education system.

Politics of Guarded Agenda: Critique of the National Educational Policy, 2016

Vikas Gupta, in an article "Politics of the Guarded Agenda of National Education Policy 2015–16" published in the *Economic and Political Weekly* (October 15, 2016, Vol. LI, No. 42, pp. 59-69) underlined the inadvertent omissions and points of overemphasis on the draft NEP, 2016. The article highlighted that the overall framework of the new NEP has been pitiable in addressing the aspects of structural and infrastructural discrepancy, economic inequality, social injustice, and cultural homogeneity. Rather than resolving them, the new NEP framework will according to him legitimise and augment these problems. The author makes it clear that the extremely constrained scope and guarded nature of the framework of the new NEP is a strategy for subverting the possibility to voice fundamental issues, for channelizing the responses in specific directions, and for co-opting some of the discursive threads likely to be created in this process to legitimise and bulldoze the predetermined agenda of the dominant classes, and to reproduce the iniquitous social order. In this sense, it is anti-poor and adversarial to the interests of most women, *Dalits, Adivasis*, disabled, and religious, linguistic, or ethnic minorities, which form the bulk of the majority of the class of "have-nots". An already weak programme for addressing social inequalities is further watered down owing to its disregard of the class phenomenon of poverty, and due to its non-recognition of the internal heterogeneity and power relations existing within each community.[7]

The new NEP as has been debated in different forums seeks to provide "minimalist" and segregated education to the impoverished masses in each community. It is at best capable of serving only the immediate interests of the upper stratum within different excluded groups and higher classes in general. It is an essential prerequisite for the co-option of community elites in the politics of hegemonic classes. Since the agenda of the new NEP champions the politics of cultural uniformity, it is also adversarial to all forms of diversity. It revives the model of "integrationalism" with the added flavour of religious "majoritarianism" of the 1950s and 1960s, and the cultural revivalism of the 19th century. It only uses the technological facade to create the illusion of its democratic nature and proclaims to have entered in "grassroots" consultations within a stiff structure and predetermined and constrained agenda so that it can continue to serve the interests of the dominant classes.[8] Ajay S. Sekhar (2016) also highlights the hidden agenda of the Government. According to the author, the Indian state makes attempts to corporatize the educational system with the adoption of the new education policy. Gender inequality in education and its nexus with caste inequality, according to the author is not even addressed by the draft. The draft NEP mentions the word gender only once in the section "Preamble to Mission". Another major omission highlighted by the Ajay S. Sekhar is that of the sexual minorities and transgenders in Indian society who are experiencing serious human rights and civil rights violations. While Sanskrit and Yoga are pushed into the draft from all corners, it keeps mum on the crucial issue of ecological crisis. The careful and cunning evasion and silence on issues such as gender, ecology, caste and sexuality are typical examples of the totalitarian and repressive regime and its social, political and ecological vision.[9] The draft policy also has the elements of saffron ideologies and if translated into reality, it would further widen the gap existed in the society instead of minimizing it.

Education for All: The Importance of Mainstreaming the Marginalised Communities

Education is a right, like the right to have proper food or a roof over your head. The article 26 of the Universal Declaration of Human Rights, 1948 states that "everyone has the right to education". Education is not only a right but a passport to human development. It opens doors and expands opportunities and freedoms. It contributes to fostering peace, democracy and economic growth as well as improving health and reducing poverty. In the year 2000, the world's governments adopted six "Education For All" (EFA) goals and eight Millennium Development Goals (MDGs), the two most important frameworks in the field of education. The two sets of goals are an ambitious roadmap for the global community to follow. They offer a long-term vision of reduced poverty and hunger, better health and education, sustainable lifestyles, strong partnerships and shared commitments.[10] The six EFA goals are:

1. Expand early childhood care and education.
2. Provide free and compulsory primary education for all.
3. Promote learning and life skills for young people and adults.
4. Increase adult literacy.
5. Achieve gender parity.
6. Improve the quality of education.

Indian state has failed miserably in realising most of the goals except for some progress in policy formulation front. India homes the largest share of stunted child in the world. According to the Global Hunger Index (GHI) released by the International Food Policy Research Institute (IFPRI), India has been ranked 97 on the list of 118, worse than its neighbours Nepal, Bangladesh and Sri Lanka, but marginally better than Pakistan. The four components that are being considered for the survey were—undernourishment, child wasting, child stunting and child mortality. The FAO data reveals that more than one third of the total population in India continues to live below the poverty line. Almost 30 per cent of India's rural populations live a life with abject poverty and hunger. India is the home to a staggering 43 per cent underweight child and 48 per cent children whose growth is stunted by malnutrition. These statistics speaks the obvious of failures of the Government and of messy politics and politicking.

Given the circumstances, a holistic approach needs to be adhered to in order to bring those communities, groups and sections into the mainstream, who have for long been deprived of their rights.

1. Expansion of Educational infrastructure: Enrolment at primary, secondary and higher levels in India is increasing constantly. Accordingly, to accommodate increasing number of students at all levels it is indispensable to have more educational infrastructures. The Right to Education Act, 2009 provided for establishment of new schools at approachable distance, but the proposed new national education policy remain silent on the issue. Physical infrastructures along with its scientific management are central to advance education for all. Enrolment at primary, secondary and higher levels in India is increasing constantly. Accordingly, to accommodate increasing number of students at all levels it is indispensable to have more educational institutes.

There has been a structural change in education sector after allowing private partnership, at higher levels in particular. This has led to private investment not only in school education, but also in tertiary education. Consequently, several private universities and colleges are opening in general education, engineering and medical education. Despite these changes, the Government and local bodies still organize more than 90 per cent of primary schools whereas the contribution of private agencies was about 9.79 per cent in 2004-05. In the case of Secondary/Senior Secondary level education, the growth of institutes under different management bodies has also increased continuously. Since 1973-74, percentage of Government Secondary/Senior Secondary schools has increased from 26.5 per cent to 33.1 per cent in 2004-05.[11]

2. Governance and Finance: Good Governance matters a lot in advancing education. The question of governance needs to be given top priority. Half cooked policies and its dispirited implementation may not yield in positive outcomes. The example of NITI Ayog's draft bill to set-up a National Medical Commission needs special mention. The release of the 92nd Parliamentary Standing Committee Report of the Ministry of Health and Family Welfare on the State of Medical Education in India captured widespread attention not only among the close circle of policy-makers, but common people also started to realise that something is not right with the Medical Council of India, the highest body to ensure high standards in medical education. The Parliamentary Committee Report also looked at the state of health care in the country, the quality of healthcare services. The report dwelled at length on the constitution of MCI, which was responsible for the rot that had set in medical education, from the process of granting accreditation to medical colleges to the mushrooming of medical colleges in the private sector and the exorbitant amounts charged under the name of capitation fees. Government looking at the nature of the issue constituted a three member committee under the NITI Ayog to examine the aspects of Indian Medical Council Act, 1956 and to suggest reforms in Medical Education. The committee came up with its recommendations including proposing a new Bill that would repeal the IMC Act and pave the way for the constitution of National Medical Commission. The Committee further recommended the establishment of private medical colleges and private healthcare what critics have labelled it as the "cure worse than the disease."[12] From this example it becomes apparently clear the intention of the Government. Since public funding becomes an issue for the Government, it tries to push for massive privatization of education. The inability of the Government to spend 6 per cent of the GDP on education speaks for itself. But whatever the bottlenecks, Indian state must shoulder the responsibility of financing educational institutions in order to develop human capital.

3. Personnel Issues: The education sector employs a huge chunk of the Indian workforce. There must be good policies in place so that the personnel involved with the profession do not face hardships. Since education is in the concurrent list of the constitution (previously it was in the state list but with the 42nd Constitution Amendment Act, 1976 the matter was transferred to concurrent list so that State Governments as well as Central Government can frame policies concerning education), therefore, there exist variations/differences in recruitment and compensation policies of the personnel. At times, it so happened that for the same services discharged, teachers are paid differently in different states. Special care and effort should be given to the primary and upper primary levels so that learners get ample scope and opportunities to develop their inner potentials.

Education for All: the North-east Indian Context

The North-east India exemplifies plurality and diversity. The region though is endowed with innumerable opportunities, but fails to translate the blessings into reality owing to multitudes of issues ranging from underdevelopment, unemployment, social unrests etc. In order to facilitate education for all, minimise gender disparity in availing education, improving gender friendly infrastructures in schools, impart democratic sentiments among the learners in a much diverged socio-cultural setting new learner-centric policies needs to be initiated. This is the time to revamp the education system starting from the schools to Universities with special focus on marginalised communities.

Three Key issues impacting education in the North-east and the way forward:

(a) The massive privatization has changed the very landscape of the education in the region. It has resurfaced the age old Indian problem of social hierarchy. The well to do families have started sending their kids to private owned schools and the low income families to the government owned schools thereby compounding the very socializing process. The values of democracy are taught in the schools as part of the curricula, but the very structure is undemocratic in nature. The students fail to comprehend the nature and character of Indian socio-cultural values of cooperation, coordination and equality. The mushrooming of the private schools and higher education institutions must be controlled (if not stopped) to promote equality and Government funded institutions must be strengthened and provided with all possible financial and managerial support. Table 2.1 explains the intensity of private penetration in education system in India.

(b) The North-east Indian States have been facing acute crisis in education funding. As per the statistics in 2012-13, the largest allocation to education (compared among all Indian states) comes in Assam (21.1%) while the lowest is in Arunachal Pradesh (8.3%). In Tripura, education spending has decreased by 3.4 per cent to 13.8 per cent making it the largest reduction compared to the previous year.[13] The Assam spent more because of the fact that it implemented the provisions of the Right to Education Act, 2009. Still there persist series of issues of starting from recruitment, infrastructural bottlenecks, poor teacher-pupil ratio which have heavily impeded on the advancement of education. State funding to educational institutions ensuring transparent spending is the key to address many ills. Shift in policy approach needs to be resorted to by the Government keeping it bay the privatization trends.

(c) Development of Syllabi keeping in mind the cultural flavour of a region needs to be ensured. The present dispensation is hinging on development of uniform syllabi in the undergraduate levels. The Choice Based Credit System (CBCS) developed for undergraduate studies in India by the University Grants Commission (UGC) only allows 30 per cent deviations from the draft module prepared for each discipline. Once implemented this would be a severe blow to the regional variance of learning and would undermine the analysis and comprehension of diversity of issues being faced in different geographical locations. The North-eastern states may find itself in a awkward position to implement these norms because of its long cherished diversity and plurality.

Table 2.1: Management of Intermediate/Senior Secondary Schools (10 States)

Sl. No.	States/Union Territories	Intermediate/Senior Secondary Schools								
		Government		Local Bodies		Private Aided		Private Unaided		Total
		Number	age	Number	age	Number	%age	Number	%age	
1.	Andhra Pradesh	1750	29.8			226	3.8	3897	66.4	5873
2.	Arunachal Pradesh	102	86.4			9	7.6	7	5.9	118
3.	Assam	2133	45.8			1960	42.1	562	12.1	4655
4.	Bihar	2295	92.1			156	6.3	41	1.6	2492
5.	Chhattisgarh	1707	57.9	26	0.9	98	3.3	1116	37.9	2947
6.	Goa	16	18.6			67	77.9	3	3.5	86
7.	Gujarat	506	8.9	147	2.6	3056	53.7	1980	34.8	5689
8.	Haryana	1558	45.3			117	3.4	1761	51.3	3436
9.	Himachal Pradesh	1318	73.8			22	1.2	445	24.9	1785
10.	Jammu & Kashmir	604	67.9			2	0.2	283	31.8	889

Source: Statistics of School Education, 2011-12, GoI.

The emerging local issues cannot be incorporated in the syllabi which would perhaps negate the very process of reform. The reform process needs to adhere to democratic principles and must uplift the marginalised sections of the society. The question of margins and marginalisation are very relative concept. It has an inherent element of comparison. Question may further arise relating to the parties with whom the comparisons be made. The entire rural pockets of the North-eastern region can be focused as marginalised compared to the urban and semi-urban localities.

Conclusion

From the above discussion, it becomes evident that the education system needs to be revamped with the added vision of equality and participation. The privatization of education needs to be stopped and Government funding must be ensured at all levels. Special focus requires to be given to the North-eastern region because of its diversity and plurality of cultures. Haphazard policy decisions are detrimental to the advancement of education and hence, the democratic sentiments and principles need to be respected. Benjamin Franklin is still right when he contemplates that funding knowledge yields manifold results and advances an egalitarian society. All stakeholders engaging in education must come forward and ensure the dawn of a healthy and peaceful society.

Notes and References

1. Vikas Gupta, "Politics of the Guarded Agenda of National Education Policy 2015-16", *Economic & Political Weekly*, October 15, 2016, Vol. LI, No. 42, pp. 59-69.
2. Government of India, Ministry of Human Resource Development, "Some Inputs for Draft National Education Policy 2016", p. 41.
3. Government of India, Ministry of Human Resource Development, Analysis of Budgeted Expenditure on Education 2010-11 to 2012-13, New Delhi, 2014 accessed from http://mhrd.gov.in/sites/upload_files/mhrd/files/statistics/ABE_2010-13.pdf
4. Corruption Catalogue: School System, accessed from http://www.livemint.com/r/LiveMint/Period1/oldpdf/93cae9d3-0b4d-4911-a87b-8ffc20c32cc3.pdf

5. Padmapriya Govindarajan, "India's New Education Policy: What Are the Priorities?" accessed from http://thediplomat.com/2016/07/indias-new-education-policy-what-are-the-priorities/
6. Rajya Sabha TV, "The Big Picture—New Education Policy: Highlights and Hitches", accessed from http://www.insightsonindia.com/2016/08/03/big-picture-new-education-policy-highlights-hitches/
7. Vikas Gupta, "Politics of the Guarded Agenda of National Education Policy 2015-16", *Economic & Political Weekly*, October 15, 2016, Vol. LI, No. 42, p. 69.
8. *Ibid.*
9. Ajay S. Sekhar, "Saffronising and Corporatising Indian Education: Critique of the National Educational Policy 2016 Draft", accessed from http://indianculturalforum.in/2016/08/10/saffronising-and-corporatising-indian-education-critique-of-the-national-educational-policy-2016-draft/
10. http://www.un.org/en/globalissues/briefingpapers/efa/
11. Naresh Kumar, Vipan Kumar and Neelam Kumar, "Educational Infrastructure in India", accessed from http://www.nistads.res.in/indiasnt2008/t1humanresources/t1hr3.htm
12. T.K. Rajalakshmi, "A Cure Worse than the Disease", *Frontline*, Vol. 33, No. 22, November 11, 2016, pp. 64-66.
13. PRS Legislative Research, "State-wise expenditure on Education", 2014.

3

Marginalised Tribal's Education History of Manipur

A Case Study of Ukhrul District

Console Zamreinao Shimrei

The Manipur state lies in latitude range 23° 50' N and 25° 41' N and longitude range 93° 2' E and 94° 47' E.[1] The state has a total geographical area of 22,327 square kilometres which constitutes about 0.7 per cent of the total geographical area of the Indian Union. Out of the total area, about 90 per cent constitute the hills area and the remaining 10 per cent that is 2238 constitute the plain or valley area. Out of this, an area of 550 square kilometres is occupied by lakes, wetland, barren uplands and hillocks.[2] The state of Manipur has three major ethnic groups namely the Meiteis, the Nagas, the Kukis and other community like Pangals (Muslim) etc. The people of Manipur are mainly Mongoloid stock who speaks Tibeto-Burman languages.

Education is the key sector to bring development in the field of socio-economic condition, moral value and enlightened people in the field of politics. Captain Gordon laid down the seed of education in Manipur. He set-up the first primary school in Manipur, but could not success due to poor attendance of the students.[3] The second attempt was made by General W.E. Nuthal in 1872, the then Political Agent of Manipur with a support of the Government of Bengal. They supported and helped them by sending books, maps and other necessities worth about Rs. 400 to Rs. 500.[4] Nevertheless, his efforts could not be succeeded due to orthodoxy of the Meitei society. James Johnstone made an attempt to establish a Middle English school, but the Durban objected and it was only in his second attempt that Maharaja Chandrakriti Singh through General Thangal permitted him to do so.

Thus, the first Middle English School known as the Johnstone Middle English School was established in 1885.[5] After the establishment of Johnstone Middle English School three Lower Primary Schools were established in different parts of Manipur; one at Sekmai in 1892, the second Lower Primary School was established at Mao in 1893 and the third one at Tera in 1894 respectively.[6] Similarly, in 1894 one school was established at Thangmeiband. However, before the inauguration of the school, all the furniture of the school was stolen and the school was started the following year.[7]

Mr. A. Porteous, the then acting Political Agent of Manipur, granted permission to enter Manipur to Reverend William Pettigrew (1869-1943). He arrived in Imphal on 6th January, 1894. After his arrival, he started his work by opening a primary school at Singjamei for boys in his name. The school is now upgraded to Junior High School is known as Pettigrew Juniour School. When the headmaster of Johnstone Middle English School resigned, William Pettigrew was given the honorary headmastership of the school of the Johnstone Middle English School and his service was highly appreciated by all sections of the people of Manipur.[8]

Indeed, Pettigrew's functions and activities strongly resented by the orthodox Hindus of Manipur. They suspected it as an attempted in-road upon the Meitei culture by means of imposing Christianity. A tension was escalated in the mind of the people. The arrival of Major Maxwell, Political Agent of Manipur set things at rest and the tense situation was brought under control. Pettigrew was asked to work in the hill areas of Ukhrul which were under the direct British administration at that time, that also at his own risk. On the other hand, the sponsorship given by the Arthington Mission was not willing to establish a permanent mission station in any particular place. So, the big question arose for him to establish school in other place or left home (England). He had no other alternative then to apply for membership to the American Baptist Missionary Union in Assam. Subsequently, he was re-designated as a Baptist missionary to Manipur. He only changed the Christian denomination from the Anglican to the Baptist only for his mission purpose.[9]

Pettigrew landed at Ukhrul on October 1895. He first came in touch with Mr. Raihao the chief of Hunphun (Ukhrul) village. The Missionary immediately proposed to open one school but the Headman flatly refused to comply with the proposal saying that the Tangkhul script was written on animal skin but a dog has taken and at the same time animal's skin was eaten-up. Thus, it was unwise to think about education for the people of Tangkhul Nagas.[10] Pettigrew wisely replied that he had met the dog on the way and had brought back the script-skin to them. He convinced Raihao. He enrolled as a first batch of students. By the time Raihao was well advanced in age, he was beyond 70 years. Indeed, there was no discipline in the classroom. Raihao was the architect of shaping the classroom atmosphere into a disciplined manner. He could manage this because he was not only respected but also feared by the local people. Raihao was taught English alphabet language by Pettigrew at the same time he was a teacher of Pettigrew as he taught Tangkhul dialect to Pettigrew.[11]

Pettigrew started his work from first February, 1896. From March to September 1896 he was engaged in the construction of mission bungalow. Maxwell's, the then Political Agent of Manipur offered of Rs. 1000 to build a new school. Parents refused to send their children to school. However, 30 students were enrolled in the school. The primary school was upgraded to the standard of Middle English School in 1906. Mrs. Alice, wife of Pettigrew greatly helped to impart education among the Tangkhul women folk. She personally visited from door to door and urging the parents to permit their daughters to attend the night school after day's work was done. She used her bungalow as Night School for the girls. Interestingly, she imparted the elementary education in the girl's dormitory. Thus, girls' hostel was constructed not only for the Tangkhul girls but also other marginalized tribal's girls at Mission School at Ukhrul. Mrs. Alice taught them how to read, to write, to sing, how to behave, how to approach people, table manner, dressing, hygiene etc. in order to grow better life.[12]

In 1919, Mission Centre was shifted to Kangpokpi now at Senapati district of Manipur. Two girl's hostels were opened. They were altogether 48 girls in 1922. Out of 48 girls, 24 girls were Tangkhul Nagas and 24 girls from Kom and Thadou Kukis tribes. Out of the nine girls, seven girls were sent for training at Nowgong, Golagat and Gauhati. After obtaining basic training they became teachers in the hills district of Manipur. One of the first lady teachers who assisted Mrs. Alice was Chorani, from Chingjaroi village, which belongs to Tangkhul Nagas, Ms. Sanamla, also belongs to Tangkhul Nagas who served as matron in the Mission school at Kangpokpi.[13]

For the implementation of SSA in Manipur, a State Level Implementation Society in the name of Sarva Shiksha Abhiyan State Authority, Manipur has been set-up and registered under the Manipur Societies Registration Act, 1989 (Manipur S.R. Act of 1990) and numbered as No. 146/M/SR/2000 dated 31/12/2000. The management structure of the Society Comprises two bodies:

(i) The general body/Governing Council at the apex for policy formulation with Chief Minister as *ex-officio* President.
(ii) The Executive Committee under the Chairmanship of the Chief Secretary to oversee the implementation of the programme.

The state-level office is headed by the director of education (School) who functions as the State Project Director (SPD). He is the Member Secretary of the General Body and Executive Committee. The first meeting of the General Body of the SSA Mission has taken place on the 3rd February, 2003 with Shri O. Ibobi Singh, Hon'ble Chief Minister of Manipur as the President. As part of SSA activities, the state has opened Block Resource Centres and Cluster Resource Centres in the state of Manipur. The lists of Resource Centres in the Ukhrul district are: (i) Ukhrul, (ii) Kamjong, (iii) Phungyar, (iv) Kasom, and (v) Chingai.

List of cluster resource centres in respect of Ukhrul district is:

(i) Ukhrul Block

1. Zonal Education office, Ukhrul
2. K.K. Leishiphanit Jr. High School
3. Tuinem High School, Tuinem
4. Mangkot Chepu High School, Mangot Chepu.

(ii) Chingai Block

1. Chingai High School, Chingai

2. Kharasom Junior High School, Kharasom
3. Raphei School
4. Paocham High School, Paocham

(iii) Phungyar Block

1. Phungyar High School, Phungyar
2. Shingkap High School, Shing
3. Ripha Junior High School
4. Sorde High School, Sorde

(iv) Kamjong Block

1. Kamjong High School, Kamjong
2. Chatrid Junior High School, Chatrid
3. Grihang Junior High School, Grihang
4. Chammu Junior High School, Chammu.

(v) Kasom Khullen Block

1. Kasom Khullen High School, Kasom Khullen
2. Kasung Junior High School, Kasung
3. Lower Junior High School, Lower Khoiripok
4. Lairam Phungka.

Alternative and Innovative Education Bridge Course (AIE)

Under the SSA, many programmes were taken-up and out of these; the AIE is one of the important programmes which were successfully implemented so far. AIE is an important institution for drop-out students between the age groups of 9-14 years old. The main aim of the AIE is to educate the children who are unable to study on various reasons.

There are two types of Alternative and Innovative Education Bridge Courses:

(i) *Non-Residential Bridge Course* called NRBC is a six month course. This NRBC is open in nine villages with twenty four centres. In each centre, there is one education volunteer and not less than fifteen students. Altogether there are around about five hundred students in NRBC. In all the centres teaching-learning materials has been provided. In a day, class has been taken for not less than four hours and in order to function more effectively, VEC (Village Education Committee) was appointed to look after the NRBC and from time to time, monthly report have been given to VEC.

(ii) *Residential Bridge Course:* In Ukhrul district, five NGOs have been appointed to implement this programme and among the five NGOs, PASDO (Participatory Action for Sustainable Development Organization) implemented this programme in September 2006. Residential Bridge Course Centre of Ukhrul district is established in Alungtang, Ukhrul. This institution mainly focuses on the education of girl who could not study at all or girls who drop-out in the age group of 12-15 years of age. As per the record of 2006, fifty drop-out students were admitted and classes started at 9.30 A.M. and continue till 2.00 P.M. To look after the students two education volunteers were appointed. As a result, they also gave vocational training like making soap, jam, jelly, pickle, bread, cards etc. and also rear pigs, learn how to maintain a kitchen garden.[14]

Under the Sarva Shiksha Abhiyan Projects very good schemes were introduced like mid-day meal, provision of free textbook from class I to class VIII etc. to the students. Recruitment of teacher for primary teachers and upper primary teachers were done and appointed to each districts of Manipur state. Various programmes of construction like class room, toilet and kitchen construction were taken up under SSA programmes. However, various schemes under SSA were not successful due to improper management and misappropriate funds by the concerned authority. In spite of its difficulty, shortcomings and lapses of its implementation of its scheme under SSA, yet it brought many changes from bad to good at least for the student's community at large.

According to Census of India 2011, the literacy rate of male and female of the Ukhrul district is 86.05 per cent and 77.47 per cent respectively.[15] According to the census of 2011, the total literacy rate of Ukhrul district is 81.87 per cent. Her population is 1,83,115 out of 27,21,756 of the total population of the State of Manipur. There are about 268 Tangkhul villages in Ukhrul district and outside the district of Ukhrul. The district has a population density of 40 inhabitants per square kilometer. Its population growth rate over the decade 2001-2011 was 30.07 per cent. Ukhrul district has a sex-ratio of 948 female for every 1000 males, and a literacy rate of 81.87 per cent out of which 77.47 belongs to female literacy rate of the Ukhrul district of Manipur.

The Government of Manipur has recognized Tangkhul language as major language in the state and therefore, Tangkhul language is being introduced as Modern Indian Language (MIL) subject up to XII class. As per the Report 2013-14 of the Zonal Education Office, the following are the existing Schools, colleges and institutions of the Ukhrul district of Manipur. There are 10 Higher Secondary Schools (5 Government + 5 Private), High Schools 67 (43 Government + 24 Private), Junior High Schools 51 (41 Government + 10 Private), Aided Schools 36, Primary Schools (under ZEO) 76, Primary (ADC) 158, Colleges 4 (1 Government + 3 Private), NIOS 3, and Central Schools.

There are 1973 Government teachers working including Autonomous District Council and Aided Schools teachers. In the private sectors, the existing teachers are only 1162. Out of the five Blocks in Ukhrul district, there are 3135 teachers as per the report. Forty eight thousand four hundred twenty two (48,422) students were enrolled from classes I-XII standard in the Ukhrul district. The students are mostly Scheduled Tribes communities. Frequent transfer of teachers from hill districts to Imphal valley was one of the major common problem of the marginalised people. They transferred even before the probation period was completed. Because some teachers preferred their own home town, and place like Imphal in order to assist and look after their families and relatives. Staying far away from home town and families was also a matter of great concern for the teachers irrespective of communities. There are no teacher's quarters in almost all the schools with exception of school like Ukhrul Higher Secondary School. Sharing room and toilet in the far flung village was a matter of great problem for the teachers. Another factor was that road communication was very bad; and in some villages there is no motorable road in the hill district of Manipur. Ukhul Higher Secondary School is the only Higher Secondary School at Ukhrul town. There is no mathematics teacher (Lecturer) for teaching in classes XI and XII. It is like fish without water.

Manipur is a beautiful multilingual state with a formation of 38 different ethno-cultural communities. They are Aimol, Anal, Angami, Chiru, Chothe, Gante, Hmar, Inpui, Koirao (Thangal), Koireng, Kom, Kharam, Lamkang, Liangmai, Mao, Maram, Maring, Mate, Meitei, Pangal (Muslim), Mizo, Monsang, Moyon, Nepali, Paitc, Paumai, Purum, Ralte, Ruangmei (Kabui), Sahlte, Sema, Simte, Tangkhul, Thangal, Thadou-Kuki, Vaiphei, Zeme and Zou. The 35 tribal language groups predominantly live in the hill district of Chandel, Churachandpur, Senapati, Tamenglong and Ukhrul with their sizeable tribal population in all valley districts of Imphal East, Imphal West, Bisnupur and Thoubal.[16]

In Manipur, the performances of Education Department with regards to instruction in mother tongue of marginalised tribal communities are completely dismal and upsetting. As such, the tribal languages are totally ignored for the growth of tribal languages like the Manipuri, English and Hindi languages. At national level, languages, especially linguistic minorities are given top priority for national integration, because India is a multilingual country. Out of the 35 tribal languages, only 10 tribal languages have been approved as major tribal dialects of Manipur. They are Hmar, Kom, Mao, Mizo (Lushai), Paite, Ruangmei (Kabui), Tangkhul, Thadou-Kuki, Vaiphei and Zou. Thus, the remaining 25 tribal language groups are deprived of the opportunity of learning in their mother tongues in the schools.[17]

The marginalised tribal mother tongues in Manipur are suppressed by the State Government. As such, the 10 tribal languages were approved by the Government of Manipur without giving proper fund. Therefore, the respective literature societies are running from pillars to posts to bring out their school textbooks in tribal languages whereas textbooks of English, Hindi and Manipuri are developed and printed at the expense of the State Government borne by the Board of Secondary Education of Manipur. There is neither maintenance grant nor any sort of financial assistance from the State Government for the growth and development of literature societies of tribal languages in Manipur.[18]

Only small amount of money was provided under Tribal Research of Institutes of Manipur Government. That was only Rs. 8 lakh (4:4 State + Centre fund) for 10 approved languages for the printing of school text book at a rate of Rs. 25,000 for the year 2010-11 and Rs. 29,000 was sanctioned for the year 2011-12.

Whereas the actual needs for printing of a single textbook of one particular language was around 1 lakh.[19]

Over 900 marginalized tribal students of Manipur University including Research scholars and other undergoing studies in various departments of the varsity sit – in protest to demand withdrawal of the resolution adopted by the Manipur University Academic Educational Institutions (Reservation in Admission) Act, 2006. Under the aforesaid 2006 Act, Scheduled Tribe (ST) students will be provided only 7.5 per cent seats in admission, Scheduled Caste will be provided only 15 per cent, and other backward classes will be provided 27 per cent. No tribal student will enter the Manipur University Campus until authorities concerned give a written assurance, stated by Manipur Tribal Students Union (MUTSO) President Mr. Thangtinlen Haokip.[20]

The marginalised tribal students' organisations like Manipur University Tribal Students' Union (MUTSU), All Tribal Students Association Manipur (ATSUM), All Naga Students Organisation Manipur (ANSAM), Kuki Students Organisation (KSO) and other tribal organisations protesting against reverting the decision of the Academic Council of the Manipur University to follow the reservation norms of 2006 in admission. According to the Central Education Institutions (CEI) Reservation in Admission Act, 2006 was amended in 2012 and as per the amendment, the reservation policy applicable in Manipur University should be SC-2 per cent, ST-31 per cent, and OBC-17 per cent. The CEI Amendment of 2012 has been in operation in Manipur University for the last two academic sessions in accordance with the directive from the UGC on October 5, 2015. Reverting to the 2006 reservation policy as decided by the Academic Council of Manipur University is not only unwarranted, but is also a serious breach of the directive from the UGC.[21]

The adoption of the reservation of 15 per cent for SC, 7.5 per cent for ST and 27 per cent for OBC was also in violation of the order passed by the High Court of Manipur which ruled that the percentages of reservation for STs, SCs, and OBCs shall be 31 per cent, 2 per cent and 17 per cent respectively for admission to various courses in Manipur University alleged by Democratic Education Students' Association Manipur (DESAM). This was also in violation of the directive of the High Court of Manipur which issued an order on September, 2015 and again reiterated it on October 3,

2016 claimed by DESAM. Stating that denying the entitled reservation share of STs in admission will be a serious deprivation of the rights of STs in Manipur. According to DESAM, as per the 2011 Census, the population of ST in Manipur was 43 per cent of the population of the state while the SCs constituted 3.8 per cent. Thus, the denial of the entitled reservation share of 31 per cent to the ST students will further increase the gap between the hill and valley people said by DESAM.[22] On the other hand, NPF (Naga People's Front) of Manipur unit categorically stated that the percentage of the Scheduled Tribes of Manipur is 45 per cent as per the latest information.[23]

Conclusion

We need to address various issues and problems of the marginalised people with holistic approach by avoiding ethnic-identity of the various communities living in Manipur. The Central and State Governments need to look into the matter very seriously in order to bring equilibrium society in respect of economy, education, politics etc. The civil societies should not emphasis of their own community rather they should also think and do needful for other weaker section of people who are living under poverty line. They should not dictate to government for their own benefits and interests. The simple reason is that the state belongs to multi-ethnic groups of communities not to a particular majority community. Think for other communities are helping to the government; because government belongs for the people.

Notes

1. Allen, B.C., 2011, *Gazetteer of Naga Hills and Manipur,* New Delhi: Mittal Publications, p. 1.
2. Gupta, R., 2014, *Manipur General Knowledge,* New Delhi: Ramesh Publishing House, pp. 35-36.
3. Brown, R., 1975, *Statistical Accounts of Manipur,* Sankaran Prakashan, Delhi.
4. Dun, E.W., 1975, *Gazetteer of Manipur and Naga Hills,* Delhi: Vivek Publishing House, p. 26.
5. Johnstone, James, 1983, *Manipur and Nagas Hills,* Delhi: Cultural Publishing House, p. 144.

6. *Administrative Report of the Manipur Political Agency for 1891-92,* Published by Government of Manipur, p. 12.
7. Minutes of Assam Missionary Conference 5th Session on 11-19, February, 1899, p. 20.
8. Shimrei, Console Zamreinao, 2014, *English Education among the Tangkhul Naga of the Ukhrul District of Manipur from 1894-2013,* in (Eds.) Bhattacharjee, J.B., Qadri, F.A., and Passah, Amena, Proceedings of North East India History Association, Simaluguri, 2014, p. 419.
9. *Ibid.*
10. *Pettigrew Report and Letters,* Champhang Jajo, 1891-91, Ukhrul, p. 8.
11. Shimrei, Zamreinao Console, *op. cit.,* p. 420.
12. *Ibid.,* p. 422.
13. *Ibid.*
14. Shangjam, Ringmichon, 2007, "*Women and Social Change in Tangkhul Society*", Unpublished Ph.D. Thesis, Department of History, Manipur University Canchipur, Imphal, pp. 139-143.
15. Shimray, U.A., "Education in Tangkhul Naga Region," *The Legacy: A Bi-Monthly Journal,* Vol. 1, p. 23.
16. Ragongning Gangmei, 2012, *State Apathy of Tribal-languages in Manipur,* Council of Tribal Languages and Literature Societies, printed at BCPW, Imphal, pp. 9-10.
17. *Ibid.,* p. 20.
18. *Ibid.,* pp. 20-25.
19. *Ibid.,* pp. 40-41.
20. *Ibid.*
21. *The People's Chronicle,* dated 12th October, 2016, p. 1.
22. *The Sangai Express,* Manipur, dated 13th October, 2016, p. 1.
23. *Ibid.,* p. 2.

4

Medium of Instruction in the Educational Development of Primary School Children

A Study Among the Tribal Children of Karbi Anglong

Hiranya Saikia

Introduction

Medium of instruction is a very important variable which determine the entire educational environment of primary school. Majority of the eminent educationists and researchers in education reveal that mother tongue is the best medium of instruction to communicate with the young children specially, at primary school stage. They can develop right concept on the subject matter and knowledge becomes permanent in teaching learning process when the teacher use mother tongue as a medium of instruction. The population structure of Karbi Anglong district is to some extent different from the other plain districts of Assam. The tribal population is the highest in the district and among tribals the Karbi placed top position according to census report. There are more than thirty two communities in the district and the present tribal population comprises more than 60 per cent of the total population of the district. There are Assamese medium, English medium, Bodo medium, Bengali medium and Hindi medium government and provincialised primary schools in Karbi Anglong. However, there is no Karbi medium government and provincialised primary school in the district. Majority of the primary schools are Assamese medium. The medium of instruction in the Assamese medium school is completely Assamese. Similarly, English is the medium of instruction in the English medium schools, Bodo is the medium of instruction in the Bodo medium schools, Bengali is the medium of instruction in the Bengali medium schools and Hindi is the medium of instruction in the Hindi medium schools. The teachers do not use tribal language as medium of instruction for the tribal student. Therefore, the investigator has an interest to know whether the tribal students those who have been studying in the Assamese, English or Hindi medium schools understand the teaching of the teachers properly or not? Do the primary school teachers face any problem in communicating with the tribal students using Assamese or English as a medium of instruction? To find out the answers of the above questions, the present study was taken up with the following objectives.

Objectives of the Present Study

In the present investigation an attempt is being made to realise the following objectives:

(i) To study the different medium of instruction used in the primary schools in Karbi Anglong.
(ii) To study whether the present medium of instruction create any problem to the tribal pupils in the primary schools of Karbi Anglong.
(iii) To suggest some remedial measures to overcome the problems.

Method of Data Collection

The survey method was used for the present study. The data required for the present study was collected from 177 tribal pupils and 177 Headmasters/teachers of 177 primary schools of Karbi Anglong. Besides, secondary data were collected from various sources such as – government office, institutions and websites to achieve the objectives of the study.

Delimitation of the Study

The present study is limited to the government, provincialised and recognised primary schools of Karbi Anglong located in rural, semi-urban and urban areas. The primary data were collected from 177 primary schools of Karbi Anglong and opinion was taken from 177 tribal pupils and 177 tribal and non-tribal teachers.

Sampling

Sampling is the process of selecting a sample from the total population. In the present study purposive sampling technique has been adopted by the investigator. There are three sub-divisions and eleven educational blocks in undivided Karbi Anglong district. Two blocks have been selected from each sub-division and ten per cent schools from each block have been selected for this study. Block-wise highest number of primary schools in the tribal dominated areas are found in Lumbajong and Howraghat block of Diphu sub-division, Bokajan and Nilip block of Bokajan sub-division, Chinthong and Rongkhang Block of Hamren sub-division. Therefore, the schools have been selected from these six blocks.

Tools

The standard and quality of research depends on the use of valid and reliable tools use for the research work. There are two types of tools generally used by the researcher for the investigation. Standardised tool and self-developed tool. In this study, the investigator used self-developed tool for the investigation.

Preparation of Questionnaire and Problem Check-List

For this study a questionnaire schedule is prepared for the primary school teachers of Karbi Anglong to collect the information regarding medium of instruction of the schools. Two problem check-lists were prepared, one for teachers and another for tribal children of primary school to check out the problems related to medium of instruction of the primary school children.

Analysis of Data

There are 1802 government and provincialised primary schools in Karbi Anglong. The majority of these primary schools are Assamese medium. Now, the tribal people demand for establishment of more and more English medium primary schools in the district and even the economically backward tribal parents also prefer to send their children to English medium primary school. Thirty five per cent government and provincialised primary schools in Karbi Anglong are English medium and other English medium primary schools are private. But economically backward parents cannot send their children to private English medium school and they demand for establishment of more English medium government school in the district. Due to the increasing demand for English medium schools, the authority of Karbi Anglong Autonomous Council has initiated converting the Assamese medium primary schools into English medium gradually and phase-wise. In table 4.1, medium-wise total number of primary school is presented.

Table 4.1: The Medium-wise Total Primary Schools in Karbi Anglong

Medium	*Number of Schools*	
	2013-14	*2015-16*
Assamese	1019	959
Bengali	46	30
Bodo	56	56
English	623	708
Hindi	28	49
Total	**1772**	**1802**

Source: SSA, Karbi Anglong Autonomous Council's Report.

The authority of Karbi Anglong Autonomous Council, Diphu introduced Karbi Language as a compulsory subject in all primary schools in Karbi Anglong district with effect from the academic session 2003-2004 *vide* Karbi Anglong Autonomous Council's notification No. KAAC/PED/138/KL/2003-04/708 (A), dated the 11th June, 2003. On the basis of the Karbi Anglong Autonomous Council's notification, the district primary education department, Karbi Anglong notified an another order to implement the Karbi language as a compulsory subject at primary school stage *vide* District Primary Education department notification No. KAAC/PED/KLA/2003/103/5990, dated the 20th June, 2003. According to this notification, the introduction of Karbi Language should be started from class-I and on phase-wise up to class-IV in all primary schools including the non-governmental primary schools, established with prior approval of Karbi Anglong Autonomous Council. The authority of Karbi Anglong Autonomous Council has strongly emphasised on the following guidelines for proper implementation of this order:

1. Students in all classes in primary schools must obtain minimum qualifying marks in Karbi Language to be eligible for promotion to next higher class.
2. No financial assistance/grant should be extended to any private school in case of non-compliance of this order.
3. The order of allotment of land and Council's recognition etc. may be withdrawn in case of non-compliance against any private school/schools.

In this regard all the Block Primary Education Officers were directed to take immediate necessary steps to implement the order and personally supervise the implementation of the order accordingly. It was also strict order to all non-governmental Lower Primary schools that their recognition would be withdrawn if they do not comply with this order.

The Karbi Anglong Autonomous Council introduced Karbi Language as a compulsory subject in all primary schools in the district, but it created some problems in the implementation of the policy. The great challenge in this respect was the preparation and construction of curriculum and textbook in Karbi language. The primary education curriculum is prepared by State Council of Educational Research and Training (SCERT), Kahilipara, Guwahati. There are lack of resource and expert person to frame and construct the curriculum of Karbi Language in SCERT. Therefore, with due permission from the Government of Assam, the authority of Karbi Anglong Autonomous Council constituted a Karbi Language Development Board *vide* Karbi Anglong Autonomous Council's notification No. KAAC/PED/KATA & PB-30/pt-1/4780, dated the 5th December, 2006 with the following officials:

1. *Chairman:* Chief Executive Member (CEM)/Executive Member (EM) i/c Education, KAAC.
2. *Vice Chairman:* Principal Secretary, KAAC.

3. *Secretary Member:* Mr. Wophong Engti, Development Officer, Karbi Language Development Board.
4. *Members:* (a) Mr. C.S. Teron, Deputy Secretary, PED, KAAC
   (b) Mr. Rowelson Rongpi, Asstt. Inspector of Schools
   (c) Mr. B.S. Teron, DEEO, Elementary Education Department
   (d) Mr. Arun Teron, SDEEO, Diphu Sub-Division
   (e) Mr. Pani Ram Engti, SDEEO, Hamren Sub-Division
   (f) Mr. Ram Sing Terang, SDEEO, Bokajan Sub-Division
   (g) Mr. Bidya Sing Kro, Educationist and Writer
   (h) Mr. Bidor Sing Rongpi, Educationist and Writer
   (i) Mr. Sarthe Singnar, Teacher
   (j) Mr. Suren Kramsa, Teacher
   (k) Mr. Samay Senar, Teacher
   (l) Mr. Benjamin Terang, Subject Teacher.

A Karbi language Text Book Preparation Committee was formed under Karbi Language Development Board and Longkam Teron was the first chairman of this Committee. This committee prepared the Karbi language textbook for primary and upper primary school and follow the guideline of national curriculum framework while constructing the curriculum and textbook. The constructed curriculum is sent to State Council of Educational Research and Training (SCERT) for approval.

The Status of the Karbi Medium Schools

The Karbi language has been introduced as a compulsory subject in all government, provincialised and private primary schools in the district since 2004, but there is no Karbi medium government and provincialsed school in Karbi Anglong. There are 28 Karbi medium primary schools in Karbi Anglong and all the Karbi medium primary schools are administered and organised by local body and Karbi Anglong Autonomous Council. The financial assistance to run these schools is provided by Karbi Anglong Autonomous Council. In some of these schools, the building grant is provided by Karbi Anglong Autonomous Council. The salary of the teachers is provided by Karbi Anglong Autonomous Council. The appointment of the teachers is given by the Karbi Anglong Autonomous Council on purely contractual basis for eleven months and every year a fresh interview is organised. The medium of instruction in the Karbi Medium Schools is completely Karbi.

Impact of Medium of Instruction on Primary School Children

The population structure of Karbi Anglong district is to some extent different from the other plain districts of Assam. The tribal population is the highest in the district and among tribals the Karbi placed top position according to census report. The teachers do not use tribal language as medium of instruction for the tribal student. In some schools, children of different tribal communities take admission and their language are different from one another. It is not possible for the teacher to use different tribal language to communicate with the children of different tribal communities. In some rural and very backward areas, the tribal children do not understand Assamese or English language properly and they understand their own tribal language only. Even their parents also do not understand other than their own tribal language. In such cases, it is a great challenge for the teacher to teach the tribal children and ultimately the medium of instruction adversely affect the teaching learning process. In Table 4.2, the opinion of the teacher respondents about impact of use of other than tribal languages in teaching-learning process on the tribal children is presented.

Table 4.2: Impact of Use of Non-Tribal Language as Medium of Instruction among Tribal Students

Type of Respondents	*Question*	*Percentage of Responses*	
		Yes	*No*
Teacher	When the medium of instruction is not tribal language, is it understood by tribal student?	71.19	28.81
Student	Do you think that if the medium of instruction is your mother tongue, it would be more comfortable for you to understand the subject matter?	89.83	10.17

Source: Field Survey.

In Table 4.2, 71.19 per cent of the teacher respondents reveal that when the medium of instruction is other than tribal language, the tribal students understand the subject matter. On the other hand, 28.81 per cent of the teacher respondents reveal that when the medium of instruction is not tribal language for the tribal students, they do not understand the subject matter of teaching properly. On the other hand, 89.83 per cent student respondents reveal that if the medium of instruction is mother tongue, it would be more comfortable for them to understand the subject matter more clearly. During the fieldwork investigator observed that the tribal children of rural areas of Karbi Anglong do not understand the Assamese or English language properly and they understand only their mother tongue. Even some illiterate tribal parents of very backward areas of the district do not understand other than their mother tongue. It was my practical experience, when I visited a very backward tribal village of Dhanshiri area, a female parent respondent from Dimasa community did not understand the Assamese language and she understood only the Dimasa language. Similarly, in a backward tribal village of Hamren sub-division where the people of only Karbi community live, an illiterate male parent did not understand Assamese language. The investigator had to take the help of translator from respective community to communicate with such parents. In rural and backward areas where the tribal children do not get the opportunity to come in to close touch with other than their own community, such children have less opportunity to learn other language. It is a great challenge for the non-tribal teacher to teach these children at the primary school stage.

Medium of Instruction and Educational and Language Background of Teacher

Medium of instruction at primary school is a controversial issue in tribal areas like Karbi Anglong. There are thirty two communities in Karbi Anglong district including a large number of tribal communities. Different tribal groups use their own language and Assamese language is used by all tribal groups to communicate with one another. There are Assamese (959), English (708), Bodo (56), Bengali (30) and Hindi (49) medium government and provincialised primary schools in Karbi Anglong district. Karbi language is not used as a medium of instruction in the government and provincialised primary schools. Children from different tribal and non-tribal communities study in the same government or provincialised primary school and it is not possible for the teachers to communicate with children using different language. So, in Assamese medium primary schools, the teacher use Assamese language as medium of instruction, in English medium primary schools the teacher use English language as medium of instruction, in Bodo medium primary schools the teacher use Bodo language as medium of instruction, in Bangali medium primary schools the teacher use Bangla as medium of instruction and so on. However, use of different languages as medium of instruction in different primary schools, sometimes create problem both for the teacher and the tribal students. During the field survey, a few teacher respondents reported to the investigator that the district authority do not appoint the teacher on the basis of educational and language background. For example, sometimes a teacher having educational qualification from English medium background is appointed in Assamese medium school, a tribal teacher is appointed in Bangali medium school, a teacher from Karbi community is appointed in a Bodo medium school, and so on. These types of appointment create a great problem in teaching-learning process. However, the opinion of the teacher and student respondents in this regard is presented in Table 4.3:

Table 4.3: Problem Statement Regarding Medium of Instruction

Type of Respondents	*Nature of the Problem*	*Percentage of Responses*		
		Always	*Most of the Time*	*Not at all*
Teacher	The present medium of instruction causes problem in communicating with the tribal students.	55.37	35.59	9.04
Student	I find difficult to understand the teaching of the teacher in the present medium.	26.55	41.24	32.20
Student	I find difficult to understand the lesson in the present medium as I have to study myself at home.	31.64	52.54	15.82

Source: Field Survey.

In Table 4.3, 55.37 per cent of the teacher respondents reveal that the present medium of instruction always causes problem in communicating with the tribal students, 35.59 per cent of the teacher respondents reveal that the present medium of instruction most of the time causes problem in communicating with the tribal students and only 9.04 per cent of the teacher respondents reveal that there is no problem in communicating with the tribal students using the present medium of instruction. Here more than 90 per cent of the teacher respondents reveal that the present medium of instruction always and most of the time causes problem in communicating with the tribal students. On the other hand, 26.55 per cent of the student respondents reveal that they always find difficult to understand the teaching of the teacher in the present medium, 41.24 per cent of the student respondents reveal that they most of the time find difficult to understand the teaching of the teacher in the present medium and 32.20 per cent of the student respondents reveal that they do not find difficult to understand the teaching of the teacher in the present medium. The primary data reveal that approximately 67 per cent of the student respondents always and most of the time find difficult to understand the teaching of the teacher in the present medium.

Major Findings

1. There are 1802 government and provincialised primary schools in Karbi Anglong. Out of these 959 Assamese medium, 708 English medium, 56 Bodo medium, 30 Bengali medium and 49 Hindi medium government and provincialised primary schools in Karbi Anglong. But there is no Karbi medium government and provincialsed school in Karbi Anglong.
2. Now, the tribal people demand for establishment of more and more English medium primary schools in the district and even the economically backward tribal parents also prefer to send their children to English medium primary school. Due to the increasing demand for English medium schools, the authority of Karbi Anglong Autonomous Council has initiated converting the Assamese and Bengali medium primary schools into English medium gradually and phase-wise.
3. 89.83 per cent student respondents reveal that if the medium of instruction is mother tongue, it would be more

comfortable for them to understand the subject matter more clearly.

4. 28.81 per cent of the teacher respondents reveal that when the medium of instruction is not tribal language for the tribal students, they do not understand the subject matter of teaching properly.
5. 55.37 per cent of the teacher respondents reveal that the present medium of instruction (Assamese and English) always causes problem in communicating with the tribal students and 35.59 per cent of the teacher respondents reveal that the present medium of instruction most of the time causes problem in communicating with the tribal students.
6. 26.55 per cent of the student respondents reveal that they always find difficult to understand the teaching of the teacher in the present medium and 41.24 per cent of the student respondents reveal that they most of the time find difficult to understand the teaching of the teacher in the present medium.

Conclusion and Suggestions

Educational status of the teacher impacts upon the educational environment of the school. The standard of education and quality of teaching depend upon the educational qualification of the teacher. Investigator collected data from 177 primary school teachers of the district and out of 177 respondents only 53 respondents qualified the basic training course. The percentage of trained teacher is only 29.94 per cent. The distribution of the teacher respondents according to educational qualification is presented in Table 4.4.

Table 4.4: Distribution of the Teacher Respondents according to Educational Qualification *(in %)*

Educational Qualification	*Percentage of Respondents*
Under HSLC (Below Class X standard)	24.86
HSLC passed (Class X standard passed)	47.46
PU/ HSSLC passed (Class XI standard passed)	19.21
Graduate	8.47
Post-graduate	Nil
Total	**100**

Source: Field Survey.

Table 4.4 indicates the distribution of teacher respondents according to educational qualification.Table 4.4 shows that the educational qualification of 24.86 per cent of the teacher respondents are below X standard, 47.46 per cent of the respondents are HSLC or X standard passed, 19.21 per cent of the respondents are Pre-University/HSSLC or XII standard passed, 8.47 per cent of the respondents are graduate and no teacher respondent is found having post-graduate degree in the primary schools in Karbi Anglong district. Table 4.4 clearly indicates that majority of the primary school teachers of the district is only HSLC or X standard passed, i. e. 47.46 per cent.

The minimum educational qualification for appointment of primary school teacher is XII standard pass in any stream. However, approximately twenty years back, due to the lack of local qualified teacher, Karbi Anglong Autonomous Council relaxed the minimum educational qualification for appointment of primary school teacher and Karbi Anglong Autonomous Council appointed some candidate even under class X standard also. Now, the syllabus and curriculum of primary school have been changed and Government of Assam also follow the instructions of National curriculum framework and the modal of NCERT curriculum. Meanwhile, the class V has been attached with the primary school since 2010 in Assam and the curriculum of class V is difficult for some teachers those who are academically and professionally underqualified. It may be mentioned that, during the field visit some teachers, confessed in front of the investigator about the inability of teaching English and Mathematics in the upper classes of primary school. Among those teachers the educational qualification of majority of the primary school teacher is below X standard, i.e. H.S.L.C. failed.

Medium of instruction is a great constraint in the development of primary education among the tribal children in Karbi Anglong. It is the responsibility of the government and policy-makers to take proper steps to solve the problem of medium of instruction of the tribal children of different tribal communities in Karbi Anglong. The experiences gained at the time of field study, the investigator felt the need of following remedial measures to be considered to remove the problem of medium of instruction among the tribal children in Karbi Anglong.

1. The environment of the schools should be improved to make school more attractive for the tribal children. The behaviour of the

teachers should be impressive and children friendly. The teachers should understand the tribal tradition and culture so as to apprehend the actual need, nature, attitude and desire of the tribal children. In this regard, the non-tribal teachers may be given the knowledge of tribal language, culture, tradition, custom, believes and attitudes and it may be included in the formal training programme. If it is not possible to include in the curriculum of the formal training programme, then short term training programme may be organised for the non-tribal teachers those who have been serving in the tribal dominated areas.

2. There is lack of trained teachers in the primary schools in the district. In service teacher training is necessary for the teachers to motivate them for quality education in the tribal areas. The non-tribal teachers may be given special training to teach in tribal areas including imparting knowledge of the tribal language. Relevant and quality teaching learning equipments should be provided to schools and the teachers should be trained to use those equipments in a proper manner.

3. Special training programme on English language may be organised for underqualified teachers in DIET or BTC. The pre-primary school section ('Ka' class) have been recently attached to the primary schools. In the tribal dominated areas separate teacher may be appointed from the respective tribal community for 'Ka' class. Preference may be given to the lady teacher for 'Ka' class.

4. Textbooks may be provided in mother tongue for the Scheduled Tribe children in the beginning of the primary education where they do not understand regional language. There is a need to develop curricular and devise instructional materials in tribal language at the initial stage. In the tribal dominated areas at least one teacher from respective Scheduled Tribe community may be appointed in each school and the responsibility of teaching in the lower classes may be given to that teacher, so that quality education can be imparted without giving the burden of learning a second language among the Scheduled Tribe children.

References

Ambasht, N.K., 1979. *A Critical Study of Tribal Education,* Delhi: S. Chand & Company Ltd., Ram Nagar.

Barpujari, H.K., 1963. *Assamese: In the Days of Company,* Guwahati: Lawyer's Book Stall.

Barpujari, H.K., 1983. *American Missionary Sakal Aru Unabingsha Satikar Asom,* Assam Sahitya Sabha.

Baruah, B., 1990. *The Karbis of the Hills,* Guwahati.

Bordoloi, Bulen Chandra, 1982. *Karbi Jatir Itibritya,* Diphu, Kiran Prakash.

Gohain, B.K., 1984. *The Hills Karbis,* Smt. A. Gohain, Diphu.

Lyall Charles, 1908, *The Mikirs,* Guwahati: United Publishers, Panbazar.

Lyall, S.C., 1997. *The Karbis,* Guwahati: Spectrum Publications.

Phangcho, Dr. P.C., 2001. *Karbi Anglong and North Cachar Hills – A Study on Geography and Culture,* Published by Author.

Rongphar, B., 2005. *Karbi Anglongor Rajnoitik Itihas,* Diphu: Phu Phu Publication.

Stack, Edward., 1908. *The Mikirs,* (Edited, arranged and supplemented by Charles Lyall), United Publisher, Panbazar, Guwahati-1.

Teron, L., 1961. *Mikir Janajati,* Asom Sahitya Sabha.

Unpublished Ph.D. Thesis

Hira, M.C. Dr., 1992. "Impact of Education on the Society and Culture of the People of the District of Karbi Anglong." Gauhati University, Assam.

Saikia, Menoka, 1987. "Development of Primary Education in the Karbi-Anglong District from 1951-1981". Gauhati University, Assam.

5

Educational Development of Tribals with Special Reference to Barmans of Assam and Tripuris of Tripura

Pranay Jyoti Goswami and *Subit Dutta*

Introduction

The Constitution of India has solemnly promised to all its citizens justices—social, economic and political; liberty of thought, expression, belief, faith and worship; equality of status and of opportunity; and to promote among all fraternity assuring the dignity of the individual and the unity of the nation. Article 19 enshrines the fundamental rights of the citizens of this country. The seven sub-clauses of Article 19(1) guarantee the citizens seven different kinds of freedom and recognize them as their fundamental rights.

Tribal population of India lags behind general population in terms of different parameters. In order to improve the lot of the tribal people, Article 46 of the Constitution of India states that, "The State shall promote, with special care, the education and economic interests of the weaker sections of the people, and, in particular of the Scheduled Castes and Scheduled Tribes, and shall protect them from social injustice and all forms of social exploitation". Articles 330, 332, 335, 338 to 342 and the entire Fifth and Sixth Schedules of the Constitution deal with special provisions for implementation of the objectives set forth in Article 46. These provisions need to be fully utilised for the benefit of these weaker sections in our society. Education as a means of advancement of capacity, well-being and opportunity is uncontested, and more so among communities on the periphery. Marked improvements in access and to some extent in quality of primary education in tribal areas have occurred, as a result of the initiatives taken by the Governmental and Non-governmental Organisations. However, the number of unschooled children continues to be several millions, mainly due to a lack of interest and parental motivation, inability to understand the medium of instruction (i.e. state language), teacher absenteeism and attitude, opportunity cost of time spent in school (particularly for girls), large seasonal migration etc. Low literacy rates in tribal communities continue to indicate a need for special support. Table 5.1 reveals that the literacy rate of Scheduled Tribe in India is much lower than that of general population.

Table 5.1: Literacy Rates among General and Scheduled Tribe Population in India

Years	*General*			*Scheduled Tribes*		
	Male	*Female*	*Total*	*Male*	*Female*	*Total*
1961	34.44	12.95	24.02	13.83	3.16	8.53
1971	39.45	18.70	29.45	17.63	4.85	11.30
1981	46.89	24.82	36.23	24.52	8.04	16.35
1991	64.1	39.3	52.2	40.65	18.19	29.60
2001	75.3	53.7	64.8	59.17	34.76	47.10
2011	84.54	60.46	72.99	68.16	49.97	58.96

Source: Selected Educational Statistics 2011-12, Ministry of Human Resource Development.

The growth rate in India has been increasing at a very rapid rate more particularly since 1995. But the benefit of growth has not been percolated to all the sections of the society. That is why the 11th Five Year Plan stressed on inclusive growth. It remarks, "Inclusive growth demands that all social groups have equal access to the services provided by the State and equal opportunity for upward economic and social mobility. It is also necessary to ensure that there is no discrimination against any section of our society. In India, certain social groups such as the SCs, STs, OBCs and Minorities have historically been disadvantaged and vulnerable. Then there are certain other groups which may be discriminated against and which suffer from handicaps. These include persons with disabilities, older persons, street children, beggars and victims of substance abuse. Our Constitution contains various provisions for the development of such marginalised groups, for instance, Article 341 for SCs, Article 342 for STs, Article 340 for OBCs, Article 30 which provides the right to minorities to establish and administer educational institutions, and so on. Their individual and collective growth, however, cannot be ensured without improving their surroundings and providing clean drinking water, toilets and educational opportunities".

Objectives of the Study

1. To discuss the present scenario of tribal educations in India with special reference to Barmans and Tripuris.
2. To discuss various supports given by Government to develop tribal education in the states.
3. To suggest measures to improve the situation so that social justice will be meaningful in our democratic state.

Methodology

The data sources of the present chapter are secondary comprising of books, journals, different reports, websites etc. For the simplicity of the analysis the chapter is divided into three sections. Section-I deals with the first objective. Section-II covers the support given by different government organizations to improve the educational scenario in the state and the last section-III concentrates on suggestion to make social justice meaningful in the states.

SECTION-I

Profile of Barak Valley of Assam

The Barak Valley region is situated between longitude 92° 15′ E and 90° 15′ E and 24° 8′ N and 25° 8′ N covering a geographical area of 6922 sq. km. The Valley is surrounded in the north by the Dima Hasao District of Assam and the Jaintia Hills district of Meghalaya, in the east, by Manipur, in the south by Mizoram, while in the west by Tripura and the Sylhet district of Bangladesh. The boundary clearly reflects that the Barak Valley is surrounded by hills from three sides and plain land from one side The Valley constitutes 8.9 per cent of the geographical area of the state.

The Barak Valley is a heterogeneous land of high hills, low lands and level plains. The Valley is the upward extension of Bengal Plains. Almost the entire area of old province of Bengal deltaic region succinctly described as new mud, old mud and marsh including Surma Valley has, however, a common structural and very similar way of life and a historic entity and linguistic and cultural unit. The entire Valley region is punctuated with high lands (locally called *tillah*) and low lands of an average height of less than thirty metres from the sea level. The highest hill range of Barail group of ranges which connects the North Manipur Hills and Khasi range along the north of Cachar district ranges between 2500 feet and 6000 feet. The average height represented by Jhiri Hill range which is the highest hill range within the jurisdiction of Barak Valley is about 7660 feet above the sea level. Some hills on the eastern side are as high as 2700 feet. Bhuban Hill which is the important range, south of Barak, runs north and south at a short distance of 700 to 3000 feet height. The Rengti Pahar range also runs north and south from the watershed between Sonai and Dhaleswari Rivers. The Tilain range also runs north and south (10 to 500 feet). The Sarispur or Sidheshwar Hill which formed the boundary of Cachar and Sylhet (before partition) varies from 600 to 2000 feet. Rest of the land of Barak Valley is flat land of an average height of 100 feet. The principal river of the Valley is Barak which rises on the southern slope of the lofty ranges of Nagaland and forms the northern boundary of Manipur.

Administratively, the Barak Valley region at present is comprised of three districts *viz.*, Cachar, Hailakandi and Karimganj. The district of Cachar alone accounts for 54.7 per cent of the total area of the Valley, the shares of the Hailakandi and Karimganj districts in the total area are 19.2 per cent and 26.1 per cent respectively. The district head-quarters of Cachar, Hailakandi and Karimganj are Silchar, Hailakandi and Karimganj respectively. Cachar is the largest and Hailakandi is the smallest district with total geographical areas of 3786 sq. km. and 1327 sq. km. respectively and that of Karimganj is 1809 sq. km. as per 2001 census. The importance of Cachar district block-wise as well as village-wise is also comparatively more than that of Hailakandi and Karimganj districts. Before the annexation of Cachar (present

Barak Valley) to British kingdom, the population was less than fifty thousand with density of 11.38 per sq. km. Gradually, the population began to expand with the development of agriculture. The colonial policy was also responsible for rapid demographic change. The partition of India and subsequent large scale influx of refugees from East Pakistan in different waves raised the population of Barak Valley, which consequently, affected the socio-economic and political dimensions of the Valley. The Valley contains 11.22 per cent of the population of state as per 2001 census. More than 15 per cent of the total population of Barak Valley is constituted by the tea and ex-tea garden labour community. Regarding average daily number of labourers employed in tea plantation, tea gardens in Barak Valley employed 69,815 labourers with an 11.29 per cent share of that of whole Assam in 2005.

The Barak Valley is mainly agriculture oriented and about 66 per cent of the working population depends on agriculture for maintaining their livelihood. The problems of agriculture in the Barak Valley are not different from that of Assam in general. The agriculture in this Valley is "characterised by many impediments such as small and uneconomic farm units, low cost intensity, low productivity, lack of proper irrigation facilities, inadequate credit. Besides, in agriculture and rural economy, tradition persisted very deep reducing the total productivity to a large extent. Excessive rain, flood and sometimes drought conditions here and there and paste attack on standing crops are some of the other problems which agriculture has to face every year." "Agriculture in the rainy months is mainly confined to the high lands which are free from waterlogging. Besides rice, jute and sugar canes are also grown here with no land available for reclamation and bringing under cultivation, agriculture cannot support more people in Cachar." The principal industry of the Valley is the Tea industry. There were 198 tea gardens with 31,894 hectares area under tea cultivation in 2005. Besides, Barak Valley produced 44,858 kg. of tea in 2005.

Growth Rate of Population

Decadal growth rate of population in Barak Valley and Assam has been presented in Table 5.2.

Table 5.2: Decadal Growth Rate of Population (1941-2001)

Years	*Total Population in the Barak Valley*	*Variation*	*Decadal Growth Rate (in %)*	
			Barak Valley	*Assam*
1941	895140	(+) 91446	(+) 11.38	20.40
1951	1115865	(+) 220725	(+) 24.66	19.93
1961	1378476	(+) 262611	(+) 23.53	34.98
1971	1713318	(+) 334842	(+) 24.29	34.95
1991	2491496	(+) 778178	(+) 45.42	53.26
2001	2995769	(+) 504273	(+) 20.23	18.92

Source: Directorate of Economics and Statistics, Government of Assam.

Table 5.2 shows that except 1941-51 and 1991-2001 decades, the growth rate of population in the Valley is always less than that of Assam as may whole. Table 5.2 also reveals that the growth rate of population in the Barak Valley has been rising very steeply since 1941-51 decade to 1991. This is perhaps because of influx of a large number of displaced persons from Sylhet and other districts of the then East Pakistan (presently Bangladesh).

Population by Religion

The population by religion in Barak Valley has been shown in Table 5.3.

Table 5.3: Population by Religion in Barak Valley

Religions	*1961*		*1971*		*2001*	
	Total	*% of Total*	*Total*	*% of Total*	*Total*	*% of Total*
Hindu	821600	59.60	1005995	58.72	1580660	52.76
Muslim	539457	39.13	683387	39.88	1362114	45.47
Christian	15178	1.12	22686	1.32	45476	1.52
Buddhist	311	0.02	308	0.02	1677	0.06
Jains	437	0.03	800	0.05	1970	0.07
Sikhs	39	0.00	141	0.01	765	0.03
Other Religion	1369	0.09	1	–	1791	0.06
Tribal Religion	85	0.01	–	–	1316	0.04
Total	**1378476**	**100**	**1713318**	**100**	**2995769**	**100**

Source: Statistical Hand Book, Assam, 1982 - 2005.

Table 5.3 reveals that the main religious communities in the Barak Valley are the Hindus and the Muslims. However, there are many Christians also in this Valley, who are mainly among the Hill Tribes like Hmar, Khasi, Tipra, Riang etc.

The Barmans of Cachar

The tribals of Barak Valley are falling into 3 (three) categories, *viz.*, (a) plain tribals, (b) hill tribals, (c) hill tribals without ST Status. (a) The Barmans (Kacharis) are recognised Scheduled Tribes in Cachar. Barmans are the Kachari community distributed mainly in the Barak Valley district of Assam. They speak in *dimasa,* which belongs to the Tibeto-Burman language family and use the Bengali script. The community is divided into eight clans and they use Thaosen, Hagjer and Barmans as surname. Both patriclans and matriclans are prevailed among them. The Barmans are non-vegetarian and rice is their staple food. The Barman practice both shifting and wet cultivation. They have accepted Hinuism long back. The Barman Kacharis are proud of their own music, dance forms, dress, folk-tales and folk-songs. They have keen interest to study. (b) The Hmars, Mizo, Kuki, Khasi and Jaintias, Nagas, Chakmas and Karbis were recognized Scheduled Tribes under Scheduled Caste and Scheduled Tribes Act, 1950 *vide* Ministry of Home Affairs, Government of India Notification No. S.R.O. 510 Dt. 6-9-1950, but not Recognised in plain district due to Areas Restriction. (c) The Bru (Reang), Tripura (including Kewa, Laitong, Gurjung, Gabeng) etc. Hrangkhol, Chorei, Sakechep, Saihriem, Aimol, Khawchung, Chiru, Vaiphei, Ranglong, Halam, Rupini (Barman). The lost tribe (clan) Rupini is a constituent of 12 Halam recognized in Tripura, but opted for Barman here in Assam. All the hill tribes are not recognised as Scheduled Tribes by the Govterment of India till date.

Profile of Tripura

Tripura is a tiny and hilly state in the North-east corner of India with an area of 10,491.65 sq. km. of land. This state is located in between 22° 56' N and 24° 32' North latitudes and 91° 09' E and 92°20' East longitudes. The state is bounded in the north by the Cachar district of Assam, in the west by Comilla and Noakhali district of Bangladesh, in the south by the district of Chittagong and in the east by the Mizo Hills of Mizoram covering about 182.4 kms in length from its north to south and 112 kms in breadth from its east to west. Of the total area of Tripura, about 60 per cent consists of hills, hillocks and hilly terrains of flat land stripped with turbulent serpentine rivulets and painted grey with barren tracts, lush green hue with wild growth. Tripura was a princely state and it was ruled by the Maharajas of Tripura. The rulers of this princely state have done many welfare works. After Independence, Tripura was merged with India on 15th October, 1949. Thereafter, Tripura was administered by the Chief Commissioner appointed by the Government of India.

Scheduled Tribes in Tripura

The Tripura Territorial Council (T.T.C.) was constituted in 1956 with total members of 32 out of which 2 were nominated members. The Government of India declared Tripura a full-fledged state on 21st January, 1972. The total population of Tripura as per 2001 census was 31,99,203, which has increased to 36, 71,032 as per 2011 provisional census report. 9,93,426 persons, i.e., 31.1 per cent of the total population of the state belonged to tribal population as per 2001 census. Diverse ethnic groups have been residing in the state. The state registered 16.4 per cent decadal growth of Scheduled Tribes population in the decade 1991 to 2001. There are 19 notified Scheduled Tribes in the state. They are Tripuri, Reang, Chakma, Jamatia, Halam, Noatia, Mog, Garo, Munda, Kuki, Lushai, Lepcha, Chaimal, Khasia, Urang, Santal, Uchai, Bhil and Bhutia.

Tripuris: Tripuris or *Tripra* is the largest tribal community in Tripura and comprises 54.74 per cent population in total tribes of Tripura. They have first migrated in this territory and could be introduced as aboriginal tribe of Tripura. Tripura was under the rule of *Tripuri* Kings till it was merged with Indian Dominion in the year 1949. *Tripuris* are mainly Animist. They worship different gods and nature. Garia, Kharchi, Ker are their main festivals. They have colourful folk dances like, Garia, Lebang, Musak surmani, and Mamita. These dances are invigorated with sweet melodies of folk songs and music flute, Sarinda, Champreng and other string instruments. *Tripuris* are now treated as an advanced tribal community among the tribes of Tripura.

Tribal Literacy in Tripura

Literacy rate of ST population in Tripura is much less than that of general population since independence. However, the rate has been rising (Table 5.4).

Table 5.4: Growth of Literacy among the ST and General Population in Tripura

Years	*Scheduled Tribes*		*General in the State*	
	Literacy Rate	*Decadal Growth*	*Literacy Rate*	*Decadal Growth*
1961	10.01	–	20.34	–
1971	15.03	5.02	30.39	6.15
1981	23.07	8.04	42.12	11.73
1991	40.4	17.33	60.39	18.27
2001	56.48	16.08	73.66	13.27
2011	NA	NA	87.8	14.14

Source: Census Reports 1961, 1971, 1981, 1991, 2001 and 2011 (Provisional). NA—Not Available

Table 5.4 depicts the picture of literacy rate among the Scheduled Tribes in comparison to overall literacy rate in the State Tripura. It clears that increase in literacy rate among Tribal over the period was slower than the other states up to 1991 census, but there was a rapid growth in literacy rate during the decade 1991 to 2001. Various reports also reveal high rate of drop-outs is prevailed among various tribal groups.

SECTION-II

Government of India as well as State Government has taken various measures in order to increase tribal educational status of the country. Pre-metric Scholarship is provided @ Rs. 40 per month for the students from classes VI to VIII and @ Rs. 50 per month for the students of classes IX to X for a period of 10 months in an academic year. Scheduled Tribe students reading in Senior basic/ Junior high/high/HS schools in Tripura shall be eligible for grant of Pre-metric Scholarship if he/she remain present at least 70 per cent of the total classes held in every month. The Post-Matric Scholarship scheme is in operation since 1944-45, and open to all ST students whose parents annual income is up to Rs. 1 lakh, to facilitate students to pursue professional courses. The students from KG-I to class X, staying in the approved Boarding Houses are given boarding House Stipend @ Rs. 30 per day per student and @ Re. 1 per day per student. There are 275 nos. of Boarding Houses altogether, out of which 111 nos. are run by the Non-Governmental Organizations as on 31st March, 2011. An amount of Rs. 58.9 crore was utilized to benefit seven lakh ST students in the Tenth Five Year Plan. The scheme of establishing Ashram schools in TSP areas provides funds for construction of school buildings as well as hostels and staff quarters. Seventy-eight Ashram schools with a capacity of 9610 seats were supported at a cost of Rs. 22.34 crore. The scheme of construction of hostels for ST boys and girls provides for the construction of new hostel buildings as well as extension of the existing hostel buildings. An amount of Rs. 57.84 crore was utilized for the construction of 120 hostels for 9884 students. The scheme of setting-up educational complexes is being implemented for promotion of education among tribal girls in 136 identified low literacy districts of the country. In the Tenth Five Year Plan, an amount of Rs. 62 crore was allotted under the scheme to set-up 76 complexes. A scheme for vocational training in tribal areas for developing the skills of tribal youth for a variety of jobs as well as self-employment is also in operation.

The Departments of Elementary Education and Literacy and of Higher Education in States have provided special incentives to ST students which include free textbooks up to class VIII and financial grant in lieu of textbooks to the students from Class IX to Degree Course. Special focus is also accorded to ST students under the District Primary Education Programme, Kasturba Gandhi Balika Vidyalaya, Mid-day meal etc. Government is also granting money in different schemes like Merit Award to Meritorious Students, Coaching for Madhyamik Final year Failed Student, Up-gradation of Merit, Establishment of Ashram School (Classes III to V), establishment of Ekalavya Model Residential School (Classes VI to XII) etc. In addition to the above mentioned facilities, Government grants stipend for Special Coaching in Core Subjects to the students of classes V to X, Coaching for Civil Service Examination/IAS/MBA, to Trainees at ITI/GNM/MPW etc.

However, the problem of adequacy of the school buildings, both in number and in facilities, still remains. The lack of education in the mother language or dialect in primary classes, ignorance of non-tribal teachers about tribal languages and ethos, delay in distribution of scholarships, textbooks and uniforms, continue to be sources of worry.

Development of Tribal Language

Right To Education by mother tongue is one of the human rights. UNESCO highlights the importance of mother tongue as part of the right to education and encourages its member states to promote instruction and education in the mother tongue. International Mother Language Day has been celebrated every year since February 2000 to promote linguistic and cultural diversity and multilingualism. This year the theme of the International Mother Language day is "Mother tongue instruction and inclusive education". Excluded population groups, such as indigenous peoples, are often those whose mother tongues are ignored by education systems. Allowing them to learn from a very early age in their mother tongue, and then in national, official or other languages, promotes equality and social inclusion.

Government of Tripura has taken various measures for promotion of Kokborok and other tribal languages. The Language Wing under Education Department in Tripura Tribal Areas Autonomous District Council (TTAADC) was started in 1994 by placing a Linguistic Officer. A humble start for development of Kokborok had taken place from that particular day. Later, activities have been extended to other tribal languages. The Kokborok is a language of Borok people who are geographically known as Tripuris. It is one of the State Languages of Tripura notified on January 19, 1979. The TTAADC has declared the Kokborok as Official language of the TTAADC on April 20, 1999. Language Wing has taken-up the compilation and publication of Kokborok Textbooks for introduction in primary schools under the control of Education Department in TTAADC. A numbers of Workshops and Seminars have been conducted for collection and compilation of Kokborok vocabulary and terminology. There is another committee separately constituted for the development of Chakma Language namely Chakma Language Development Committee. SCERT is also working for Development of Tribal and Minority Languages of Tripura. For this purpose Advisory Committees for Development of other languages have been constituted.

Kokborok is a recognized State Language. It has been recognized as official language from 19-1-1979. It is being taught as a medium of instruction in more than 1000 primary schools, Bishnupriya Manipuri Language is being taught as a subject in 36 (thirty six) schools and Manipuri Language is being taught as a subject in 21 (twenty one) schools in Tripura from classes I to V. Chakma textbooks and Halam Kuki Language textbooks for classes I to IV are being prepared and ready for publication. As a result there is much improvement of literacy rate in many tribal villages. The survey of two villages *viz.* Duski Village and Magrai Sardar village having 20 households under Khowai District of Teliamura Sub-Division reveals that all the children at the age of 6-14 years are now admitted in the school.

SECTION-III

From the foregoing analysis it is clear that the Government of India has taken various measures for improvement of educational status of the tribal population of the country. In the higher education seats are also reserved for different disadvantaged groups. The intake capacity of different educational institutions has been increased. As a result, the opportunities and access of the tribal students in all types of education has increased. But still they are far from social justice. There is much discrimination in the delivery of quality education in different institutions. Many minor tribal groups are still deprived of studying even in the primary school level through by their mother tongue. The social justice will be realised when all the people of the country will get equal opportunity for their development; the expansion/development of one group will not hinder the progress of another group and every person can compete freely to achieve his/her desired goal. On that day, India will be free from caste, creed and religion politics; merit and efficiency will be rewarded and everyone will work as per his/her ability and proficiency. The annual OECD "Education at a Glance" report shows that countries vary considerably in the proportion of young children who have access to good quality care, in the proportion of students completing secondary education, in participation in post-secondary education and in opportunities for adult education and workplace learning.

The following measures should be taken to accelerate the educational progress among the tribal population as suggested in the document of the Eleventh Five Year Plan:

- In the deficit areas, the requisite number of primary schools needs to be established. Specific norms for middle schools and high schools for tribal areas should be evolved and deficiencies made-up. All schools should have proper school buildings, hostels, water, toilet facilities (particularly for the girls' schools).
- Residential high schools for ST boys and girls will be set-up at suitable places. At the Gram Panchayat-level, ensuring girls' hostels will be attached to the existing primary/elementary schools that do not have hostels, wherever it is feasible to do so.
- Textbooks in tribal languages, especially at the primary level, will be produced to enable better comprehension by ST students in classes up to III. Side by side, adequate attention will be paid to the regional language so that children do not feel handicapped in higher classes.
- Efforts will be made to set-up Industrial Training Institutes (ITIs) in the TSP areas. Other training centres will include community polytechnics, and undertaking rural/ community development activities in their proximity, through application of science and technology.
- Efforts will be made for timely distribution of fellowships, scholarships, textbooks, uniforms and school bags to students. Adult education should be paid adequate attention.
- The ICDS/*Anganwadi* schemes for tribal areas should be evaluated and shortcomings eliminated. Steps to be taken to promote tribal languages, culture and heritage through adaptation of pedagogical methods, community participation in school management and so on.
- Special coaching classes should be organized. Eleventh Five Year Plan suitably aided to enable ST students to compete in entry-level competitive examinations for professional courses.
- There is a need to constitute a special committee composed of eminent sociologists, anthropologists, educationists, administrators, representatives of ST communities, and so on, to comprehensively assess the educational development of the tribals.

References

Choudhury, Jayanta and Das, Manoshi (2011): *Halam Tribes of Tripura—A Status Analysis*, Tribal Research and Cultural Institute, Government of Tripura.

Das, Pran Gopal (2002): *History of Political Thought*, New Central Book Agency (P) Ltd., Calcutta.

Debbarman, Suren (2006): "A Short Account of Tripuri Society", *Jnan Bichitra*.

http://www.oecd.org/education/educationeconomyandsociety/38692676.pdf

http://www.tripuraschooleducation.in/Language_Dev.htm

Language Wing under Education Department Tripura Tribal Areas Autonomous District Council KHUMULWNG, TRIPURA http://ttaadc.nic.in/LANGUAGEWINGWEB%20VERSION.pdf.

Planning Commission, India, Eleventh Five Year Plan.

Statistical Hand Book, Assam, 2009.

www.ttaadc.nic.in

www.destripura.gov.in

www.twdtripura.in

Zajda, Joseph *et al.*, 2006 : *Review of Education*, Springer.

6
Marginalisation and Social Exclusion of the Muslims in Assam

Prafulla Kumar Nath

The Muslims in Assam constitute a major chunk of the population of the state, which is almost one third of the 30 million state populations. There are two categories of Muslims found in Assam *viz.* the Assamese Muslims and the immigrant Muslims. The immigrant Muslims are popularly referred as *Miya* in a much derogatory sense. These people started migrating to Assam during the colonial period especially from the first decade of the 20th century for various reasons from East Pakistan (presently Bangladesh). Despite their significance contribution in the state economy, agriculture and other sectors of the society and altogether in the formation of the Assamese nationality for more than one hundred years; probably the East Pakistan origin Muslims are one of the most marginalised and socially excluded groups in Assam even now also. Frequently, they are referred as illegal Bangladeshis by the affluent caste Hindus and most often by the tribal population of the state also. Chakraborty opines, "Fact-findings about upheavals, riots or any disturbance ultimately generate a situation where citizens suddenly view each other through the exclusivist prism of "indigenous" and "foreigner" identities. The clichés such as "influx of foreigners", "loss of culture", "identity-crisis", "demographic invasion", "loss of economic livelihood", "politics of appeasement" etc., boil down to notions about cultural exclusivism that hide the dialectic of cooperation and assimilation, adoption and acculturation evident in the march of human civilization" (2012: 21).

The Assamese nationality discourse although seems to be secular in nature, unfortunately, it has blurred the distinction between the old settler and the new settler. However, such tendency is not very new in Assam. The coming and settling of the immigrant Muslims in Assam was a serious concern among the Assamese gentry in the colonial period also and the same stance continued in the post-colonial period too for which a majority of the population are away from the mainstream society. As a result, the social exclusion of this population converts every Muslim man and woman as a new settler or a potential illegal immigrant of Bangladesh. This further leads to marginalisation of them as a whole in one hand and on the other exclude them from various rights as a citizen of the state.

By and large, this population came in various phases to Assam. The first batch came during colonial period, secondly when India got independence and partition occurred in 1947 a considerable section came and settled and finally in 1971 when Bangladesh got sovereignty, a good number of people came and settled in Assam. After six years of the Assam movement, which demanded deportation of the illegal citizens from the state, the Assam Accord was signed in 1985 through which the various sections of the state accepted 1971 as the cut-off year to deport the illegal foreign nationals from the state. As a result, apart from the pan-Indian situation where identifying and deporting of illegal foreign national is 1951, in case of Assam it is 1971.

However, the dubious nature of the Assamese middle class, which hardly differentiate between the old settlers and the new, and the continuous ranting of the said section along with the media converts every Muslim a potential Bangladeshi. A shared xenophobia of "ubiquitous Bangladeshi" is thus a common phenomenon throughout the state. In this chapter, it is argued how such tendency is not only marginalising a huge number of populations, but also excludes them repeatedly from the mainstream society. Within such gaze, they become victim of suspicion in every now and then and are deprived of quality education, healthcare and other basic rights.

Migration of Muslims to Assam and Assamese Nationality Discourse

The migration of the Muslims from East Pakistan has been a central question in the Assamese nationality discourse from the early 20th century. The state witnessed heavy influx of Muslim peasantry from East Pakistan from the early 20th century. The large scale abandoned wetland (*char*) available in the Brahmaputra Valley however attracted the peasantry. The colonial Government also encouraged such influx, although in times some officials showed their concerned also. The xenophobia of Assamese nationalism started with the coming of this East Pakistan origin Muslim population. The colonial rulers themselves encouraged Muslim migration to the Assam province. Butler in *Travel and Adventures in the Province of Assam* (1855) wrote that Assam was a less populated province full of forests and "immense tracks of forests still remain untilled" and there was no hope of "a dense population for ages to come" (Baruah, 1999: 45). Baruah holds that "In the early parts of 20th century a new commercial agriculture through colonisation of land by immigrant agriculturalists became the principal way of supplying food grains and other agricultural products to the growing "modern sectors". The colonisation of land by settlers from East Bengal began in a big way in the second decade of the twentieth century, and on a reduced scale continued well beyond the partition of the subcontinent in 1947" (47).

The Assamese middle class, the newly educated tribal leaders as well as some colonial officials showed their apprehension towards the huge influx during colonial period. The demographic scenery already started changing in Assam as "non-indigenous elements came to constitute (around) one quarter of the population of Assam proper in 1901" (Guha, 2006: 39; Sharma, 2016:91). Manik Ch. Baruah, member of the Assam Legislative Council in 1915 raised concern about the large-scale migration from East Sylhet and appealed the Government to take the measures so that no conflict could take place between them and the villagers. Mr. Llyod in the Census Report of 1921 mentioned:

> "In 1911, few cultivators from Eastern Bengal had gone Goalpara....... in the last decade (1911-1921), the movement had extended far up the valley, and the colonists now form an appreciable element in the population of all the four lower and central districts....... In Goalpara nearly 20 per cent of the population is made of these settlers. The next favourite district is Nowgong where they form

> about 14 per cent of the whole population. In Kamrup, wastelands are being taken-up rapidly, especially in the Barpeta sub-division. In Darrang, exploration and settlement of the colonists are at an earlier stage. They have not yet penetrated far from the banks of the Brahmaputra river....... Almost all the trains and streamer brings parties of these settlers, and it seems likely that their march will extend further up the Brahmaputra valley and away from the river before long" (Census Report of 1921, quoted in Das, 1986: 28-29).

C.S. Mullan, the Superintendent of 1931 census, wrote—

> "Probably the most important event in the province during the last twenty five years which seems likely to alter permanently the whole future of Assam and to destroy. the whole structure of Assamese culture and civilisation – has been invasion of a vast horde of land hungry Bengali immigrants; mostly Muslims, from the district of Eastern Bengal some time before 1911. Nevertheless, as we now know, the Bengali immigrants censused for the first time on their *char* islands or Goalpara in 1921 were merely the advance guard – or rather the scouts – of a huge army following closely at their heels. By 1921, the first army cops had passed into Assam and had practically conquered the district of Goalpara. Wherever the carcass, there will vultures be gathered together. Where there is wasteland, thither flock the *Mymensinghiahs*". In fact, the way in which they have seized upon the vacant areas in the Assam Valley seems almost uncanny. Without fuss, without tumult, without undue trouble to the district revenues staffs, a population which must amount to over half a million has transplanted itself from Bengal into the Assam Valley during the last twenty five years ...the only thing I can compare it to is the mass movement of large body of ants ...it is sad by no means improbable that in another thirty years Sibsagar district will be the only part of Assam in which an Assamese will find himself at home" (*ibid.*, 30 and Sharma, 2009: 26-27).

The anxiety on the part of the Assamese middle class and some of the colonial officials seeded the rise of national consciousness in Assam. Some Assamese elites like Ambikagiri Rai Choudhury and others also raised this anxiety over the encroachment of the alien cultural groups through their writing. Guha considers such apprehension of the Assamese middle class as the rise of the little nationalism. He writes,

> "This apprehension sustained a powerful lobby of little nationalism both inside and outside the Assam Congress during the three pre-Independence decades. Assamese little nationalism no longer remained during these decades just a middle class or a nascent bourgeois phenomenon. It was fast reaching out to the peasantry, constituted of both autochthons and immigrants, and divided it" (Guha, 1984: 42-65).

The emerging tribal political organisations also demonstrated their serious concern and opposition to the increasing migrations. Accordingly, the Colonial government introduced the Line System in 1920 to protect the land from the outsiders. It was initially applied in Nowgong district and Barpeta sub-division of Kamrup, gradually spread to some other districts of lower Assam. Through the Line System, the villages were divided into three types: Open Villages, Closed Villages and Mixed Villages. In open villages, immigrants could settle freely. In close villages, immigrants were not allowed to settle and in mixed villages, a line was drawn where immigrants could settle on one side of the line (Das, 1986: 31). The Line System was later converted to Tribal Belts and blocks after continuous pressure from the Tribal League – a conglomerate body of various tribal groups formed in 1933. The creation of belts and blocks are continuing now-a-days also where in those belts and blocks non-tribal cannot settle, buy, or sell lands.

The trepidation of the Assamese middle class and of the tribal leadership since the colonial period to the post-colonial times created the binary of indigenous and outsider in most of the ethnicity discourses of Assam. In various ongoing ethnicity movements in Assam, the East Bengal origin Muslim peasants become the soft target whom are considered as illegal migrants and have occupied "our land". The Nellie Massacre (1983) and the conflicts in Bodoland (2008, 2012) can be cited here.

The various nationalistic organisations give various figures of illegal Bangladeshis in Assam who entered after 1971, which are not backed by substantial evidences. However, a kind of fear psychosis of illegal Bangladeshi is prevalent among masses for which the old settlers are also looked with suspicion. The media have also contributed a lot in creating such assumptions. This kind of conjectures produce multiple nuances in terms of Muslim politics, ethnic politics etc.

Social Exclusion, Marginalisation and Education

As mentioned, the issue of immigration has been a serious issue in Assam, but Assamese nationality discourse largely has blurred the distinction of old and new settlers and has failed to incorporate the Muslims in Assamese fold. It has always considered Muslims as other. Although a tiny progressive section in Assam accepts the contribution of the Muslims and has slotted them in but that is not sufficient to mainstreaming the population.

Here, I will discuss two specific situations that how the idea of insider-outsider, or indigenous-outsider binary circulated among the masses affects entire social life of this population. The process of social exclusion and marginalisation of the Muslims also largely affects the school children and their education. Construction of a collective conscience like Muslims as Bangladeshi by the Assamese middle class has pushed them to the margin and the xenophobia, the notion of ubiquitous Bangladeshi etc. has been a dodgy drift in Assam. This can be best understood once we see the educational scenario in *char* or in Muslim dominated areas. To corroborate my argument, the example of two Muslim villages, i.e. Khagrabari and Banderdubi are discussed below. These two villages got considerable media attention in 2014 and 2016 respectively. In Khagrabari, Bodo militant group massacred almost 42 people in 2014. Banderdubi is a fringe village of the Kaziranga National Park. Assam Government evicted the village in 2016 following an order of Gauhati High Court. However, no compensation was given to the villagers though they were evicted from their *myadi*[1] land. In both the villages, the school-going children were largely affected in the name of ethnicity and nationalism.

"The Specter of Memory" and Khagrabari

"Due to erosion the school had to be shifted for four times in just 10 years and finally it is here now. I have been working here since 1983 without any salary, as it was a venture school. In 2013, the school was provincialised. Two years ago, there were almost 71 families at Khagrabari village and total enrollment was 72 in five classes in my school. "The massacre changed everything", Azad Ali — the school teacher said. Ali then started weeping and said "sixteen school children of my school were killed in that day within 30-60 minutes. I was almost mad. Everybody was searching for dead bodies. The frightened villagers went to the deep jungle of Manas National Park to save themselves from the bullets of the Bodo miscreants. Later, when Police came announcement was given in mike and appealed the villagers to come out. But the escaped villagers scared".

It was a catharsis — though everybody gets prepare who visits Khagrabari. A 15 x 20 square feet dilapidated room is the only LP school in Nanke Khagrabari which is made of bamboo, wood and tin. The co-teacher was absent on the day I visited Khagrabari due to some official reasons. Azad Ali was teaching the five primary classes alone — mathematics to one class, spellings to the other and English alphabets to some students. The properties of the school are 10 pairs of desks and benches, a blackboard and a pair of table and chair. A battalion camp was established after the massacre for the security of the village. The only *pakka* house in the village is the school kitchen – that is occupied by the Police officer of the Battalion camp as his bedroom.

Khagrabari LP School is not only the decrepit government school in Assam. There are thousands such schools found in the *char* areas or in villages or in jungle areas of Assam. However, Khagrabari suddenly became popular on the evening of the 2nd May, 2014 as 42 people (22 children) were killed within 30-60 minutes duration by some Bodo insurgents using automatic weapons where some armed personnel of the Forest Department of the Government of Assam actively participated in the massacre. The then Government officials, Ministers, AUIDF Chief Badaruddin Azmal visited the place, promised relief and compensation. The then local BJP MLA of Sarabhog constituency never visited the place. Even in the last Assembly election, also he did not go for campaigning there.

The continuous branding of Muslims in Assam as Bangladeshis marginalising them by the ethnic politics in the state is a common phenomenon. The Nellie massacre is still alive to each Muslims where chauvinist Assamese killed almost 2000 Muslims in a single day at broad daylight in 1983. The popular slogan of NDA during the 2014 General Election campaign could not bring *achhe din,* but brought nightmare to every family of Khagrabari. The specter of memory – the massacre has been haunting every individual of the village every day. It happened just after 2014 General Election poll. Chandan Brahma was the MP candidate of the Bodoland People's Front (BPF), a sitting MLA of the Party. Sansuma Khungur Bismutiary the sitting MP of BPF could not manage the ticket from the Party and contested as independent candidate. Various non-Bodo communities and parties in the election supported Naba Sarania, a pro-talk faction ULFA leader. The Bodos of lower Assam have a long history of struggle for self-determination. It has its own discourse of Assamese hegemony and exploitation. From the Udayachal movement, to the autonomy movement and movement for separate state are incorporated with democratic protest and insurgency since 1970s. The Bodo movement has witnessed several fratricidal killings and ethnic conflicts so far in the name of ethnicity and exclusive homeland. However, it ignores the considerable presence of the non-Bodos in their imagined homeland. The Assamese nationalism or the other ethnic politics in the state have failed to manage the minorities in their larger spectrum of nationality discourse and in their ethnic spaces. As a resultant consequence, various non-Bodo groups in lower Assam had formed an organisation called *O-Bodo Suransha Mancha* (Non-Bodo Protection Forum) to counter the Bodo chauvinism.

Erosion Erodes Villages — Creates Bangladeshis

A resident of Khagrabari, after 5 minutes of our interactions in the long embankment of Beki river cried and shared his experience of discrimination and gaze of Assamese caste Hindus towards the Muslims including the official levels too. He screamed that when the erosion of Beki river was going on, people were forced to come to the road side and nearby to the embankment. A government official visited to see the flood and erosion and quite casually said "how come these Bangladeshis have built their houses here". He repeated, "we are not Bangladeshis. We have never gone or seen Bangladesh, but we frequently heard the word. People were fighting for their lives and we were branded as Bangladeshis. Why they cannot catch the real Bangladeshis and harass us always?"

The people of Khagrabari are luckless. The present small village Khagrabari once was a resourceful one. However, erosion of Beki river, started in 2004 taken away almost all the cultivable land and pushed them towards the Manas National Park. The agrarian community lost their agricultural land and some moved to the other side of the river. Though, Beki river took everything from them at the same time it created new sources of income to them along with Manas National Park. Stone and sand carried by the flow of Beki is one of the major income sources during winter and woods come from the hills of Bhutan and Manas National Park are other sources of livelihood in summer.

However, not all the Muslims in Assam are fortunate people like the people of Khagrabari in terms of livelihood. Most of the population residing in the riverside areas or in the *chars* of Assam suffer from landlessness due to erosion for which they have to shift to different places, occupy government land, forest land or move to the town areas as daily wage labour or for other menial job frequently. The Jingoism of Assamese nationalism converts them into Bangladeshis. Their settlement in a new area — the unfamiliar faces in a locality, and the common gaze and xenophobia of the ethnic communities become easy to term them as Bangladeshis. The search for a new settlement for livelihood is the horizontal expansion of the population, which is not necessarily growth of the total population, but such expansions is interpreted as "Bangladeshi everywhere".

Displacement and Marginalisation

Now-a-days, the villagers of Khagrabari carry memories. The memories of last 30 years — sometimes created by neighbouring community and sometimes by the nature those haunt them every now and then. In 1994, the Bodo movement displaced the people of Khagrabari and nearby villages of Narayanguri area. Their houses were burnt down by some Bodos in the name of Bodo nationalism for creation of an exclusive Bodo space. In 2004, the story of erosion started which again displaced them and finally in 2014, the massacre by some Bodo insurgents has taken away everything.

Miya is quite common and derogatory word pointed towards the East Pakistan origin Muslims in Assam. For last long 100 years almost all the Muslims in some way or the other in his/her lifetime faces the discrimination to be a Bangladeshi. They are yet to be brought or counted in the mainstream. Traditionally, Muslims were the vote bank for the Congress. However, with the rise of Muslim Politics in Assam, the AIUDF could manage their influence among them. Still they are gazed as Bangladeshi, they have to prove their citizenship in every now and then. The Assamese Media frequently call AIUDF as the party of the Bangladeshis.

Ethnic conflict is not a new phenomenon in lower Assam. The Bodos who have been demanding for a separate exclusive Bodo homeland, the lower Assam has witnessed a series of ethnic conflicts. The erstwhile East Pakistan origin Muslims have been the soft and hard targets for the Bodo chauvinist including the insurgent groups. During colonial period sometimes with the patronization of the Government or sometimes, self-willingly a good number of Muslims came from present day Bangladesh and settled down in different riverine areas of lower Assam. The Muslim is one of the most hardworking communities in Assam — they are found in every sector including agriculture, menial work, as labour in construction sites and so on. Like the Assamese nationality discourse, the different ethnic groups of Assam who carry their own nationality discourse have the similar gaze towards the Muslims as Bangladeshi. Any man with long beard with a *lungi*[2] is a Bangladeshi for such nationalists. In one sense, they are the most vulnerable group in Assam.

The river Beki, has separated Khagrabari from the rest of the world. On the other side, it is Manas National Park and Manah river. Beki river is also a pain and source of livelihood for the people of Khagrabari. Erosion pushed the villagers towards west and northern side, i.e. towards Manas National Park. Local people said Beki river destroyed almost 600 acres of land. A villager said, "Beki is flowing in our land". On 2nd May, 2014, around 3:30-4 PM most of the males went to the market crossing the river Beki. Two days ago, Bodo gunmen killed two men in a nearby village of

Narayanguri, the other side of the Beki. The ruling BPF party of the Territorial Council could feel the pulse of the election that they are going to lose the Kokrajhar Parliamentary seat. After series of conflicts from 2008 onwards in BTAD, the relationship between these two communities became bitter day-by-day. Finally, Khagrabari massacre happened. After the massacre, every family got compensation from the Government. Out of 42 deaths, 22 were children, who did not know what nationalism is or a homeland even!

The people of Khagrabari are still there. Some have moved to 'safe places', some are living with the specter of memory and some are regular visitors. The local BJP MLA did not come for election campaign in the last Assembly election also. Badaruddin Azmal came to the place and promised a house to every affected family, but he did not keep the promise and gave to a few families only. Badaruddin Azmal who emerged as saviour of the Muslims himself lost the Assembly election in 2016. The BPF never came to Khagrabari for either campaigning of election or even did not make a visit after the massacre.

Education and Health at Khagrabari

The horrific incident compelled many families to leave Khagrabari. But those who are staying at Khagrabari are in pathetic condition. There is no medical facility in the village. There is only one primary school located inside the boundary of the mosque with two teachers. There is no separate room for different classes or any office room for the teachers. Lots of experimentation have been done on primary education including methodology, teaching aid etc., but these are a far cry at Khagrabari. The children are deprived of quality education, pure drinking water and other facilities. Their childhood, their education are victims of the nationalistic jargons of the middle classes where no one has the time to take care about them. Their childhoods are victims of conflicting nations and religions.

Banderdubi: Encroachment and the Kaziranga National Park

On 19th September, 2016 following an order of the Gauhati High Court, the Assam Government carried out eviction drive in three fringe villages of Kaziranga National Park, *viz.* Banderdubi, Deocharchung and Palkhuwa. Most of the evicted villagers were East Pakistan origin Muslim peasants who migrated to those villages during 1950s. The eviction was highly communalised by a section of the caste Hindu Assamese and also by the local media. The popular media coverage of the eviction was that the lands of the Kaziranga National Park was encroached by the illegal Bangladeshis and they become threat to the park. It was also popularised in social media that the villagers were engaged in rhino poaching. As usual, there was no credible evidence to substantiate such claims.

Kaziranga was declared as a National Park on 11th February, 1976. Interestingly, the evicted villages were set-up much before than the park was declared as National Park. For example, the Banderdubi Mosque was set-up in 1951 and the LP School was provincialised in 1966. Hence, the village was never part of the National Park. Moreover, the Banderdubi village was a revenue village of the Assam government where the residents of the village carried *myadi patta* document of their land. Unfortunately, during the time of eviction, 2 persons were killed in police firing when the villagers registered massive protest demanding proper re-settlement and compensation before eviction. But the Government did not listen to their plea and evicted the villages.

The Assamese middle class and the local media through their coverage branded the population as encroachers and illegal Bangladeshis. Akhil Gogoi, the leader of the *Krishak Mukti Sangram Samittee* (a peasant organisation of the state) was trolled in social media for his support to the evicted masses. The evicted villagers clearly mentioned that they were ready to vacate the villages for the sake of the Park, but they demanded compensation and rehabilitation before eviction.

The post-eviction politics was highly communalized from various sections of the state. It was tried to prove their alleged involvement in rhino poaching, encroachment of land, question on their citizenship and finally it was popularly circulated that the village was an animal corridor. But none of the above allegations came true. The map of the village prepared in 1966 by the revenue department of Assam, the voter lists of 1951, 1966 were circulated in the social media widely. The issue of illegal poaching, and Banderdubi was an animal corridor etc. were also could not be proved.

Once eviction was completed in those villages, at Banderdubi, Assam Battalion occupied the government school and no villager was allowed to enter into the village. The teachers of the schools were transferred to nearby schools. During the time of eviction, there were 160 students in Bandrdubi primary school. Though officially it was announced that the school children were admitted in the nearby schools, but the ground reality was quite murky. The students were denied admission by the nearby schools citing lack of infrastructural facility, lack of teachers etc. Thus, most of the school children lost their academic year. After the eviction, the people were compelled to camp in the road by themselves, as the Government provided them no alternative. Unfortunately, in the camps also no government facility or aid such as food, drinking water or medical facilities were provided. The Government did promise compensation against the *myadi* land within forty days, but that was also never fulfilled.

Though initially common people had a suspicion over the citizenship of the evicted people, but several reports came latter which dismissed such allegations. When I talked to the evicted people it was seen that some well-to-do families sent their children to their relatives for continuing the education. But majority of the school children whose parents were poor had to stay in the camps leaving their schools. The All Assam Students Union (AASU), the most influential students body of the state never visited those people or issued any statement or demanded the basic rights for them. The Asom Sahitya Sabha (Assam Literary Society) or no any leading organisation paid any attention to the evicted masses in general or raised any concern for the school children. Thanks to the local media also who could form a consensus through their nationalistic and jingoistic tune among the masses how harmful the evicted people were. Many school children held that along with the houses the administration also burnt down their books and school kits.

Conclusion

From the above two cases what we have seen that the bigoted, narrow, communal and discordant nationalism of the affluent caste Hindu Assamese has not only marginalise or exclude the East

Bengal origin Muslims, but at the same time kids, women, school children also suffer largely from such prejudices. The gaze of the Assamese caste Hindus of ubiquitous Bangladeshi, blurring of the distinction between old and new settlers, have affected the secular foundation of the Assamese society. Such perceptions have multiple nuances where a particular section is pushed to margin time and again, and in various social situations they are denied the basic human rights also. It thus weakens the very essence of the democratic values of a society.

Notes

1. Official landholding document.
2. Ankle length wrap around wear by men.

References

Baruah, Sanjib (2001): *India against Itself: Assam and the Politics of Nationality*. New Delhi: Oxford University Press.

Butler, Major John (1855): *Travel and Adventures in the Province of Assam, during a residence of Fourteen years*. London: Smith, Edler & Co.

Chakraborty, Gorki (2012): "The 'Ubiquitous' Bangladeshis", *EPW*, Vol. xlvii, No. 38, pp. 21-23.

Das, J.N. (1986): "Genesis of Tribal Belts and Blocks of Assam." In *Alienation of Tribal Land and Indebtedness*. Guwahati: Tribal Research Institute.

Gauhati High Court (2015): PIL (*suo motu*) 66/2012, 67/2012, and WP(C) 648/2013 and 4860/2013.

Guha, Amalendu (2006): *Planter Raj to Swaraj: Freedom Struggle and Electoral Politics in Assam 1826-1947*. New Delhi: Tulika.

Sharma, Chandan Kr. (2016): "Immigration, indigeneity and Identity: The Bangladeshi Immigration Question in Assam." In Gogoi, Dilip and N. G. Mahanta. (ed.) *Unheeded Hinterland Identity and Sovereignty in Northeast India*. Oxon: Routledge Publications.

—— (2008): "The issue of illegal migration in Assam and the State". In Sarma, Debabrata (ed.) *Migration and Assimilation*. Jorhat: Jorhat College.

SECTION-II

Right To Education

7

Border Barrier and Right To Education in No Man's Land

A Study of the Border Inhabitants of Cachar District

Ameera Yasmin Mazumdar

1. Introduction

International borders are political boundaries between two nations that separate one nation from another. In between the border of two countries, certain breadth of land is left vacant. The width of this land according to international convention may be one hundred fifty yards inside the territory from the zero point or as agreed between the countries. This tract of land is left over for preventing commotion between the uninformed personnels of the two nations. It is a neutral tract along the international border over which neither country have any right. This tract of land is known by different nomenclatures in different parts of the world, such as buffer zone, neutral zone or in the Indian context as "no man's land".[1] The term "no man's land actually dates back to 14th century and to London during the months preceding the plague, when the bishop of London purchased land outside the city to prepare a mass grave ahead of the bubonic plague."[2] No man's land in Latin is known as "*terra nullius*". "*Terra nullius*" is a Latin expression deriving from Roman law meaning "nobody's land". This term is used in international law to describe territory which has never been subject to the sovereignty of any state, or over which any state or over which any prior sovereign has expressly or impliedly relinquished sovereignty.[3]

India is a vast nation with various cultures, communities and beliefs. The country shares land borders with Pakistan in the west, China in the north, and Bangladesh, Myanmar and Bhutan in the east. Of the 29 states, the assortment of eight states commonly known as the north-eastern states shares more than 4000 kilometres of international borders with China, Myanmar, Bhutan and Bangladesh.[4] Of these eight states, Assam shares international borders with Bangladesh and Bhutan. With Bangladesh, Assam shares a length of 267.5 kilometres (approximately) of international border. The district of Cachar shares 36.8 kilometre of international boundary with Bangladesh.[5]

The border fencing with barbed wires started in 2005 and as per international norm the fence needs to be 150 yards away from the zero point. But at places, 200 to 400 kilometres of land have been left over for erecting the wired fence. As a result, a number of families who were Indians were left beyond the fence which is considered as the "no man's land". Around 174 families of Cachar district are reported to be living along the 36.8 km India-Bangladesh border.[6] The State Government have decided to allot 89 *bighas* of land under the Katigorah block for rehabilitation of these families[7], but it has not yet been materialised. When the Deputy Commissioner of the district along with other officials visited the area, earlier, he interacted with the local residents. From reports it is revealed that young students are irregular in school, as they go to help their parents earn a living. The reports further reveal that student of higher classes are unable to take tuitions after dusk, on the other side of the border as gates remain closed after 5 p.m.[8]

According to the protocol between India and Bangladesh, no houses or defence set-up would be erected beyond the barbed wires. Hence, government services in the region are unavailable. In Cachar residents of Mahadevpur, Nij, Jelalpore, Rongpur, Pirnagar and Nathanpur village share this fate. The government has abdicated its sovereignty over these lands. The residents in these areas live like prisoners. They can cross the 8.5 feet wall only four times during the day, that is, 6 to7 am, 9 to 10 pm, 2 to 4 pm and 5 to 7 p.m.[9] Their entry and exit are recorded in a register maintained by the Border Security Force (BSF), the fenced areas have no schools and children's are forced to attend schools in the mainland.[10] The inhabitants cannot sell their products outside as the gate timings and market timings differ. No government aided scheme is present in the villages. The villagers have to show their identity card while going to vote. No banks give them loan or other credit. Electricity facility is also not available in the area. Government schemes like Indira Awas Yojana, Pradhan Mantri Gram Sadak Yojana, NREGA, or any other employment generation policy of the government are also excluded.

2. Objective

The main objective of this study is to analyse the fundamental right to education of Indian citizens who are residing near the Indo-Bangla border. The residents are deprived of their fundamental rights despite being the citizens of this country. The right of children to free and compulsory education have been discussed keeping in view the plight of children of the area under study. The study also throws light on the laws, policies and schemes relating to education prevailing in Assam. The study tries to find how the rights and privileges which are enjoyed by other citizens are denied to this section of the population. The duty of the government to rehabilitate them is under process. The different government laws and policies to rehabilitate them have also been discussed. The study is an attempt to find out the plight of children living in no man's land, their right to free and compulsory education and their future prospects from thc light of fundamental and statutory rights.

3. Research Methodology

The study is doctrinal and conducted through the perusal of secondary data. The available reports, data, legislations etc. have been analysed to find answers to the research queries. The descriptive study is based on secondary sources of information. Internet as a source of information has been used.

4. Types of International Borders

International borders are political boundaries which separate one nation from another nation. To demarcate the political boundary of onc nation from another, some types of International borders exists. These are:

A. Controlled Borders

This is the most common type of border persistent throughout the world. In this type of border, there exists official border crossing points. This point checks the documents and goods seeking to move to the other side of the border. Passports and visas are checked by the border officials of each country. The individuals crossing such border have to satisfy these officials with proper documents. The Immigration department and custom department examines the goods and documents thoroughly. These borders are closed in whole length and if any individual enters through means other than the gate than it will be an illegal entry.

The Indian-Bangladesh border at Sutharkandi, Karimganj is an example of controlled border.

B. Closed Border

Closed borders are those borders where no public or goods traffic is allowed. These restrictions can be imposed by both the countries or by anyone country primarily for security reasons. Borders may also be closed for political reasons.

C. Open Borders

Open borders are those borders where there exists gates but citizens are allowed entry to the other country on verbal permission from the border guards and are allowed to move up to a distance of three kilometres only. The person who enters the other country must return before sunset or before the time set by the border guards of the concerned nation. Movements of goods in bulk are not permitted without permission of the authorities. If one intends to move further then permission of respective government is required. The Indo-Bhutan and Indo-Nepal borders are examples of open borders.

D. Imaginary Borders

Imaginary borders implies some borders which were declared by the British officials during the British regime in India. These borders were named after the administrators who declared some international boundaries as imaginary borders. These borders were declared imaginarily and capriciously. Such declarations caused immense misery to common man. One such declaration was the Radcliffe line which divided India into India and Pakistan. As the line was arbitrarily declared, the inhabitants suffered immensely because their houses were divided between two countries. Many villages were also divided. Division affects people in a number of ways. Rights and duties are no exception.

5. Right to Education is a Fundamental Right under the Constitution of India.

Right to education flows directly from the right to life.[11] Right to education stand above other rights. Right to education is recognised as the most important, "as one's ability to enforce one's fundamental rights flows from one's education."[12] Right to education is a Fundamental Right under Article 21A of the Constitution of India. The right to education was not a fundamental right until 2002. It was a Directive Principle under Article 45 of the Constitution. It was made a fundamental right by the 86th Amendment of the Constitution in 2002. This Amendment added Article 21A to the Constitution. Accordingly, Parliament passed "The Right of Children to Free and Compulsory Education Act, 2009". The Act provides for state's responsibility in providing neighbourhood school so that each and every child may be admitted in the schools. Prior to it, right to education was a Directive Principle of State Policy under Article 45 which required the state to provide free and compulsory education to all children until the age of 14 years. This directive was to be implemented by the states within ten years from the date of commencement of the Constitution. But only few states made endeavour to fulfil this directive, which included the state of Assam also.

Right to education was also made a Fundamental Duty under Article 51A (k) by the 86th Constitutional Amendment Act, 2002. This amendment imposed a duty on parent or guardian to provide opportunities for education to his child or as the case may be, ward between the age of six and fourteen years. This Article refers to citizens only. Education promotes good and dignified life. In Superstar Education Society *vs.* State of Maharashtra[13], the

Supreme Court has held that it is the duty of the State Government to provide access to education. In Mohini Jain *vs.* State of Karnataka[14], the Supreme Court while reading Article 21 with the Directive Principle of State Policy contained in Articles 38, 39(a), 41 and 45, reiterated that, "the framers of the Constitution made it obligatory for the State to provide education for its citizens." The Court further ruled that, "the right to education flows directly from the right to life" and that the right to education is concomitant to the fundamental rights, "the state is under a Constitutional mandate to provide educational institutions at all levels for the benefit of the citizens, we hold that every citizen has right to education under the Constitution". Hence, right to education is a Fundamental Right, a Directive Principle as well as a Fundamental Duty.

6. Governments Policy on Education in Assam

Education in Assam developed since ancient times. Accounts of Chinese pilgrim, Hiuen Tsang reveals the prevalence of education system in Assam during the reign of King Bhaskarvarman in the 7th century. Religious leaders Srimanta Sankardev and Madhabdev also played crucial role in spreading education in Assam. *Pathsalas, Tols, Maktabs, Namgars* and *Satras* were some prominent place of learning during the ancient time.[15] After the annexation of Assam by the British in 1826, Mr. David Scott started eleven schools to promote indigenous education. The first compulsory primary education Act was passed in 1926. After independence, basic education was considered as the national pattern of elementary education in Assam. Accordingly, the Assam Basic Education Act was passed in 1954. This Act increased governments control over elementary education in Assam. To provide free and compulsory education, the Assam Elementary Education Act, 1962 was passed. Secondary education in Assam was started in 1835 with the establishment of an English school by Captain Jenkins known as "Guwahati Seminari" which is now known as Cotton College.[16] The literary scenario improved from 1912 onwards when the number of schools increased. After independence, the government adopted several measures to improve the standard of education in the state. Changes were introduced in the administration, curriculum, evaluation system etc., the Mudaliar Commission (1952-53), the Kothari Commission (1964-66), the National Education Policy, 1986, framed by the Government of India made tremendous contribution to the development of education in Assam also. The Secondary Education Act passed in 1961 established the Board of Secondary Education in Assam to regulate the secondary stage in education in the state. The National Education Policy, 1968 recommended the government to make strenuous effort towards fulfilling the objective enshrined in Article 45 of the Constitution. In 1986, a New Education Policy (NEP, 1986) was formulated. It emphasised on universal enrolment and retention in primary schools, to improve the quality of education in schools, to provide non-formal education and to prevent school drop-outs among others. To evaluate the effectiveness of this policy, the government constituted a committee. It emphasised on improvement of education in backward districts. Accordingly, District Primary Education Programme scheme was formulated in 1993. Initially district projects were prepared for 44 districts of eight states which included districts from Assam also. This scheme aims at providing access to all children of primary education, to reduce drop-outs, to reduce gender and social-group gap and to increase learning achievement by 25 per cent.[17] Currently in Assam this scheme is going on in nine districts which does not include the district of Cachar. The Sarva Shiksha Abhiyan, another scheme was formulated by the Central Government in 2000 to Universalise Elementary Education (UEE).[18] The scheme aims at absolute enrolment within a time frame, absolute five years of primary-level schooling, universal retention among other objectives. In Assam, the Mission was started in 2002. In 2011, the overall literacy rate in Assam was 73.18 per cent while in 2001 it was only 64.28 per cent. Male education percentage was 78.81 per cent and that of female was 67.27 per cent while in 2001 male literacy rate was 71.93 per cent and that of female was 56.03 per cent. In Cachar district, the average literacy rate according to 2011 census was 80.36 per cent. The rate of male literacy in 2011 was 85.85 per cent while for female it was 74.62 per cent. Most of the population were concentrated in the rural areas which was 81.80 per cent of the total population. Literacy rate in the rural areas was 78.14 per cent while that of urban areas it was 89.77 per cent. The Government has been making continuous efforts to improve the education scenario in the country. The State Government in Assam is also not lagging behind. Accordingly, many Acts were passed despite prevalence of Central Acts and schemes.

The Assam Elementary Education (Provincialisation) Act, 1974 was enacted with the spirit to provide free and compulsory education to all children until they attain the age of 14 years. Under Section 21 of this Act, no guardian or person can utilize the services of the child whether on remuneration or otherwise, in any manner which will interfere with the attendance of the child in school. Contravention of the provision attracts penalty of fine not exceeding two rupees and an additional fine of 50 paise if the contravention continues. But from reports it is revealed that young students in the border areas are irregular in school, as they go to help their parents earn a living. Moreover, there are no Government schools in existence in those areas.

The Assam Right of Children to Free and Compulsory Education Rules, 2011, provides the limit that, within a walking distance of one kilometre a school shall be established for children studying in classes I-V.[19] and for children studying in classes VI-VIII, a school shall be established every 3 kilometres. The Act further provides that in respect of areas with lack of roads or danger for young children in approach from their homes, the government shall locate the school in such manner as to avoid such dangers by reducing the limit prescribed for schools in earlier sections.[20] The Act further provides that for children from small villages, where no school exists, the government shall make adequate arrangements such as free transportation, residential facilities and other facilities for providing elementary education in a school.[21] Under Rule 27, the Act ensures that for better coordination of academic matters, the Government shall make a thorough review on the existing management, planning and administrative mechanism right from the grassroots level to state level and organise steps for its strengthening.

7. Education of Border inhabitants: Problems and Prospects

The inhabitants on the other side of the border have restricted entry into the mainland where government school exists. Reports reveal how the student of higher classes are unable to take tuitions after dusk, on the other side of the border as gates to the mainland remain closed after 5 p.m. thereby effecting their pursuit for higher studies. Poverty forces the young ones to miss schools. The children are forced to assist parents earn a livelihood in tender years. There are no transportation facilities in those areas unlike the mainland. Though the number of children are less yet report shows that there exist children below the age of fourteen years, not to speak of children who have grown to adults since fencing started, dividing them. These children suffer a fate not by choice but by chance. The children suffer inadequate security problems as no government facility operates in no man's land. Reports reveal how due to lack of security, some of these areas have become flourishing centres of crime like dacoity. The social functions are conducted in silence. The security threat for women and girls are notable. The government policy which inflicted misery on them must also rehabilitate them. The right of the government to defend the country implies duty towards its citizens also. Rights and duties are correlative.[22]

According to Article 300(A) of the Constitution, "no man shall be deprived of his property save by authority of law." Law in this context means "an Act of Parliament, or of a state legislature, a rule or a statutory order having the force of law that is positive or state made law." The Land Boundary Agreement, 1974, between the two nations facilitated a better demarcation of land between India and Bangladesh, but inflicted untold miseries on a section of the population living on the boundary land in issue. The inhabitants had been torn between two parts of the boundary. Some of them have their houses on one side of the boundary, while farm land on the other side. This action also effected not only lives, but also property of those citizens. The fenced land has also lost its market value as there is no potential purchaser now.

The National Rehabilitation and Resettlement Policy, 2007, has been prepared by the Government of India to rehabilitate families effected by acquisition of land in any government projects.[23] The policy provides for rehabilitation of families where land acquired is private land and purpose is government project.

The Preamble to The National Rehabilitation and Resettlement Policy, 2007 states that rehabilitation and resettlement is provided for persons involuntarily displaced by government's legal action. Appropriate government for rehabilitation purpose is "the Central Government if acquisition is for purpose of the Union Government or in relation to a project executed by the Central Government agency or undertaking or by any other agency on the order or direction of the Central Government.[24] But if it is in relation to the acquisition of land for purposes other than those mentioned above, than the State Government is to rehabilitate the affected families.[25]

The Right to Fair Compensation and Transparency in Land Acquisition and Resettlement Act, 2013, provides that, land acquired by the government and used for public purposes only is subject to rehabilitation and compensation. "Public purpose" is explained as, defence and national security, roads, railways, highways and ports built by either the government or under public private project etc. In every case of acquisition, rehabilitation and resettlement must be undertaken. An administrator must be appointed after publishing the preliminary notification for acquisition. The Administrator shall then conduct a survey and prepare a scheme for rehabilitation and resettlement. The scheme must be discussed with local authorities and sent to the Commissioner for approval. The Commissioner send it to the government for further action.

As per latest report[26], the Cachar district administrator sent a proposal worth Rs.15 crore to the government for constructing a town area rehabilitating 176 Indian families who were barricaded out during construction of the barbed wire fencing along the Indo-Bangla border in Cachar district as per the government's plan to rehabilitate them as The National Rehabilitation and Resettlement Policy, 2007 provides that the resettled area must be provided with infrastructural facilities like roads, drainage, drinking water, grazing lands etc., but it has not yet been materialised. The proposal lying in the government office is in process since years. Such delay is bound to destroy the future citizens of this country living in the *terra nullius*. The rehabilitation activity needs to be fastened before another group of minor turn to adults.

8. Conclusion

The study throws light on the plight of people especially children living in the no man's land. The population though meagre suffer from untold miseries. Their fundamental rights under the Constitution of India become a misnomer. Right to education is no exception. Unless they are rehabilitated in the mainland, their plight is bound to increase rather than decrease.

Accordingly, the following suggestions may be put forward:

(i) Report of presence of inhabitants in no man's land is failure of the Sarva Shiksha Abhiyan scheme of the government as universal admission and retention cannot be a reality in a place where government cannot exercise jurisdiction upon its own citizens. Hence, this marginalised group must be rehabilitated as soon as possible to ensure better implementation of education schemes of the government.

(ii) The strict border gates rules and timings for school students residing in no man's land, if any, must be relaxed so that they can pursue their right to education effectively. Adequate compensation must be secured to the inhabitants of no man's land after rehabilitation so as to ensure them their right to social justice under the Constitution.

(iii) Skill education must be imparted to those whose schooling have been already effected due to non-implementation of rehabilitation scheme of the government so that they become eligible for employment.

(iv) Employment under several government employment generating schemes must be ensured to the elderly in the family after rehabilitation so that their children do not miss school on ground of helping parents earn a livelihood.

Notes

1. Dhar, Bibhash and Ganesh Ch. Ojha (2014): *International Boundaries in North East India: Community, Culture and Stress* (Lakshi Publishers and Distributors, New Delhi), p. 20.
2. *Isaac, Tumusiime: No Man's land...principles in international law,* viewed on 25th October, 2016*(htt://www.academia.edu)*
3. No Man's Land: viewed on 15th April, 2017 (*https://en.m.wikipedia.org.*).
4. *Supra note* 1 at p. 3.
5. Gupta, Arindam (31/12/2015): Land Cheers for people along Indo-Bangla border, viewed on 2nd November, 2016 (*www.assamtribune.com.*)
6. *Ibid.*
7. *Ibid.*
8. *Ibid.*

9. Singh, Daya Nath (20/03/2012): Captive Citizens of No man's Land viewed on 2nd November, 2016 (*https://www.assamtimes.org*)
10. *Ibid.*
11. Mohini Jain *vs.* State of Karnataka, [AIR 1992, SC1858(1992)3SCC 666].
12. Ashok Kumar Thakur *vs.* Union of India [2008 6 SCC 1: (2008) 5JT, per Dalveer Bhandari J. at p. 646.]
13. (2008) 3SCC 315.
14. AIR 1992, SC1858 (1992)3SCC 666.
15. Introduction to primary education commission of 1952-53, viewed on 4th November, 2016 (*www. kkhsou.in.*)
16. Introduction to education in Assam, viewed on 4th November, 2016. (*www. kkhsou.in*)
17. *Supra* note 14.
18. *Ibid.*
19. PART III, Rule 4.
20. Rule 4(3).
21. Rule 4(4).
22. Agarwal, Prof. (Mrs.) (2007): *Jurisprudence, Legal Theory* (Allahabad: Central Law Publications), p. 142.
23. Fenced Indians pay for National Security politics (23/03/2015) viewed on 4th November, 2016 (*https://www.ukessays.com.*).
24. Sec. 3.1 (f).
25. *Ibid.* (f).
26. Cachar project proposal for rehab of 176 families(19/10/2016) viewed on 1st November, 2016 (*timesofindia.com)*

Bibliography

1. Books

Agarwal. Dr. H.O. (2014): *International Law and Human Rights* (Central Law Publications, Allahabad).

Agarwal,. Dr. H.O. (2014): *Human Rights* (Central Law Publications, Allahabad).

Agarwal, Prof.(Mrs.) (2007): *Jurisprudence, Legal Theory* (Central Law Publications, Allahabad).

Basu, D.D. (1965): *Commentary on the Constitution of India,* S.C. Sarcar & Sons, Calcutta.

Dhar, Bibhash and Ganesh Ch. Ojha, (2014): *International Boundaries in North East India, Community, Culture and Stress* (Lakshi Publishers and Distributors, New Delhi).

Jain, M.P. (2014): *Indian Constitutional Law* (Lexis Nexis Butterworths Wadhwa, Nagpur).

2. Online Sources

Isaac, Tumusiime: No Man's land...principles in international law, viewed on 25th October, 2016 *(htt://www.academia.edu)*
No Man's Land: viewed on 15th April, 2017 (*https://en.m.wikipedia.org.*).
Gupta, Arindam (31/12/2015):Land Cheers for people along Indo-Bangla border, viewed on 2nd November 2016 (*www.assamtribune.com.*)
Singh, Daya Nath, (20/03/2012): Captive Citizens of No man's Land viewed on 2nd November 2016 (*https://www.assamtimes.org*)
Introduction to primary education commission of 1952-53, viewed on 4th November, 2016 (*www. kkhsou.in.*)
Introduction to education in Assam, viewed on 4th November, 2016. (*www. kkhsou.in*)
Fenced Indians pay for National Security politics (23/03/2015) viewed on 4th November, 2016 (*https://www.ukessays.com.*).
Cachar project proposal for rehab of 176 families (19/10/2016) viewed on 1st November, 2016 (*timesofindia.com)*

3. Cases

Ashok Kumar Thakur *vs.* Union of India, [2008 6 SCC 1: (2008) 5JT, per Dalveer Bhandari J. at p. 646.]
Mohini Jain *vs.* State of Karnataka, [AIR 1992, SC1858(1992)3SCC 666]
Superstar Education Society *vs.* State of Maharashtra, (2008) 3SCC 315.

4. Bare Act

The Assam Elementary Education (Provincialisation) Act, 1974.
The Right of Children to Free and Compulsory Education Act, 2009.
The Assam Right of Children to Free and Compulsory Education Rules, 2011.
The Right to Fair Compensation and Transparency in Land Acquisition and Resettlement Act, 2013.
The Land Boundary Agreement, 1974.

8

Education and Marginalised Children and Right To Education in Assam

Tarun Dutta

Background

India is trying to provide quality education since 1990 through Education For All (EFA) programme. EFA is indeed an ambitious onus to strive at providing quality elementary education for 1.4 billion children. After that last two decades saw much action in educational reforms—definitely in terms of formulation of quite a number of schemes, programmes, projects etc. In selective instances and at certain times it manifested as sincere efforts at field-level leading to perceptible changes in classroom practices too. Post-Jomtien and Dakar conferences, the country committing itself to the Millennium Development Goals, along with rest of the world, the universalisation of Elementary Education became a major focus area for India. If the 1990s was the decade of various experimental projects like Lok Jhumbish, Andhra Pradesh Primary Education Project (APPEP), Bihar Education Project (BEP), Uttar Pradesh Basic Education Project (UPBEP), District Primary Education Project (DPEP) etc. which targeted districts/regions identified as having low female literacy, the next decade went for the massive all-encompassing effort—Sarva Shiksha Abhiyan (SSA). The goals were more or less the same to provide quality primary education to all the children, especially those coming from various disadvantaged groups.

In Assam, too, SSA was launched in 2001 along with rest of the country and the state mission which was coordinating the DPEP in nine districts of the state took over the SSA Mission. SSA has completed ten years of its project period and now SSA has taken the form of Right To Education (RTE) Act, 2009 and a new Rashtriya Madhyamik Shiksha Abhiyan (RMSA) and Rashtriya Ussotor Shikshya Abhiyan (RUSA) focusing on secondary and Higher education respectively are being launched.

The Genesis of RTE in India

In the 86th Constitutional Amendment Act (2002) *via* Article 21A it proceeds that a child in between 6 years to 14 year age group has the right to get a free and compulsory education. As a stakeholder, the Government schools shall provide free education to all the children and the schools. According to the Act, the management will be done by School Management Committees (SMC), constituted as per the Act. It has also been said that the Private schools shall admit at minimum 25 per cent of the children in their schools without any fee. A commission shall be formed by the National Commission for Elementary Education to monitor all aspects of elementary education including quality. After the amendment of the constitution in December 2002, first draft of the Bill was prepared in October 2003 and circulated for public comments. After receiving comment and taking it consideration in 2004 the revised draft was prepared as "Free and Compulsory Education Bill, 2004" and the draft Bill submitted to MHRD by CABE (Central Advisory Board of Education) in June 2005. But on 14th July, 2006, the Bill was rejected by the Finance Committee and Planning Commission for lack of funds and sent a Model Bill to all State Governments for their own arrangement. But in 2009, the Bill was passed in both Houses of Parliament, which received President's assent in August 2009 and subsequently, the Act came into effect from 1st of April, 2010.

Implementation of RTE 2009 in Assam: A Quantitative Report

As part of the nationwide stocktaking of RTE organised by National RTE Forum, ActionAid Northeast too, which too is part of the forum, participated in a detailed quantitative survey on the status of implementation of the RTE Act in the schools of Assam and Manipur. The methodology, questionnaire, and the sample size were designed at the national-level. The agreed sample for Assam was 155 (Among them Government aided 16 and unaided

13) schools in the districts of Kamrup, Bongaigaon, Dhemaji, Golaghat and Barpeta. The sample included children from upper primary as well as lower primary-level. And a total number of children covered was 10,189 (Girls 10,055 and Boys 20,645) Special care was taken to include urban as well as rural schools in the sample. ActionAid Northeast conducted these surveys through its partner NGOs and some volunteers, which took place in the year 2012-13. Here some findings are mentioned below, which are some basic requirements of the RTE 2009.

Education Incentives

As per RTE, the children are entitled to certain educational incentives such as Free textbook, Uniform, Mid-Day Meal, and Disability aid for disabled children. Our study tried to find out whether they are available. Here are our findings—

(a) Availability of Free Textbooks (In the First Month of the Academic Session)

It was found that textbook for a student of SC category boys only 42.6 per cent was available to all children, 0.66 per cent it was available to some children only, 1.94 per cent it was not available all and 54.8 cases question was either not applicable or the information not available. For SC girls, the findings are not much different from boys. For the ST, 42 per cent boys and 40 per cent girls received it in all schools, 1 per cent was available to some children only, 2 per cent it was not available at all and 56 per cent cases question was either not applicable or the information not available. For the OBC, 39 per cent boys and girls received it in all schools, 1 per cent was available to some children only, 3 per cent it was not available at all and 57 per cent cases question was either not applicable or the information not available. For the CWSN, 13 per cent boys and 15 per cent girls received it in all schools, 1 per cent was available to some children only, 1 per cent it was not available at all and 84 per cent cases question was either not applicable or the information was not available for disabled. For the Muslim, 45 per cent boys and girls received it in all schools, 1 per cent was available to some children only, 2 per cent it was not available at all and 52 per cent cases question was either not applicable or the information not available. In the case of General children, 37 per cent boys and 36 per cent girls received it in all schools, 1 per cent was available to some children only, 1 per cent it was not available at all and 36 per cent cases question was either not applicable or the information not available.

It can be seen that the emerging pattern is more or less similar here except the per cent being low in case of disabled and general children.

(b) Availability of Free Uniform

It was found that uniform for the student of SC category Children only 27 per cent was available to all children, 18 per cent it was available to some children only, 18 per cent it was not available at all and 54 per cent cases question was either not applicable or the information not available. For the ST, 30 per cent boys and 27 per cent girls received it in all schools, 1 per cent was available to some children only, 14 per cent it was not available at all and 55 per cent cases question was either not applicable or the information not available. For the OBC, 39 per cent boys and girls received it in all schools, 4 per cent was available to some children only, 17 per cent it was not available at all and 40 per cent cases question was either not applicable or the information not available. For the CWSN, 13 per cent boys and 14 per cent girls received it in all schools, 0 per cent was available to some children only, 5 per cent it was not available at all and 80-82 per cent cases question was either not applicable or the information not available for Disabled. For the Muslim, 30 per cent boys and girls received it in all schools, 1 per cent was available to some children only, 15 per cent it was not available at all and 54 per cent cases question was either not applicable or the information not available. In the case of General children, 23 per cent boys and girls received it in all schools, 1 per cent was available to some children only, 15 per cent it was not available at all and 62 per cent cases question was either not applicable or the information not available.

(c) Availability of Free Mid-day Meal

The meal for mid-day was available during the survey period only in 37 per cent of schools. Seven per cent of school were not available at that time and 56 per cent of schools either have no response or no records provided. In available schools, only 56 per cent of school follow the Mid-day meal menu chart and other are not aware or not followed the same.

Profile of Teachers

(a) Category

In 155 schools, total 994 teachers were found out of them 454 were female. Among these teachers, 4 per cent belong to SC, 15 per cent ST, 38 per cent OBC, 10 per cent Muslim and 33 per cent general category.

(b) Qualified or not

According to the RTE guideline teachers of the surveyed schools are Qualified fulltime 78 per cent, Unqualified fulltime 7 per cent, Qualified part-time 4 per cent, qualified full-time contractual 11 per cent for classes I to V and for Classes VI-VIII and Qualified full-time 75 per cent, Unqualified full-time 11 per cent, qualified full-time contractual 14 per cent.

(c) Availability of Teachers

As total 155 schools, we found following types of schools, no teacher are 4, Single teacher 1, Double teacher 24, Three to four teachers 43, Five to six teachers 29, Seven or more teachers 54.

Availability and Accessibility

(a) Neighbourhood Norms and Connectivity

One hundred two (69%) numbers of School are established as per Neighbourhood norms; 110 (71%) schools are connected by all weather roads.

(b) Type of School Building

Out of non-permanent 39 schools Mud build school is 7 (18%), Thatched with leaves/grass is 3 (8%), Tin shed 28 (72%), and Open space 1 (2%).

(c) Drinking Water

Drinking water is available in 60 per cent schools, Not available in 25 per cent schools, Available but not accessible in 9 per cent of Schools.

(d) Sanitation

Functional toilets with water for girls is available in 43 per cent schools, not available in 39 per cent schools and available but not accessible to girls 11 per cent, No response 7 per cent.

(e) CWSN Facility

In most of the schools, CWSN friendly toilet is not available. (71%). Others are not available or not accessible for CWSN.

Ramp with handrail is available in 44 per cent schools and other schools have no such facility.

Status of Teaching Staff According to RTE Norms

PTR norm available in 44 per cent schools and other schools either not followed or not responded.

One hundred fifty number of teachers engaged in non-teaching activities out of 994 teachers (15.09%).

Social Exclusion in Education

During admission, most of the schools insisted for identity proof, but no such incident like denial of admission due to lack of such document was reported.

But from 16 per cent school charges money for admission and other purposes which are violation of RTE Act, 2009.

Facilities for CWSN is not available in schools most of the schools. Very few schools provided such facilities and so drop-out ratio is high among this category children.

Teaching in Mother Tongue

Out of total 35 per cent tribal children concentrated schools, only 10 per cent of tribal children taught in the mother tongue.

Summing-up

India is a country of 1.4 billion children. The Government has certainly onus to contribute a lot towards these children and RTE is a reflection of that responsibility. But the half-hearted approach of the implementing stakeholder to the implementation of RTE Act progress still looks gloomy. Indeed it is interesting to note that the *mantra* of Free and Quality has failed to attract students in government schools. Such ideals merely remains a slogan and are yet to be translated and requires a much more resolute political will.

According to RTE and otherwise, quality is an intriguing aspect of education. The study found that the concerned authority not take care for that. Even the other stakeholder are not continued to remain loyal in their defunct institutions unless there is an improvement in the quality input.

RTE emphasised on equal opportunity for CWSN children to access quality education. The study reveals that education for this category of children remains a huge challenge. RTE Act suggests an inclusive approach to mainstream these vulnerable children. But in the visible absence of physical upgradations towards disable friendly schools and environment, it remains a dream to think of absorbing CWSN in the neighbourhood schools. It is also interesting to note that providing special teachers on population ratio completely defiles.

Bibliography

Annual Status of Education Report (Rural). 2014. New Delhi.

Centre for Civil Society. 2014. RTE State Rules Matrix. New Delhi.

Free and Compulsory Education Bill. 2004. New Delhi: MHRD, Government of India.

National Education Policy. 1986. New Delhi: Ministry of Education, Government of India.

National Education Policy. 1992. New Delhi: Ministry of Education, Government of India.

NEIPA and UNESCO. 2003. *Different Approaches for Achieving EFA: Indian Experience*. New Delhi.

Salam Jeebanlata. 2013. *State, Civil Society and Right to Education*. New Delhi: Rawat Publications.

Sarva Shiksha Abhiyan. 2011. SSA Framework of Implementation in the Light of Right to Education Act, 2009. New Delhi: MHRD, Government of India.

The Right of Children to Free and Compulsory Education Act, 2009. New Delhi: Universal Law Publishing Co. Pvt. Ltd.

UNICEF. 1994. *The Right to be a Child*. New Delhi.

9

Right To Education for Persons with Disabilities in the North-east India

K. Mema Singha, Sumita Sinha and *K. Nirupama Singha*

Introduction

It is well known that an ideal society is not possible unless the various individuals, that constitute it, are perfectly rational in their outlook and behaviour. In order to prevent society from the various unpleasant and undesirable situations which involves the breach of peace and harmony in social life, it is absolutely necessary that every individual be so trained and disciplined that he/she will naturally think and behave rationally. Education has precisely this as its primary aim. Education, in real sense, is to humanize humanity, and to make life progressive, cultured, and civilized. It is very important for the progress of individual and society. It is through Education that a person develops his/her power of thinking and reasoning, problem solving and creativity, intelligence and aptitude, positive sentiments and skills, and good values and attitudes. Education is one of the major indicators of development in today's world. Education is generally considered as a cornerstone of socio-economic and cultural development of a society or country. Education spreads not only awareness, but also informs us about our rights and the services that we can access. Education helps to bridge the gap between the different sections of society.

In India, the constitution guarantees values which are based on the principles of equality, liberty and fraternity, and ensures the dignity of an individual irrespective of his/her caste, creed, political, economic or social status. But these can be achieved only in an atmosphere of justice and fair play. The educational scene in the country has undergone major change over the years, resulting in better provision of education and better educational practices. The Kothari Commission (1964–66), the first education commission of independent India, observed: "the education of the handicapped children should be an inseparable part of the education system." The Commission recommended experimentation with integrated programmes in order to bring as many children as possible into these programmes (Alur, 2002).

The medical model defines disability scientifically, as a physical, medically-diagnosed deficit which handicaps (Giffard-Lindsay, 2007). Article 1 of the Convention on Rights of Persons with Disabilities (CRPD, 2006) describes persons with disability (PWD) as "those who have long-term physical, mental, intellectual, or sensory impairments which in interaction with various barriers may hinder their full and effective participation in society on an equal basis with others". But it should be mentioned here that disability is a multidimensional and complex construct and there is no single universally accepted, unproblematic definition of disability. And as such it is very difficult to find reliable data about the prevalence of disability. As per the World Bank and World Health Organization's first "World Report on Disability" (June 11, 2011), one billion people are suffering from some sort of disability (Chakma, 2015). The World Health Organization (WHO) estimates that 10 per cent of the total population is disabled (Thomas, 2005). Among the marginalised groups, disabled persons remain the most excluded, discriminated not only because of their disability, but also because of the lack of understanding and knowledge about its causes, implications and stigma.

Disability issue has not received substantial attention in India, especially when it is in the North-Eastern States of India. There exists some service providers, associations of parents, disabled and self advocates in this region that are taking care of the disabled. However, the life of the disabled persons remains unchanged; their aspirations for a decent livelihood are a distant dream in the North-East Region.

Education is one of the most effective ways to break the cycle of discrimination and poverty that persons with disability often face. Moreover, when children with disability (CWD) do attend school they rarely progress beyond the primary level, leading ultimately to lower employment chances and long-term income poverty. Their access to school is often limited by the lack of understanding about their needs, lack of teacher training, unconducive school environment, classroom support and learning resources and facilities. Even though various efforts have been made in the recent past, both the rates of educational participation and outcomes of education, remain very poor for children and young adults with disabilities. Illiteracy rates for this group remain much higher than the general population and school attendance continues to lag behind that of non-disabled peers.

Education as a Right of the Persons with Disabilities

To ensure that all people enjoy their basic human rights without discrimination, disability inclusion should be mainstreamed in all policies and plans and this applies to education system also. Persons with disabilities have a right to education. Since the UN Universal Declaration on Human Rights was released in 1948, there has been legislation on providing education for all children. Disability is recognised as one of the least visible yet most potent factors in educational marginalisation. Persons with disabilities remain one of the main groups being widely excluded from quality education.

The education of children with disabilities and special needs in India was initiated in the late 1800s, with the establishment of special schools for the Deaf in Bombay in 1883, and for the Blind in Amritsar in 1887. By 1900 numerous special schools for the visually and hearing impaired children were set up across the country. This initiated the tradition of special schools in the country and till the 1970s, this was the dominant mode of service delivery for Children with Special Needs (CSN).

The Convention of the United Nations on the rights of persons with disabilities says that persons with disabilities have the right to inclusive education. Inclusive education is "a process of addressing and responding to the diversity of needs of all learners through increasing participation in learning, cultures and communities, and reducing exclusion within and from education. It involves changes and modifications in content, approaches, structures and strategies, with a common vision which covers all children of the appropriate age range and a conviction that it is the responsibility of the state to educate all children" (UNESCO, 2005). Inclusive education is not a marginal issue, but is central to the achievement of high-quality education for all learners and the development of more inclusive societies. This means that persons with disabilities have the right to go to regular schools and learn new things together with persons without disabilities.

Persons with Disabilities in North-East India

The North-East (NE) region of India is home to 44 million persons who live in eight states – Arunachal Pradesh, Assam, Manipur, Meghalaya, Mizoram, Nagaland, Sikkim and Tripura. The NE region has been affected by numerous conflicts for decades, which continue to flare up periodically. Due to all these reasons, the development of infrastructure, institutions, communication and services is lagging behind the rest of the country. Significant challenges affect the disability and rehabilitation services in the North-East. Lack of accessible information about disability and rehabilitation services is another key issue that makes it difficult to understand the gaps and the challenges. Apart from the data collected during national censuses, very little statistical information is available about the lives of PWDs and their families in the region. "Sarva Shiksha Abhiyan", a Government programme promoting Universal Access to Education, is often the only source of periodic reports on this theme, though these reports focus only on the children, including the children with disabilities, of the school-going age (*Disability and Rehabilitation in North East India,* 2016).

The past decade has seen important progress in the NE region in terms of services for PWDs, including the setting up of offices of the State Disability Commissioners (SDCs) and District Disability and Rehabilitation Centres (DDRCs). Slowly there are efforts in different states of the North-East to provide disability certificates and access to various government schemes aimed at poor families and those with PWDs.

The national census carried out in India in 2011 collected information about persons with eight categories of disability (seeing, hearing, speech, movement, mental retardation, mental illness, multiple disabilities and any other disabilities). Through the census, a total of 26.8 million persons with disabilities were identified in India in which around 15 million are men and 11.8 million are women. Rural areas have higher proportion of disabled persons than urban areas. Disabled persons constitute 2.13 percentage of the total population of the country. In 2001-2011, percentage of disabled persons has been increased in the country. Globally, the states with the highest and lowest prevalence of persons with disabilities were both in the North-East India – Sikkim with 2.98 per cent and Mizoram with 1.38 per cent. Table 9.1 presents an overview of 2011 census data regarding persons with disabilities in the North-Eastern states.

Table 9.1: Basic Demographic Information about PWDs in the North-East

States	*Total PWDs (% of the total population)*	*Men with disabilities*	*Women with disabilities*	*Children below 18 yrs.*
Arunachal Pradesh	27,634 (1.93%)	14,245	12,489	8,438
Assam	4,80,065 (1.54%)	2,57,385	2,22,680	1,34,479
Manipur	54,110 (2.11%)	28,783	25,327	16,181
Meghalaya	44,317 (1.49%)	23,326	20,991	17,413
Mizoram	15,160 (1.38%)	8,198	6,962	3,748
Nagaland	29,631 (1.50%)	16,148	13,483	7,740
Sikkim	18,187 (2.98%)	NA	NA	NA
Tripura	64,346 (1.75%)	35,482	28,864	16,509

Source: Census of India, 2011.

The census data does not always coincide with other data collected by the states. For example, according to the 2011 census, there were 44,317 PWDs in Meghalaya. However, according to the Annual Report of the State Disability Commissioner (SDC Meghalaya, 2009-13), in 2012-13, there were 39,089 PWDs in the state. This may be due to different definitions and methodologies used for identifying PWDs at different points in time.

Access to Education for Persons with Disabilities in the North-East India

The Government of India has made outstanding efforts to ensure the access of persons with disabilities to a range of poverty alleviation and employment generation programmes with the aim of achieving inclusive development. But despite the government's initiatives persons with disabilities in North-East India are still among the most marginalised and excluded population groups and the need remains to continue joint efforts towards an inclusive society.

The 86th Constitutional Amendment of the Constitution of India in 2002 made the Right to Education a Fundamental Right, by providing the right to free and compulsory education to all children between the ages of 6 and 14 years. Sarva Shiksha Abhiyan (SSA) is a national programmes launched and implemented in 2001, in collaboration with State Governments for promoting universal access to basic education for children between 6 to 14 years of age. Among other things it promoted right to primary education for children with disabilities by promoting mainstreaming and inclusive education. For children with severe disabilities who were unable to access local schools, it proposed home-based education.

The impact of SSA was evaluated in 2008 in eleven states, including Assam (both in urban and rural areas) from the North-East. Regarding the overall impact of SSA on children with disabilities, the report of this evaluation (PEO, 2010) concluded that "An impressive increase was also observed in the enrolment of differently abled children with their share rising from 0.43 per cent of the total enrolment in 2003 to 1.17 per cent in 2007 in rural areas. In urban schools, their share declined during the reference period. Though the children were provided financial and non-financial incentives, few schools had individualised education plans." The evaluation report mentioned that under the scheme "Integrated Education for Disabled" training was provided to teachers on teaching techniques and for preparation of individualised education plans, children were provided assistive devices such as hearing aids, spectacles, wheelchairs, braille kits etc.

A regional meeting on SSA and inclusive education in the NE was held in Shillong in 2013 (SSA-NE, 2013). The workshop concluded that the inclusive education strategy in NE needed to focus on capacity building of general teachers and acknowledged huge gaps in data collection on children with disabilities. Annual Report of Human Resources Development Ministry at national level for the year 2013-14 informs that under SSA they provide Rs. 3000 for the integration of each child with disability in the school and cover actual costs for assistive devices, books and stationery, uniform and transport. This report also provides a long list of various schemes and services to support education for children and young adults with disabilities (MHRD, 2015).

Students with Disabilities in Higher Education in the North-East

Since 2011. Ministry of Human Resource Development has also initiated a survey on higher education at university level. This also provides information about students with disabilities enrolled in universities in India. A review of the annual reports of this survey between 2011 and 2014 provides the following information about total students with disabilities in Higher Education institutions in the North-East. In 2011-12 they were 663 (66% male and 34% female); in 2012-13 they were 867 (66% male and 34% female); and in 2013-14 they were 2,182 (61% male and 39% female). Thus, between 2011-12 and 2013-14, there has been more than 100 per cent increase in enrolment of students with disabilities in the universities in the North-East and this increase has been much higher for female students (AIHES, 2015). However, if we look at the data from individual states of the NE, the increase in enrolment in higher education has occurred mainly in Assam and Tripura, and to a lesser degree in Manipur and Meghalaya. In Mizoram and Nagaland, the increase was minor and the total number of students was also very small. While in Arunachal Pradesh and Sikkim, the number of students with disabilities in higher education has actually decreased. Table 9.2 presents the detailed data from these survey reports.

Thus, the specific attention shown by Ministry of Human Resource Development and State Governments has had a positive impact in enrolment of students with disabilities in higher education in some States of the North-East. In future, it will be important to see what percentage of students with disabilities complete school and what percentage joins the institutes of higher education compared to non-disabled students.

Conclusion

In spite of all the efforts taken at various levels to include children with disabilities in the learning process, there are a number of

Table 9.2: Students with Disabilities in Higher Education in the North-East

States	Students with Disability in higher education		
	2011-12	2012-13	2013-14
Arunachal Pradesh	53	32	31
Assam	384	517	996
Manipur	80	93	150
Meghalaya	24	106	63
Mizoram	9	13	12
Nagaland	10	10	15
Tripura	96	92	914
Sikkim	7	4	1
Total	**663**	**867**	**2,182**

Source: Annual Reports of All India Survey on Higher Education 2011-12, 2012-13 and 2013-14.

factors that still hamper their progress. Many times persons with disabilities are still not accepted by society as equals and have to make great effort to realize even their most basic rights. If education of the persons with disabilities is to become a reality in North-East India, the training of teachers has to become a top priority. The teachers need to be provided with intensive training to work with various disabilities. It is essential to address issues related to infrastructural facilities, curriculum and educational materials for education of children with disabilities. It is also necessary to establish an alternative system of examination for persons with disabilities. Students in this system should be asked to do activities that demonstrate their abilities rather than disabilities. There is no doubt that the dream for discrimination free and equal education for the persons with disability may require a comprehensive change in the institutional arrangements and legal provisions, but the most important change has to come in our minds, in our thinking and attitude towards the disabled. Removing barriers to accessing education and to learning for children with disabilities are prerequisites for the realization of "Education For All". To ensure that all children have access to quality education, education policies and practices must be inclusive of all learners, encourage the full participation of all. Diversity is to be regarded as a resource, rather as an obstacle. Inclusive education will pave the way to prosperity for individuals and for the society.

References

AIHES (2015), Annual Reports of All India Survey on Higher Education 2011-12, 2012-13 and 2013-14 (provisional report) <http://aishe.nic.in/aishe/reports;jsessionid=76ADC9772C7569D2A61866DF46CB88E0>

Alur, M. (2002), "Special Needs Policy in India", in S. Hegarty and M. Alue (eds.), *Education and Children with Special Needs: From Segregation to Inclusion*. New Delhi: Sage Publications.

Census of India (2011)Data on Disability, <http://www.censusindia.gov.in>

Chakma, Namita (2015), "Trend of Disability in North-East India, 2001-2011: An Assessmen", in *International Journal on Recent and Innovation Trends in Computing and Communication*, Volume 3, Issue 11, <http://www.ijritcc.org>

Convention on Rights of Persons with Disabilities, 2006, <www.un.org/../conventionfull.shtml>

Disability and Rehabilitation in North-East India (2016) prepared by Dr. Sunil Deepak, as a consultant to Mobility India, 2016 February, <http://globaldisability.org/wp-content/upl...>

Giffard-Lindsay, Katharine (2007), *Inclusive Education in India: Interpretation, Implementation, and Issues*, UK: CREAT.

MHRD (2015), Annual Report 2013-14, Department of School Education and Literacy, Ministry of Human Resource Development, Government of India, New Delhi.

PEO (2010), Evaluation Report on Sarva Shiksha Abhiyan, Programme Evaluation Organisation, Planning Commission, Government of India, New Delhi, May 2010.

SDC Meghalaya (2009-13), Annual Report 2009-10, 2010-11, 2011-12, 2012-13, Office of the Commissioner for the Persons with Disabilities of Meghalaya, Lower Lachumiere, Temple Road, Shillong-793001, Meghalaya.

SSA-NE (2013), Sarva Shiksha Abhiyan – Minutes of the Regional Workshop on "Consolidation of CWSN Academic Support Structures and Activities", Shillong, Meghalaya, 9-10 July, 2013.

Thomas, P. (2005), *Disability, Poverty and the Millennium Development Goals: Relevance, Challenges and Opportunities for DFID*, London: Disability Knowledge and Research, <http://disabilitykar.net/research/pol_final.html>

UNESCO 2005, *Guidelines for Inclusion: Ensuring Access to Education for All*, Paris.

SECTION-III

Understanding Great Educationist

10

Understanding Gandhian Perspective on Transition Through Education

Archana Barua

When everywhere around us there is tremendous impact of dehumanising effects of "impersonal systems" in many forms, we have to look back to Gandhi for providing positive "humane system" and for building a better world, a new system that would be free from any sort of violence at the individual as well as at the social level. Gandhi provided a scheme how to distinguish true form of education from indoctrination. Mahatma Gandhi, Rabindra Nath Tagore and many other visionaries were concerned not only that there should be wider opportunities for education across the country (especially in rural areas where schools were few), but also that the schools themselves should be more lively and enjoyable. If education is a process that causes real change, not just in one's ability to manipulate symbols, but in every respect of one's being, then what today's educators are called upon to do may be many things, but it is not education. Tagore himself had dropped out of school early, largely out of boredom, and had never bothered to earn a diploma. Gandhi Ji provided a scheme how to distinguish true form of education from indoctrination. To Gandhi, therefore, education means "an all round drawing out of the best in child and man—body, mind and spirit."

Education as Ecstasy

What then is the purpose, the goal of education? George B. Leonard, the senior editor of 'Look' magazine, the Vice President of the Esalen Institute in San Fransisco, and Big Sur, California, and an educational consultant to the USA, suggests one: "a large part of the answer may well be what men of this civilization have longest feared and most desired: the achievement of moment of ecstasy. Not fun, not simply pleasure as in the equation of Bentham and Mill, not the libido pleasure of Freud, but ecstasy, *ananda,* the ultimate delight."[1] That education can and should often be ecstatic may seem an exaggerated and even shocking suggestion. If education is a process that causes real change, not just in one's ability to manipulate symbols, but in every respect of one's being, then what today's educators are called upon to do may be many things, but it is not education. In those class rooms "some pupils learn how to day dream; others, how to take tests".[2]

Tagore himself had dropped out of school early, largely out of boredom, and had never bothered to earn a diploma. He wrote extensively on how schools should be made more attractive to boys and girls and thus more productive. His own co-educational school at Shantiniketan had many progressive features. The emphasis here was on self-motivation rather than on discipline, and on fostering intellectual curiosity rather than competitive excellence. But the intelligence tests in our laboratories have little to do with our ability to educate. Gandhi laments: "The schools and colleges are really a factory for turning out clerks for Government. The real difficulty is that people have no idea of what education truly is. We assess the value of education in the same manner as we assess the value of land or of shares in the stock-exchange market. We want to provide only such education as would enable the student to earn more. We hardly give any thought to the improvement of the character of the educated. The girls, we say, do not have to earn; so why should they be educated? As long as such ideas persist there is no hope of our ever knowing the true value of education."[3] To Gandhi, therefore education means "an all round drawing out of the best in child and man—body, mind and spirit."[4]

Education for Liberation: Empowerment of the Girl-child

Literacy is not end of education or even the beginning. All literate men may not be truly educated while the "illiterate rural masses" at times may cultivate refined sensitivity and progressiveness that "true education" is supposed to bring out. "Rural areas are less literate, but have a better, more balanced gender ratio than urban areas. The harsh truth is that modern education has increased social discrimination instead of eradicating it. It is generally believed that the gender ratio is adverse (in favour of men) in those states where the literacy rate is lower and the gender ratio is more balanced where the literacy rates are higher. This is a completely false interpretation. According to census data the gender ratio in India has steadily fallen from 972 (in the year 1901) to 929 (in 1991), while the literacy rate has been steadily going up from a low of 5.39 per cent in 1901 to a high of 52.21 per cent in 1991."[5] When Gandhiji assumed India's leadership the average life span of an Indian woman was only twenty seven years. Babies and the pregnant women ran a high risk of dying young. Child marriage was very common and widows were in very large number. Only 2 per cent of the women had any kind of education and women did not have an identity of their own. In North India, they practiced the *purdah* system. It is in this context that we have to recognize the miracle of Gandhi's work. "Gandhiji always advocated a complete reform which he called '*Sarvodaya*' meaning comprehensive progress. He believed that the difference between men and women was only physical and has expressed several times in his writings that in many matters especially those of tolerance, patience, and sacrifice the Indian woman is superior to the male. Gandhiji declared that there is no school better than home and there is no teacher better than parents."[6]

He said men and women are equal, but not identical. "Intellectually, mentally, and spiritually, woman is equivalent to a male and she can participate in every activity." Indian society is a mâle dominated one. Gandhiji has illustrated in his autobiography (*The stories of my experiments with truth*) how early in his marriage he too wanted to dominate his wife. He often said that paternal society is the root cause of inequality. In his book, there is a very touching chapter about when he asked his wife to clean a public toilet and the resulting conflict between him and his wife. He has written how ashamed he was of himself, and how he took care not to hurt her anymore for the rest of his life. "Womanhood is not restricted to the kitchen", he opined and felt that "Only when the woman is liberated from the slavery of thc kitchen, that her true spirit may be discovered".[7] We may address this issue from feminist perspective; as well. A feminist perspective is one that addresses women related issues from a woman's point of view. The way

Gandhi had sensitive approach to the caring and the nurturing traits of women, modern feminists emphasis on the experiences of motherhood, a woman undergoing experiences of trauma/rejection etc. as victims of rape, sexual harassment etc. add another dimension to her knowledge. Gandhi glorified woman as mother and also for her capacity to undergo suffering and to emerge wiser out of that experience that is provided by the "laboratory of life."

In the United States, Jane Roland Martin was one of the first professional philosophers of education to bring a feminist perspective to her work. Gandhi will have full support for her feminist concerns that the "very definition of education and the educational realm adopted implicitly by the standard texts in philosophy of education excludes women"[8] (Martin, 1999: 150). Apart from referring to certain woman related issues like sexual harassment, feminist authors have focused on gender linked approaches to knowing their implications for teaching (Belenky, 1986) in its various manifestations. In addition, feminist scholarship has sparked philosophical analyses of types of relationships and practices that in the past were generally ignored by philosophers of education. For instance, Sara Ruddick has argued that mothering constitutes a kind of practice driven by the aims of preservation, growth, and social acceptability (Ruddick, 1989).[9] Engaging in the practice of mothering, Ruddick argues, fosters certain metaphysical attitudes, cognitive capacities, and conceptions of virtue.

From a perspective such as Ruddick's, mothering appears to be of profound educational significance. Gandhi emphasized on attitudinal change that should come from education in its true sense of the term. Gandhi does not mean that women should not cook, but only that household responsibilities be shared among men, women and children. He wanted women to outgrow the traditional responsibilities and participate in the affairs of nation. He criticized Indian's passion for male progeny. He said that as long as we do not consider girls as natural as our boys our nation would be in a dark eclipse.[10] We may relate it to situational mode of knowing that differs from decontextual mode of knowing. Gandhi comes close to the former.

Between ecstasy and order: *Education is a process that changes the learner.*

With our more emphasis on artificial intelligence and computers in school learning, we are optimist that education now is on the right track. It gives more emphasis on "doing", where "doing", unlike in Gandhi, is more mechanical and robotic. "Doing" now means mostly proving mathematical theorems and writing computer programmes. In the field of AI the criterion of "what works" is straightforward, clear, and objective in the manner of engineering design; arguments and criticisms from outside the field can make no claim at all against it. It is this type of thinking that makes humans imitate machine thinking; it keeps no scope for any indecisiveness of the human thinker: there is no grey area; everything is either black and white. This mechanical way for testing intelligence makes us *'mantra vid'*, one who knows all the formulas and have all the required information in one's field, but education here fails to make us *'ātmā vid'*, one who is aware of what lies beyond the surface experience, of values and ideals, the drives and the motivating force that inspires us to 'know'. Gandhi comes close to Dewey in this regard. In an address entitled "Education for the Rank and File", David Snedden drew on the social Darwinism of Herbert Spencer in asserting that society, like nature itself, was governed by often harsh natural laws that must be obeyed. Snedden saw the ultimate aim of education as "the greatest degree of efficiency." This meant that for "the rank and file", that is, "those who do duty in the ranks..., who will follow, not lead", efficiency required "utilitarian training which looks to individual efficiency in the world of work."[11] Dewey thought he saw a social class dualism in David Snedden's distinction between vocational education for the rank and file and liberal education for the few that would lead.[12] For Dewey, all meanings emerged from socio-cultural linguistic transactions. Concepts are cognitive meanings. Dewey warned against hypostatising concepts abstracted from everyday practice. The distinction that Dewey wants to draw is between education through the occupations, something he supports for the kind of philosophical reasons discussed by Hickman, and education for the occupations, a kind of social pre-destinations he entirely rejected. For Dewey, the most important distinction to be drawn was not between liberal *versus* vocational education, but between liberating *versus* enslaving education.[13]

Mahtama Gandhi understood this simple truth long time back when he understood creativity as the basic instinct in men that makes him dynamic and living. Gandhi's conception of basic education was concerned with learning that was generated within everyday life which is the basis on which informal educators work. It was also an education focused on the individual but reliant on co-operation between individuals. The dehumanizing effect of any education system may preserve order, but it will not provide new weapons to survive at a time of change and transition, from localization to globalization, certain changes which just happen to us and which is unavoidable. It is only in an environment, which fosters innovation that borderless minds can be formed and borderless thinking can flourish. It is only breaking up those walls and opening-up those windows of mind will bring that fresh wind that will build the "Innovative India" of our dreams.

Empowering the Poor: Liberation For All—Gandhi sought to safeguard the human dimension of our existence and in this dialectic, man represented the whole of mankind, not just India, and the machine represented the industrialised. This alternate model of development will be decisive in his education policies. Gandhi wanted to re-order priorities, he was not against machine and industry, but he was against the mechanisation of humans and dehumanising effect of it on society. He visualised that the burden of cities should be heavy on villages, of larger cities on smaller ones. Gandhi revolutionised the basic concept of education with more focus on an alternate model of development that will also empower the poor and the village along with benefits to the elite and the cities. No one rejected colonial education as sharply and completely did by Gandhi, which was unprecedented. Instead of Gandhi proposed a radical alternative on educational curriculum based on vocational and training. But this is not just a usual stereotyped response that one can easily interpret Gandhi's an search for an alternate education system as a kind of xenophobia. "It would be equally wrong to see it as a symptom of a subtle revivalist dogma. If it were possible to read Gandhi's "basic education" plan as an anonymous text in the history of world education, it would be conveniently classified in the tradition of Western radical humanists like Pestalozzi, Owen, Tolstoy and Dewey. It does not lend itself to be read in the context of the East-West dichotomy that Gandhi did deal with in some of his other writings."[14]

Yet the fact remains that Gandhi wanted education—reconstructed along the lines he thought correct—to help India move away from the Western concept of progress, towards a different form of development more suited to its needs and more viable, for the world as a whole than the Western model of development. Adequate definitions of "development" and "under-development" must necessarily be linked to a form of self-reliance rooted firmly in the capacities and interests of the working people. Re-defining development in terms of an expansion of capabilities, or freedoms to lead a life which is valuable (Sen, 1993), Nobel laureate Amartya Sen defines development not in terms of GDP, but in terms of "the real freedoms that people enjoy."[15] In the true sense of the term, development must embody five elements: political freedoms, economic facilities, social opportunities, transparency guarantees and protective security. Basic education or *Nai Talim* is based on the fundamental principle of "learning by doing". Gandhi is essentially a doer than a thinker and, therefore, his concept of basic education can be classified as activity method or practical method. It is primarily a method of co-relation of book learning, craft and like-situations. He lays great emphasis on the necessity of training student for manual work under the supervision of teachers. Gandhi is of the opinion that education should be imparted through crafts like gardening, weaving, spinning, carpentry etc., a realistic scheme of education must be closely integrated with the physical and social environment of the student.

Gandhi sought to keep the centrality of the *charkha* in our education system. This he did in order to revolutionize entire teaching programme that traditionally associated productive handicrafts with the lowest groups in the hierarchy of castes. This now kept room for "radical restructuring of the sociology of school knowledge in India, where knowledge of the production processes involved in crafts, such as spinning, weaving, leather-work, pottery, metal-work, basket-making and book-binding, had been the monopoly of specific caste groups in the lowest stratum of the traditional social hierarchy. Many of them belonged to the category of 'untouchables'. India's indigenous tradition of education as well as the colonial education system had emphasized the skills (such as literacy) and knowledge of which the upper castes had a monopoly."[16] The social philosophy and the curriculum of "basic education" thus favoured the child belonging to the lowest stratum of society. It sought to alter the symbolic meaning of 'education' and thereby to change the established structure of opportunities for education. Schools must be self-supporting, as far as possible, not to be dependent on the contributions from the poor students, and also self-sufficiency will protect schools from dependence on the State and from interference by it. Financial self-sufficiency was linked to truth, and autonomy to non-violence.

"Gandhi had established in South Africa, Phoenix Farm, started in 1904, and Tolstoy Farm, which was established in 1910, provided him with a lasting interest and faith in the potential of life in a rural commune. John Ruskin's 'Untothis' apparently inspired the first of these experiments last. Gandhi learnt three lessons from this book, or rather, as Louis Fischer has explained, Gandhi read three messages from the book. The first message was that the benefit of all is what a good economy is all about; the second was that earnings from manual work (such as that of a barber) have the same value as mental work (such as that of a lawyer); and the third one was that a life worth living was that of a labourer or craftsman."[17] In the context of education too he seemed reluctant to commit himself to a purely secular position, but the fact remains that his basic education plan provides no room for religious teaching. In June 1938, he had to explain the matter in some detail because a delegation of educators demanded to know precisely what his view was on this matter. His answer was: "We have left out the teaching of religion from the Wardha scheme of education because we are afraid that religions as they are taught and practiced today lead to conflict rather than unity. But on the other hand, I hold that the truths that are common to all religions can and should be taught to all children. These truths cannot be taught through words or through books—the children can learn these truths only through the daily life of the Teacher. If the teacher himself lives up to the tenets of truth and justice, then alone can the children learn that Truth and Justice are the basis of all religions."

Conclusion

Dr. Karna Singh speaks out on our behalf when he says: "I belong to the Post-Gandhian generation, but it does seem to me, that as time goes by many of us who, when we were younger, tended to dismiss Gandhiji's ideas as being unrealistic and hopelessly idealistic, are now beginning to realize that perhaps in the long run those ideas can be of great value to the emerging global civilization."[18] In Rio de Janeiro in 1992, the Earth Summit, there were thousands of green activists who drew their inspiration not from Marx, not from Lenin, not from Adam Smith, but from Mahatma Gandhi. There were young people there who had been influenced by the thoughts of this man, who spoke to them across the gulf of decades. Gandhi's emphasis on the individual rather than the machines and on small-scale village production rather than large scale factory manufacture can bring about peace, freedom and socio-economic development in a reasonable period. I conclude with the following words of Arya Bhushan Bharadwaj," We have to look back to Gandhi. After the near failure of both communism and capitalism, we have to look for a Third Power which could provide a better and more positive "humane system" for building a better world, a new system that would be free from any sort of violence at the individual as well as at the social level. Here comes the relevance of Gandhi who advocated a new socio-political system based on human values of love and compassion."[19]

Notes

1. George B. Leonard (1968). *Education and Ecstasy*. New York: Delacorte Press.
2. *Ibid.*
3. M. K. Gandhi, True Education on the NCTE sit Veeraraghavan, "Education and cultural diversities; An opportunity for Adult Education in the post-modern world", in LITERARY ONLINE http://www.literacyonline.org/products/ili/webdocs/raghvan.html
4. *Ibid.*
5. *Ibid.*
6. Jyotsna Kamat, "Gandhi and Status of Women", Mahatma Gandhi Album Page Last Updated: September 08, 2006: http.www.kamat.com/mmgandhi
7. *Ibid.*
8. Martin, J.R. (1999). "Women, Schools, and Cultural Wealth". In Titone, Connie and Maloney, Karen E. (Eds.), *Women's Philosophy of Education: Thinking Through our Mothers*. Upper Saddle River, New Jersey: Merrill, 149-177.
9. Ruddick, S. (1989). *Maternal Thinking: Toward a Politics of Peace*. New York: Ballantine.
10. Gandhi, M.K. (1977). *The Collected Works*, Ahmedabad: Navajivan. (Talk to Khadi Vidyalaya Students, Sevagram, Sevak, 15 February, 1942, *CW* 75, p. 269).

11. "Education for the Rank and File", Snedden Cited by Walter H. Drost in *David Snedden and Education for Social Efficiency*, (Madison: University of Wisconsin Press, 1967), p. 43.
12. John Dewey, *Democracy and Education*, in, *The Middle Works, 1899-1924*, Vol. 9, (ed.) Jo Ann Boydston (Carbondale: Southern Illinois University Press, 1916, 1980), p. 316.
13. *Ibid.*
14. Veeraraghavan, "Education and cultural diversities: An opportunity for Adult Education in the post-modern world", in LITERARY ONLINE http://www.literacyonline.org/products/ili/webdocs/raghvan.html
15. *Ibid.*
16. *Ibid.*
17. *Ibid.*
18. Gandhi, M.K. (1977). *The Collected Works*, Ahmedabad: Navajivan. (Talk to Khadi Vidyalaya Students, Sevagram, Sevak, 15 February, 1942, *CW* 75, p. 269).
19. The Emerging Order For Regional Peace and International Security. Arya Bhushan Bharadwaj. http://www.mkgandhi-accesed:October 2006.

11

Gandhi's Concept of Basic Education

A Sustainable Solution

Pranay Deb

Introduction

Mahatma Gandhi is considered as one of the greatest teacher of India, who has left his valuable imprint on us. His role has been imparted as a reformer of ancient thought to conform to the requirements of the modern world. Gandhi realised the necessity of educational reconstruction for the general and political regeneration of his country. In the present study, an attempt has been made to explore the basic characteristics given by Gandhiji about the *Basic Education* and an attempt would be made to emphasise on its implication towards a sustainable solution, which can definitely give a new dimension to our educational system.

Now-a-days, environmental crisis is a global issue. The large-scale industrial development is responsible for environmental pollution and producing threat to the ecology. To solve this problem, Gandhi advocated for a sustainable society, which works in partnership with nature and conserves natural resources. It is the society which integrates the environment, development, economic and social dimensions. A sustainable society has faith in science and technology merely as an instrument to environment-friendly social and economic change. Economic growth must not be at the expense of ecological assets. There is concern for the environment, how to combat environmental pollution, and avoiding depletion of non-renewable resources. In this sustainable society, use of natural resources depends not merely on the ways of their use, but more importantly, people's equal access to those resources. It is a developmental model that promotes ecological sustainability, social equity, community ownership and management of resources, gender equality and equality among nations.[1] It is based on the social awakening of individuals to realise "equal rights to all". In this regard people must be aware of his harmonious relationship with the nature. This task would be fulfilled by the proper education of man.

Education for Sustainability

Human development has no meaning without moral values. The moral values place an important role in the human life. It builds a strong foundation on which human society develops. Modern technology has developed in such an aggressive way that it has become its own enemy. The modern development has increased inequality. The rich have become richer and the poor have become poorer. Unfortunately, human knowledge instead of becoming an instrument of peaceful world has become instrument of domination, exploitation. True education should promote morality, character and spirituality. Education should provide both physical knowledge for living and spiritual knowledge for understanding the nature which sustains life.

Gandhi placed his faith in the power of *'Nai Talim'* (Basic Education). Through this he visualised to restore the objectives of education and help to create a non-violent society. He realised the necessity of educational reconstruction for the general and political regeneration of his country. This education process should be in the mother tongue, through the medium of village-craft and should aim at self-reliance. Gandhi structured the educational process by saying,

> Craft, art, health and education should all be integrated into one scheme. *Nai Talim* is a beautiful blend of all the four and covers the whole education of the individual from the time of conception to the moment of death. Therefore, I would not divide village uplift work into watertight compartment from the very beginning but undertake an activity which will combine all four. Instead of regarding craft and industry as different from education, I will regard the former as the medium of the latter.[2]

Every individual has to be trained and educated in such a manner that the ideal of *Rama-Rajya* is reached conveniently.

Concept of Basic Education

According to Gandhi education means "an all-round drawing out of the best in child and man—body, mind and spirit."[3] As such, education becomes the basis of personality development in all dimensions—moral, mental, and emotional. Every individual is born with certain qualities which can be developed to the fullest extent for the benefit of individual and society by proper education. Education enlightens the moral values in man, which gives emphasis on the complete and harmonious development of individual personality. It will make the way to transcend the finite nature of man and finally to attain the state of spiritual unity of all. Everybody would be able to realise the element of goodness present in every man. Gandhi emphasised the need for living in intimate kinship with nature.

Therefore, the goal of education, according to Gandhi should be character-building; the development of strength, courage, virtue, the ability to forget oneself in working towards great aims. All-round development is possible only if education is combined knowledge with work, percept with example. Gandhi says, "I hold that true education of the intellect can only come through a proper exercise and training of the bodily organs, e.g., hands, feet, eyes, ears, nose etc. In other words an intelligent use of the bodily organs in a child provides the best and quickest way of developing his intellect."[4] His intellectual education would include knowledge of mathematics and the various sciences and to be added by literature. Then it would give him a perfect well-balanced, all-round education, which will constitute an individual into a natural, harmonious whole. This is what is known as Basic Education.

To build good character moral education is necessary. Gandhi's concept of basic education is based on moral and ethical knowledge. Any education system that lacks these two cannot be termed as good. This lays down the philosophy of the basic education. The reason behind such a thought is that, without morality and without ethics, no student, in a real sense, can be considered to be healthy in mental and physical terms. A person who is not a moralist and who does not differentiate between right and wrong cannot rise to the essential level of a true student. On the other way we also prove the same thing, because when we consider education as a means of attaining salvation and also as a means to liberation, we cannot differentiate it from spiritualism.

Craft-centred Practical Education

Education has to be through a craft, not merely through books and abstractions. Gandhi emphasised on practical aspect of education, which includes manual work. Therefore, he recommends that a student is taught to use his organs of knowledge and action harmoniously in learning some basic handicraft, *e.g.* carpentry, spinning, weaving or any other similar kind. So, he says, "You have to train the boys in one occupation or another. Round this special occupation you will train up his mind, his body, his hand-writing, his artistic sense, and so on. He will be master of the craft he learns."[5] This type of education will supply them intellectual background as well as the solution of problems arising out of such manual work. By doing so individual will develop interest in his work and will be able to give out his best. Then only the learner would enjoy the education, instead of bearing the burden of education. By this way "...students would be made physically efficient, intellectually alert, practically useful, and possessed of self-confidence."[6]

The ultimate purpose behind Gandhi's attempt was to make young men and women self-reliant in the economic field. All branches of knowledge and integrating them with manual work done by the students would fetch some income to them, which will be benefited for them as well as for the state. Gandhi conceived this method primarily for the villages. In other words, Gandhi's educational philosophy was borne out of his intense need to better the condition of rural India. As Kumarappa puts it, "Gandhiji saw that the only way of saving the nation at that juncture was to revive village economic life and to relate education to it. Education was to be based on village occupations. The child was to be trained to be a producer."[7]

Gandhi foresaw the mad race of the luxuries of industrialised urban societies. This blind race of the modern society leads to the enslavement of the individual by the modern consumerist society. Gandhi advocated solution to this problem in the form of rational approach to our wants. Let us voluntarily reduce our wants to a genuine-level. Gandhi had conviction in plain living and high thinking. We have to make remarkable few demands on the earth. Once Gandhi said, "...the secret of happy life lies in renunciation. Renunciation is life. Indulgence spells death."[8] The attitude of renunciation, self-sacrifice, and self-transcendence must be the essence of Gandhi's educational thought.

Gandhi's theory is against the prevalent model of higher education because it alienates the student from society and stuffs him with largely irrelevant imported information. Such an education merely gives instructions or makes man literate, but literacy is not education. In Gandhi's type of education, the individual will find that the things that he learns are of actual use in life. But unlike Gandhi's concept, the higher education that is imparted today in Indian Universities is mere intellectual training unrelated to the real needs of the society and the individual. So, he wrote, "I would therefore begin the child's education by teaching it a useful handicraft....Only every handicraft has to be taught not merely mechanically as is done today but scientifically, i.e. the child should know the why and the wherefore of every process."[9] Even in the modern perspective, his idea of *buniyadi* or basic education is applicable and it does not clash with the concept of today's job-oriented or technical education.

This kind of education will help an individual to be confident. Then it will become the power-house of a silent social revolution and will make individuals skilled in their own arts and they will choose their own destiny. The establishment of scientific and efficient cottage industries would eliminate the evils of industrialisation and it will prevent the decay of village culture and the lust for city-life. As Kumarappa puts it, Gandhi "...was convinced that machine civilisation brought enslavement and exploitation of vast sections of a nation and of industrially backward peoples."[10] Gandhi's educational ideals were thus meant to transform backward, illiterate, exploited, desperately poor peasants into self-confident and self-respecting citizens of a new community and nation. In that sense, Gandhi was the least elitist and most practical of our major educational thinkers of this century.

Conclusion

The basic system of education is still in an experimental state in

India. Gandhi's dreams of making the villages self-reliant on the basis of some basic craft and agriculture remain mostly unrealised. Gandhian educational ideas, founded as they are on certain eternal principles, will not lose their fundamental relevance in the years to come. His education system are greatly emphasising the culture of peace, sincere work, dedication of the cause to the nation, social minded, friendliness, right feelings, economic advancement, physical improvement and socio-cultural progress. He believed in the necessity of study, research and experiment without bias, to discover truth from all sources, ancient and modern, Eastern and Western. Our planners will have to think of a self-supporting primary education, which will improve the lot of the poorest of the poor. That is why Gandhi's concept of Basic Education has far-reaching consequences in the modern ego-centric world. We have to apply Gandhi's thought according to the present circumstances of our country and also as per the demands of our present time.

Notes

1. Mishra, Anil Dutta & S. Narayanasamy (2009): *World Crisis and the Gandhian Way*, New Delhi: Concept Publishing Company (P) Ltd., 161.
2. Gandhi, M.K. (1960): *Village Industries* (Ahmedabad: Navajivan Publishing House), p. 19.
3. Gandhi, M.K. (1937): *Harijan*, 31 July.
4. Gandhi, M.K. (1937): *Harijan*, 8 May.
5. Gandhi, M.K. (1937): *Harijan*, 18 September.
6. Datta, D.M. (1968): *The Philosophy of Mahatma Gandhi* (Kolkata: University of Calcutta), pp. 19-30.
7. Gandhi, M.K. (1951): *Basic Education* (Ahmedabad: Navajivan Publishing House), p. iii.
8. Gandhi, M.K. (1946): *Harijan*, 24 February.
9. Gandhi, M.K. (1937): *Harijan*, 31 July.
10. Gandhi, M.K. (1951): *Basic Education* (Ahmedabad: Navajivan Publishing House), p. iv.

References

Bose, Nirmal Kumar (1978): *Studies in Gandhism* (Ahmedabad: Navajivan Publishing House).

Datta, D.M. (1968): *The Philosophy of Mahatma Gandhi* (Kolkata: University of Calcutta).

Dayal, P. (2006): *Gandhian Theory of Social Reconstruction* (New Delhi: Atlantic Publishers and Distributors).

Diwakar, R.R. (1965): *Gandhi: A Practical Philosopher* (Mumbai: Bharatiya Vidya Bhavan).

Gandhi, M.K. (1962): *Hind Swaraj* (Ahmedabad: Navajivan Publishing House).

Gandhi, M.K. (2011): *India of My Dreams* (Ahmedabad: Navajivan Publishing House).

Gandhi, M.K. (1954): *Sarvodaya* (Ahmedabad: Navajivan Publishing House).

Gandhi, M.K. (2011): *Towards New Education* (Ahmedabad: Navajivan Publishing House).

Gandhi, M.K. (1951): *Basic Education* (Ahmedabad: Navajivan Publishing House).

Gandhi, M.K. (1962): *Village Swaraj* (Ahmedabad: Navajivan Publishing House).

Gangal, S.C. (1997): *Gandhian Thought and Techniques in the Modern World* (Delhi: Deep & Deep Publications).

Mishra, Anil Dutta (1996): *Gandhian Approach to Contemporary Problems* (New Delhi: Mittal Publications).

Prabhu, R.K. & U.R. Rao (ed.) (1960): *The Mind of Mahatma Gandhi* (Ahmedabad: Navajivan Publishing House).

Ramachandran, G. & T. K. Mahadevan (ed.) (1967): *Gandhi: His Relevance for our Times* (New Delhi: Gandhi Peace Foundation).

Sharma, D. (2012): *Gandhi—Thought and Philosophy* (New Delhi: Arise Publishers & Distributors).

12

Craft-Based Moral Education

A Prospect To Restore Women's Dignity

Achhiya Begam

Introduction

Moral education and economic self-dependence are two essential prerequisite for the empowerment of women. It is a fact that a large section of rural people (particularly women) of North-East India had no opportunity to have a glimpse of education. As a result they have high level of unemployment, which is adversely affecting the quality of life of rural women. The proper education increases the economic, social, and political opportunities available to women. While moral education helps to uproot gender disparities, crimes against women prevailing in our rural society. To restore women's dignity, it is important to modify social attitude and social value towards women.

Swami Vivekananda and M.K. Gandhi as two major social reformers emphasised on the role of education to emancipate women from miseries. According to them, education can change evil social attitude, which would not only be basic and vocational, but must be moral. This chapterr is an attempt to give emphasis on the importance of proper education to bring social justice. It is aimed at reviewing the dignity of women and finding out a proper status of women in the light of Swami Vivekananda and M.K. Gandhi.

Education and Women Empowerment

North-east India is known for its unique indigenous culture and rural flavour. People of this land are very close to Mother Earth and lead an uncomplicated life far away from the speedy chaotic life of the cities of mainland India. In this regard craft-centred education will make them economically stable and self-dependent.

Education increases the economic, social and political opportunities available to women. It leads to direct economic benefits in the form of higher lifetime earnings for women. Society and community is benefited from the higher productivity of their labour. Besides improving human capital and increasing economic growth, female education also reduces the fertility rate. Keeping women illiterate clearly retards economic growth. Societies that do not invest in girls' education pay a price for it in terms of slower growth and reduced incomes. Investments in female education start a virtuous cycle that leads to improved levels of income, growth and gender equality.

The economic development of women through their employment gives their family an economic advantage and it also gives them to feel more confident about their personal life. Hence, they can take their personal decisions like future career, marriage etc. by their own. Moreover, women want freedom of work. This freedom leads to greater openness, generosity and tolerance. This monetary independence leads them to the way to empowerment. So, employment emancipates women from the subordination and domination by others.

The system of education is the medium to enrich oneself with right knowledge. Various educational policies, educational institutes and educated individuals are increasing day by day, although injustice, crime, exploitation are also increased in alarming rate. The question raises automatically that, what requirement is being fulfilled by the present educational system? Material satisfaction is not enough to lead a more acceptable and peaceful society where an individual can cultivate the quality of unselfishness, which can give him spiritual satisfaction, that is only possible through moral education. Moral education helps one to know about self-duty, performance of duty in a right way, respect for others, right which is very much essential to establish social justice. So, it is important to include moral education in all branches of knowledge.

Cottage Industries and Women Empowerment

In North-East India, cottage industry is very much popular. Especially, tribal women are expert in producing Handloom product, bamboo product etc. Handloom and weaving is a popular household activity among women. Some popular craft of north-east India are handloom and handicrafts, woodcrafts, needlework, agro-based cottage industries, forest based industries, textile based cottage industries etc. In this regard craft-based education system will help them to realise their inner potentiality. Realising in this practicality will bring in self-confidence in the mind of the individual in such a way that, whatever act is performed will be of the highest order. This will play a significant role to the economic development of a nation. Education has to be through a craft, not merely through books and abstractions. All-round development is possible only if education is combined knowledge with work, percept with example. It would give a perfect well-balanced, holistic world-view, which will constitute an individual into a natural, harmonious whole. This is what is known as Gandhi's *Basic Education.*

Education is the main important factor in the developmental process of a nation. It improves the quality of a life leading to the formation of human resources. Education acts as a catalyst that makes individuals and communities to move out of poverty and ignorance into a life of prosperity and wisdom.

Gandhi on Women Education

Mahatma Gandhi believed that there is an element of goodness essentially present in every man. To realise it, there is need of proper education. Gandhi insisted on the craft based moral education to students of both at the school and at the college levels. According to Gandhi, education means "an all-round drawing out of the best in child and man—body, mind and spirit."[1] Every individual is born with certain qualities which can be developed to the fullest extent for the benefit of individual and society by proper education. Gandhi's educational theory puts greater emphasis on the complete and harmonious development of individual personality, so that everybody would be able to realise the element of goodness present in every man and would be able to realise spiritual oneness of the whole universe. Therefore, the goal of education, according to Gandhi should be character-building and self-dependence; the development of strength, courage, virtue, the ability to forget oneself in working towards great aims.

Gandhi also gave great emphasis on practical aspect of education, which includes manual work. Therefore, he recommends that a student is taught to use his organs of knowledge and action harmoniously in learning some basic handicraft, e.g. carpentry, spinning, weaving or any other similar kind. By doing so individual will develop interest in his work and will be able to give out his best. It would lead learner to enjoy the education, instead of bearing the burden of education. The ultimate purpose behind Gandhi's attempt was to make young men and women self-reliant in the economic field. But unlike Gandhi's concept, the higher education that is imparted today in Indian universities is mere intellectual training unrelated to the real needs of the society and the individual. So, he wrote, "I would therefore begin the child's education by teaching it a useful handicraft....Only every handicraft has to be taught not merely mechanically as is done today but scientifically, i.e. the child should know the why and the wherefore of every process."[2] Even in the modern perspective, his idea of *buniyadi* or basic education is applicable and it does not clash with the concept of today's job-oriented or technical education.

This kind of education will help an individual to be confident. Then it will become the power-house of a silent social revolution and will make individuals skilled in their own arts and they will choose their own destiny. Gandhi's educational ideals were thus meant to transform backward, illiterate, exploited, desperately poor women into self-confident and self-respecting citizens of a new community and nation.

Vivekananda on Women Education

According to Vivekananda, "the uplift of the women must come first, and then any real good comes about for the country. All nations have attained greatness by paying proper respect to women. If any country or nation do not give respect to women have never become great, nor will be in future."[3] For example, in

Pakistan women are in very unfortunate condition, and which affect on their national progress. If women have the chance to rise themselves then only they can raise the future of their children, through which nation, otherwise with her, everything fall down. Vivekananda realised, "If the women are raised, then their children will by their noble actions glorify the name of the country— then will culture, knowledge, power and devotion awaken in the land."[4] There is no hope of rise of that family or country where there is no estimate of women, where they live in sadness. For this they have to raise first.[5] Vivekananda believes in self-help, through which women can come out from their misery. He said, "Have faith in yourself—all power is in you, be conscious and bring it out. Arise, awake and find the ideal, the goal."[6] All this is possible through education. All the wealth of the world cannot help one, unless one is not taught to help themselves.[7]

Through education women could understood their inner power, which will help them to solve their problems. If women have the proper education then they can reform the situation. Besides this, in present day, women must need to learn some hand work to earn some living in case of need, *i.e.* painting, sewing etc. It will make one self-dependent, which is necessary to be free. Craft-centred moral Education among woman has given them chances to improve their self-consciousness, to think independently and to choose their carriers as it has been prescribed in Vivekananda's thought.

Conclusion

Happiness and welfare of the human society is based on promoting freedom and equality of all individuals. The desire to uplift others becomes well-established only when the lower self of an individual is erased and community consciousness promoted. If we want to do justice to the women we should change our outlook and attitude and treat the women as dignified as men. Swami Vivekananda laid emphasis on social unity for socio-economic-spiritual upliftment of all people. Hence, it is through the spiritual upliftment that all kinds of discrimination, inequality and oppression can be removed and we can build-up a liberated, free society open to all, which will move forward through every individual's equal efforts. Gandhi's view point on education is to the development of physical, mental and after all inner spirit of an individual. Thus we, who are concerned with education, need to think over their views on education. We have to apply the thought of those great thinkers according to the present circumstances of our country and also as per the demands of our present time.

Small scale and cottage industries are no doubt very important for the development of economic status of north-east region in particular and the economy of India as a whole. Recognising the importance of small scale industrial sector, both the Central and State Government have to take active steps to develop, promote and foster their growth. Small scale and cottage industries are suffering from a number of problems; because of the over-dependence on large-scale mechanistic industrial society. Opportunities are vast in the region, but we still need a holistic approach for overall development of the economy of North-East.

Notes

1. Gandhi, M. K. (1937): *Harijan*, 31 July.
2. *Ibid.*
3. Vivekananda, Swami (1993): *My India, The India Eternal* (Kolkata: Ramkrishna Mission Institute of Culture), p. 36.
4. Vivekananda, Swami (1964): *The Complete Works of Swami Vivekananda*, Vol. 7 (Kolkata: Advaita Ashrama), p. 220.
5. *Ibid.*, pp. 214-215.
6. Vivekananda, Swami (1993): *My India, The India Eternal* (Kolkata: Ramkrishna Mission Institute of Culture), p. 111.
7. Vivekananda, Swami (1964): *The Complete Works of Swami Vivekananda*, Vol. 7 (Kolkata: Advaita Ashrama), p. 504.

References

Bank, Barbara J., (ed.) (2007): *Gender and Education: An Encyclopaedia* (London: Praeger Publishers).

Datta, D.M. (1968): *The Philosophy of Mahatma Gandhi* (Kolkata: University of Calcutta).

Dayal, P. (2006): *Gandhian Theory of Social Reconstruction* (New Delhi: Atlantic Publishers and Distributors).

Gandhi, M.K. (1951): *Basic Education* (Ahmedabad: Navajivan Publishing House).
Gandhi, M.K. (2011): *Towards New Education* (Ahmedabad: Navajivan Publishing House).
Lal, B.K. (2005): *Contemporary Indian Philosophy* (Delhi: Motilal Banarasidass Publishers Pvt. Ltd.).
Pramanik, R.N. and A.K. Adhikary (2006): *Gender Inequality and Women's Empowerment* (New Delhi: Abhijeet Publications).
Pruthi, R.K. and Archana Chaturvedi (2009): *Mahatma Gandhi and Women* (Commonwealth Publishers).
Ramachandran, G. and T.K. Mahadevan (ed.) (1967): *Gandhi: His Relevance for our Times* (New Delhi: Gandhi Peace Foundation).
Siddhinathananda, Swami (1988): *Wealth and Wisdom of India* (Bombay: Bharatiya Vidya Bhavan).
Vivekananda, Swami (2011): *Letters of Swami Vivekananda* (Kolkata: Advaita Ashrama).
Vivekananda, Swami (1993): *My India, The India Eternal* (Kolkata: Ramkrishna Mission Institute of Culture).
Vivekananda, Swami (2004): *Practical Vedanta* (Kolkata: Advaita Ashrama).
Vivekananda, Swami (1964): *The Complete Works of Swami Vivekananda* (Kolkata: Advaita Ashrama).

13
Bertrand Russell and Vivekananda on Education

Bimal Chandra Pal

Introduction

In every society the function of education is to realize the ideals of manhood. This realization is possible only in human society. No society is static. It is in a state of change and hence reconstruction is necessary. It is only because of a great disparity between the ideal and the factual, between the unrealized potential and the realized situation, there arise a conflict and crisis in society. In such a crisis situation, the society badly needed a way out of a solution to that crisis. The role of education then is very urgent in this situation.

The function of education is inevitable for giving direction to this social reconstruction that we need desperately to solve our social problems and realize our ideals. Education must develop individuals who are cooperative in their means and constantly engagedabout the ends they desire and provide positive actions in behalf of future goals. In this chapter, I want to present the role of education for moulding our nature and ultimately how it reconstructs our society for the welfare of human being. I also put here a special reference of Vivekananda and Bertrand Russell in respect of their views on education.

Russell's View on Education

The greatest task of education is to reform the human mind. It is the key to the new world. It is the unfolding the divine nature in man. In the same tone Vivekananda also says that education is the manifestation of perfection already in man. Education is misnomer unless it trains the will of man; it is the training by which the current and expression of the will are brought under control for the reconstruction of society.

Russell also believed that right education can play an enormous role in developing the right type of individuals. The right outlook of the individual will help to reconstruct the society in which they live. According to Russell man is the Centre point of everything. The development of good society depends upon the good individuals. Education helps or trains a man to be a right type of man. Children at birth are neither good nor bad, yet with the help of education they can be made either. So, education is a process of moulding our nature.

Russell is not agreed with the Rousseau and the orthodox Christian view of education. The view of Rousseau is that children are born good, but society spoil them. Christians are opposite of this view. According to them children are born sinners and that the school have the duty of purify them. According to Russell man is driven by both positive and negative instincts. Positive instincts are called constructive e.g. play, love, co-operation, sympathy and negative instincts are called destructive instincts e.g. fight, jealousy, rage, competition etc. The role of education is to cultivate the positive instincts and connects the negative instincts to harmless outlet like sports, discovery and adventure. The function of education is to spread kindness and constructive emotion towards reconstructing of a good society.

The above nature of education turns a man into a good man. That is why an educated person always helps the people to establish peace and harmony in the universe. He possesses a strong mental courage, sensitivity or kindness to the other. These qualities are called the ideal character of an educated person.

Individual Freedom and Education

Education should aim at creating intelligent and free individuals. Nothing will be imposed upon them. The good of the individual should not be ignored. And natural growth of man is required for the good society. "Men, like trees, require for their growth and right soil and a sufficient freedom from oppression."[1] Students should be free to do their duty. It is bad enough if education prepares the students only for examination, but it is worse still if it prepares them for national wars. That is why Russell says, education should be pupil-centred, individually oriented. Students should be treated as ends in themselves and not as means to some national or religious ends. Hence, the present educational system is not matched with Russell's view of education.

The aim of education is the growth of individuality. "The object of education ought not to make all men alike, but rather to see that each person attains the fullest expression of his personality."[2] The teacher should treat each pupil as an end in himself with his own rights and his own personalities. Reverence for the human personality is the beginning of wisdom in every social question, but above all in education. So, each and every pupil's individuality should be fostered so that they may be creative and inventive.

The education helps us to make us creative and inventive. In the light of education man began to think freely and not only to believe what is being told. Everything will be accepted after experimentation. The spirit of scientific inquiry is spread everywhere. Now, people should not be concealed by blind faith. The main characteristic of an educated person is that he should be loyal to the truth alone and not to this or that entity. Everything should be judged by scientific inquiry. There is no finality in human affairs. Debates should be arranged between persons of opposite views and conclusion will be made after hearing all sides of the issue.

Religion and Education

The discovery of new knowledge acts as a weapon in the reformation and reconstruction of society. It was the cause of the decay of the dogmatic religion. Religion, according to Russell, snatches the power of the individual so that they cannot think or act freely." The mediaeval theory of life broke down through its failure to satisfy men's demands for justice and liberty."[3] In that time, Martin Luther protested against the authority that man's religion could not be determined for him by authority, but must by the free choice of the each individual. Due to this anti-scientific temper, Russell is not in favour of giving religion any place at all in education. His other objections against religion are as follows:

(a) Religious beliefs are put forth dogmatically.
(b) Religious teaching involves superstitious belief.
(c) An orthodox person cannot tolerate the opinion of others.
(d) Religion praises virtue but not intelligent at all. All intelligent people are agnostic and religious people cannot tolerate them.

Russell put the above charges against religion and concluded that Church and the State are the enemies of intelligence. The education can prosper only when it is freed from the influence of both.

International Outlook and Education

The proper function of education is to lead a good life. That is why it is essentially constructive and requires some positive conception of a good life. Russell wants education to be international in character from the political point of view. According to Russell, patriotism should not be taught in the school because it makes us feel that mutual hatred and mutual murdering are our sacred duties.[4] If the aim of education is good for all then it must not enclose in the national boundary. Therefore, education is international in character. The teaching of the idea of national superiority should not be taught in the school because it increases the hatred to the other nations and instigates wars. The civilisation at present are exposed by the gravest danger of patriotism. The conception of man as one family should be taught in the school. The aim of education is to spread and cultivate the international awareness and not to increase conflict and hatred. The people should be educated to remove the wickedness, ignorance and folly from the world. The teaching of Socrates, Buddha and Newton are the example of right education.

If man wants to survive in the world they should fight against chaos without any darkness within. The truly human activity will be international in character and it should be through the scheme of education.

According to Russell, the greatest task of education is to reform the human mind. Vivekananda's view of education is not different from this one. Now, we see what Vivekananda says about education.

Vivekananda's Educational Philosophy

Vivekananda's philosophy of education is based on universal principles of morality and ethics. Regarding the ultimate value of education, he says, that it must centred on the requirement of the human mind. Education keeps the soul in environment in which it would develop well. It initiates the citizen into the spiritual life of the nation. In other words, we can say that the general and special aim of education have a single function of enriching the people's personality. It requires the training of the soul which should be imparted by the teacher showing a model by living a spiritual life. Here Vivekananda creates a metaphysical synthesis reconciling the claims of spirit and matter, and makes it one of the chief bases of his educational philosophy.

Education and Social Reconstruction

Vivekananda's View of Education is mainly a man-making education. His aim is to unite the all sections of the society. So, he wants a new system of education on the strength of the Vedantic ideal.

In the latter half of the 19th century, Indian society was facing a very great cultural crisis. Vivekananda realized that in this time it is very urgent to spread education throughout the country for uniting and reconstructing the scattered races and wanted them to think of India as a whole. He uses education as a weapon for that purpose. He taught the people of India that they should have faith in themselves. He not only stood for spiritual freedom, but also wanted the external freedom of man. Besides talking about political freedom and social justice, he talked about the concept of strength and fearlessness. He justified his theory of fearlessness on the ground of philosophic Vedantism. He firmly believed this strength must come to the nation through education.

Man is the unit of society. Any changes in society are meant for the benefit of man. So, man will decide for what type of change he requires. His action is creative. He fights for his individual freedom. Education plays an important role to mend the nature of man. So, education is not only the information that is put into the brain, it is a creative activity of man. We must have life building, man-making, character making education in our life.

Vivekananda suggests that education should give proper emphasis on creativity, originality and excellence. To him the aim of education is to unveil the divinity in man. Real education means to cultivate the sense of humility. This sense of humility is the basis of man's character, the true mark of a balanced personality.

Education and Religion

Vivekananda takes religion as the innermost core of education. He says, "Religion is as the rice and everything else like the curries. Taking only curries causes indigestion, and so is the case with taking rice alone."[5] Religion signified to him the eternal principal of life and death and of spiritual progress. Religion is self-culture and self-culture is true education.

According to Vivekananda, all religions are for the good of mankind. The basic aim of education is universal brotherhood of man through mutual love and respect. Though the ways are apparently to be different, all religions have the same destination. Unity in variety is the plan of the universe and religion alone can lead mankind to that unity. Education in the right line will lead man to the true sense of religion and help him to acquire knowledge about the perishable nature of human body and the eternity of the soul in it. That is why Vivekananda relates education with religion. He suggests the techniques of self-religion through *Raja Yoga* for concentration and meditation because for him the very essence of education is concentration of mind, not the collecting of facts.

Yoga and Education

Education is the learning process which requires the deep concentration of mind. The more the power of concentration, the greater the knowledge is acquired. According to Vivekananda, the science of Yoga helps us to strengthen our power of concentration. From the lowest man to the highest *yogi*, all have to use the same method to attain knowledge. It is the great practical things and the secret of all education.

The practice of *Yoga* requires a high degree of concentration. When a man tries to concentrate on a particular object then thousands of undesired impulses may rush into the brain and disturb the mind. Hence to check the impulses and control the mind *Raja yoga* is the most perfect way. Vivekananda says that this *yoga* will help the student to develop his inner qualities like fearlessness, love, sympathy etc., and equip him to lead an ideal life.

Universal Religion

The practice of *yoga* makes a man holy or a saint. These holy men sustain the world by their conduct. That is why Gandhi says that politics must be spiritualized. Saints are the pathfinder of the society. They are of three categories. Meditative saints are those who ponder in isolation over the infinite and seek their own personal salvation. Devotee saints are in love with God and they bother neither about their own salvation nor about that of the society. But there is a third variety of saint who preaches religion and strives for the salvation of the society. Vivekananda is one of those missionary saints of India.

He believes in the unity of religion and hence advocated the ideal of a universal religion. His outlook was rational. He believed not only in reason, but also in the freedom of thought, expression and action. He remarks that the same method of investigation which we apply to science and knowledge outside should be applied to the science of religion.

Vivekananda realized that due to conflict among different religions more blood is shed in the name of religion in human history. That is why, there is greater need of religious tolerance or the integration of all religions. The integration of all religions is possible only when we realize the sense of oneness of the end of all religions. Vivekananda took this idea from his master sage Ramakrishna. According to his master, to realize the infinite or God is the mission of human life. The many names of God and infinite the forms lead us to know the supreme reality. This idea of oneness of the end of all religions that the idea of a universal religion has occurred to Vivekananda.

Universal brotherhood is the fountain-head of a universal religion. The universal feature common to all religions is the pursuit of the divinity. Unity in diversity is the plan of the universe, many God is one. Thus, variety being the innate nature of the universe, Vivekananda says that by the idea of a universal religion does mean a universal philosophy, or universal mythology, or a universal religion. According to him, truth is one. It can be expressed in a hundred thousand ways, and each of these ways is true. Hence, we formulate a harmonious religious creed to make all religions come together in love.

Religion is realization, not talk, not doctrine, nor theory. Professor R.D. Ranade also believes in this idea of religion being self-realization. This is the ideal of universal religion preached by Vivekananda. He practiced this universal religion throughout his life.

Education and International Understanding

Vivekananda wanted the gradual and peaceful changes through good system of education and by enlightening the people. He always insisted on the absolute conquest of fear. Being a spiritual monist he was essentially an internationalist.

Vivekananda basically preached the concept of spiritual freedom. But his words had always the spell of political freedom and international understanding. His political ideas are found in his various lectures both in India and abroad. Mahatma Gandhi and Aurobindo have also influenced by his inspiring words. He always pleaded for human expansion and unity and taught his countrymen that without the divine remarking of human nature their civilization would be doomed forever, the aim of true education is self-expansion.

The creed of nationalism was not narrow and fanatical, but was only a necessary stage in the social and political evolution of man. If man is guided by the divine, if he performs his duties with a total sense of detachment then nationalism will not be an obstacle towards internationalism.

The self-expansion is possible only when a man renounces actions even after his realization of supreme knowledge. A man's duty is to do good for others. He preached the principle of *Gita* that only duty is the concern and not the fruit. Finally, the ultimate aim should be to establish international peace and security by strengthening the spiritual foundations of different nations.

Conclusion

We have seen that both the educational philosophy of Vivekananda and Russell, the general and special aim of education is the single function of enriching the people's personality. Education according to Russell is a kind of process by which one can mould his nature. He insisted on the power of individuals which is conducive to the reconstruction of society. Regarding religion he directly denies its support in education. He says the religious outlook should find no place at all in education.

On the other hand, Vivekananda believes that by uniting *karma* with religion he could enlighten the people to think of religion in the right way. He reconciled life and religion. Religion signified to him the eternal principles of life and death and of spiritual progress. True education means training of the soul and it requires a master. It is not only worked out by reading of books. That is why he relates education with religion.

Religion makes people aware about the spirituality which reform the human mind. A deep faith is necessary to push forward a nation in the march of civilisation. This faith comes from the core of religion. So, religion is must in education. Vivekananda says, "education should unveil the divinity in man and this divinity should be seen in everything that is connected with human life."

Lastly, we can conclude that both the thinkers are common in certain aspects of educational thought. They believe that education is the best means to reconstruct our society because it can reform the human mind. In Russell's words, we can say that education is a key to the new world. It has an international and universal outlook.

Notes

1. Russell, Bertrand. 2010, *Why Men Fight*. Indian Edition, Routledge, Delhi, p. 13.
2. Russell, Bertrand. 1932, *Education and Social Order*. George Allen & Unwin Ltd., p. 42.
3. Russell, Bertrand, 2010, *op. cit.*, p. 13.
4. Russell, Bertrand, 2010, *Fact and Fiction*. Indian Edition, Routledge, Delhi, p. 63.
5. *Complete Works of Swami Vivekananda,* Vol. V, Kolkata: Advaita Ashrama. p. 366.

References

Bandishte, D.D., 1984, *A Study of The Ethics of Bertrand Russell.* Indore: Lipika Prakashan.

Lal, B.K., 2005, *Contemporary Indian Philosophy.* Delhi: Motilal Banarasidass Publishers Pvt. Ltd.

Russell, Bertrand. 1932, *Education and Social Order.* George Allen & Unwin Ltd.

Russell, 2010, Bertrand. *Fact and Fiction.* Indian Edition, Routledge, Delhi.

Russell, 2010, Bertrand. *Why Men Fight.* Indian Edition, Routledge, Delhi.

Sen, Amiya P. (Ed.) 2006, *The Indispensable Vivekananda—An Anthology for Our Times.* Ranikhet: Permanent Black.

Sengupta, Pradip Kumar (ed.). 1995, *The Philosophy of Swami Vivekananda.* Calcutta: Progressive Publishers.

Vivekananda, Swami, 2008, *Complete Works of Swami Vivekananda,* (Vols. I-IX). Kolkata: Advaita Ashrama.

Vivekananda, Swami, 1993, *My India, The India Eternal.* Kolkata: Ramkrishna Mission Institute of Culture.

SECTION-IV

Need Based Education

14

Common School System

An Alternative System Towards Multi-Ethnic Democracy for North-east Region of India

Thokchom Surjit Singh

North-Eastern Region (NER) of India comprising of eight States, *viz.* Arunachal Pradesh, Assam, Manipur, Meghalaya, Mizoram, Nagaland, Tripura and Sikkim is a multi-ethnic, multi-lingual and multi-religious region. Diversity in absence of plurality is the essence of the region. In the post-1947, the region has been experiencing ever increasing socio-political partitioning. The issues and problems are multifaceted and much beyond the Hindu-Muslim binary. Unfortunately, caste-based discrimination has been increasingly imported in the region. This trend is more acute now under the new regime.

The region has population density as thin as 17 per sq. km. in Arunachal Pradesh and as dense as 398 per sq. km. in Assam with more than 200 languages and dialects. The literacy rate ranges from 54.74 per cent in Arunachal Pradesh to 91.58 per cent in Mizoram. Within each state, there are numbers of languages with one or two official language(s) marking the hegemony of particular dominant group(s). In Nagaland and Arunachal Pradesh, the official language is English. In term of religion, though Hinduism has the largest number of followers, the Hinduism practiced in the NER is distinctively different from rest of India. Christianity and Muslim have very prominent presence in the region. Buddhism's presence too is of very high significance. The revivalist groups of pre-Hindu religion of the region are now having very strong influence in the psychosocial domain of the young people. Following Table 14.1 gives a broad picture of the region's diversity.

Table 14.1: Profile of the NER's States

(in %)

States	*Population*	*Languages*	*Official language(s)*	*Literacy*
Arunachal Pradesh	1382611	Nyishi, Dafla, Miji, Adi, Gallong, Wancho, Tagin, Hill Miri, Mishui, Monpa, Nocte, Aka, Tangsa, Khamti etc.	English	54.74
Assam	31169272	Assamese, Bodo, Manipuri, Bisnupriya-Manipuri, Bengali, Dimasa, Mishing, Karbi, Rabha, Tai Phake, Tai-Aiton, Tai-Khamtim etc.	Assamese, Bengali, Bodo, English	73.18
Manipur	2855794	Meiteilon, Tangkhul, Hmar, Paite, Lushai, thadou/kuki + 29 recognized languages	Meiteilon & English	79.85
Meghalaya	2964007	Garo, Khasi and Pnar + several languages of smaller groups	English	74.43
Mizoram	1091014	Lushai, Aso, Chho, Halam, Hinar, Lai, Mara, Miu, Khumi, Paite, Thadou, Paite, Kuki, Chakma, Bru etc.	English & Lushai	91.58
Nagaland	1980602	More than 60 languages out of which 16 are recognized.	English	79.55
Tripura	3673917	Bengali, Kok-Borok, Halam, Rangkhal, Chakma etc.	Bengali, English	87.75
Sikkim	610577	Nepali, Bhutia, Lepcha, Limbu, Newari, Rai, Gurung, Mangai, Sherpa, Tamang, Sunwar etc.	Nepali & English	85.42

Source: www.mdoner.gov.in; www.censusindia.gov.in (the data is not exhaustive).

The different communities of the region have very diverged histories of how it became a part of India. The folklore and oral narratives are not well connected with the prescribed histories (in textbooks) about origin, affinities and patriotism of the people. The majority of the tribes/communities of the region were neither a part of the ancient India nor significant parties to the collective freedom struggle of Indian Nation. The diversity in history of the region could be traced back to both pre-British and post-British period. As most of the complication of the NER started with the British-India's policy, we would like to trace a broad historical framework of the region from British period onward. The British established their rule in 1826 over the Assam plain. Gradually, it was expanded to Cachar plain in 1830, Khasi hills in 1833, Jaintia plain in 1835, Mikir Hills (now Kabi Anglong) in 1838, North Cachar Hills in 1854, Naga Hills during 1866-1904, Garo Hills in 1872-73 and Lushai hills (now Mizoram) in 1890. It was in 1921, Assam became a Governor's province under the provision of the Government of India Act, 1919. The region had never experienced a united fight against the British. In fact, a fight against British by one group would subdue by British using another group. As such, there was and still is a missing link between the ethnic nationalism as visible today and Indian Nationalism as a legacy of freedom struggle. And this missing link is evident within the psychosocial characters of the region. In the post-Independent period, the notion of the NER itself has been remained as an imposition. A closer examination reveals that the much-talked democratic social set-up amongst the tribes of NER is a myth. Of course, comparing with caste ridden Indian society, the caste-based discrimination is very less in the region. However, this does not mean the people in the region are more democratic.

There is nothing called North-East till date in the people's collective consciousness. During the British period, the region was broadly divided into fully governed area, partially excluded area, excluded area and princely States under British paramouncy. In the partially excluded and excluded region, there were demands for self-determination in the later part of British period and these demands were basically generated out of concern for dominance by the newly perceived Indian Nation. In case of princely state like princely state of Manipur, she declared herself as independent country just before India got free. There were short of intentions of becoming a part of free India by almost all the part of the region. What happens after India got Independent in North-East Region is now a part of folklore of the region. Just after Independence, the partition in 1947 kept the NER at the extreme periphery. The formulation under 6th Schedule and the like, allowing to follow customary laws without having space for critical examination of the same pushed the region more in the periphery.

As the region is in a strategic location and after China's attack in 1962, coupled with the Naga Armed Movement, the region's political status had been forced to change a lot for worse (or better!). Nevertheless, whatever the steps taken till date by the Government of India, it seldom initiates a people-to-people dialogue in the region. With the coming of Bangladesh as a free country, the region's demography was heavily affected by the obvious result of refugees in India. Today, the word illegal Bangladeshi becomes a most frequently mentioned terms in the popular discourse of the region. In a situation like this, with accumulated unfulfilled promises of the Indian State, being neither a part of ancient India nor a part of modern India, the region, unfortunately remains a Reluctant India. These realities of NER gives us sufficient ground to propose for an alternative process of nation building exercise in place of prevailing process of mainstreaming or forcing into Indian Nation. Each state has her own story, sometimes very painful stories about how she became a part of India. The process of state making is an unfinished task till date. Table 14.2 may give us a broad overview of how states in NER become states of India.

Today, we could see multiple statehood demands as a poor substitute of earlier aspiration of sovereignty. Within the federal polity of Indian State, the demand for statehood was to negotiate with the Central Government. The history of becoming a state has to do something with inter communities' conflicts. Many of these problems thought to be resolved with the creation of smaller states have been remained unresolved or unattended and in the meantime, the formation of new states or new autonomous councils created newer issues and newer problems. All the communities/tribes demands till date are based on the assumption that a singular mono-ethnic smaller unit of governance would fulfil the long standing ethnic aspiration. Does such an approach qualify to call it as a democratic, humane and egalitarian approach? Shall our education be given adequate dialogical space to build-up an understanding of what democracy is all about ?

Table 14.2: Overview of NER's States

States	*Pre-independence*	*Post-independence*	*Statehood*	*Prevailing agenda*
Arunachal Pradesh	North-eastern Frontier Agency (NEFA)	NEFA→ UT → statehood	20th Feb., 1987	Sino-Indian Border issue, Chakma problem etc.
Assam	British administered colony	Full statehood since 1947	15th Aug., 1950*	Assam Accord, Bodo State demand, Tea tribes.
Manipur	Princely State under British paramount power	Part C state → Statehood	21st Jan., 1972	Hills *vs* valley, self-determination
Meghalaya	Part of undivided Assam, Shillong being the capital.	2 districts of United Assam → statehood	21st Jan., 1972	Garo *vs* Khasi, Self - determination etc.
Mizoram	A part of undivided Assam	A district of Assam → statehood	20th Feb., 1987	Catching up, Mizo nation etc.
Nagaland	A part of undivided Assam	A District of Assam → statehood	1st Dec., 1963	Naga integration, link language
Sikkim	Princely state	A princely state → statehood	16th May, 1975	In defence of ancient glory
Tripura	Princely State under British paramount power	Part C state (1951) → UT (1956) → Statehood	21st Jan., 1972	Twipra state demand, Chakma repatriation etc.

* From the time of Independence in 1947 along with India Assam became independent, since from early it was a independent province. But adoption of Constitution in 1950 is considered as year of Constituent Statehood.

Source: www.mdoner.gov.in

Today, the NER is partially militarized zone. The people are sandwiched between the state forces and the non-state actors. At least in three states, Armed Forces Special Power Act, 1958 is still promulgated. The scheduled areas are partly or fully governed by the traditional councils. There are good numbers of non-state actors too. Each of these actors occupies the people's mind. And people have to submit to all of them for survival. The consequences of these unfortunate realities are the partitioning of mind. The people's mind particularly the young generation's mind is partitioned into four compartments: tradition and religion, non-state actor, Indian State and the neo-liberal force. One has to keep these partitions off and on depending on time, situation and location. An individual's identity under these circumstances becomes confused and very much a blurred one. That is the reason why the young minds are confused, dichotomous and broken from within. Without resolving this dichotomy, he or she remains a distorted person from within. Education must be necessarily mandated to resolve this dichotomy. Our classroom must be the location for this historical task.

People in the region have an inner quest to free themselves from the dichotomous life. And many a time, they take a conscious but short-sighted decision to free from the dichotomy. The phenomenon of walking out of school in protest by children or withdrawal of children from school by parents is an attempt to free from the dichotomy. It gives them a temporary impression that they are now integrated with the world of work as per tradition. Sooner or later they are to pay a heavy price of being alienated to and isolated from larger state structure. The price is as heavy as how much of local economy has been dismantled and how much of it has been replaced by moneyed economy as per Nehruvian model of development and further accentuated with the neo-liberal model of development. It is a catch 22 situation. The writing in the wall, "Khasi by birth and Indian by accident", phrases like "our friend from India" are examples of how societies in NER have an embedded social conscience of non-state actor. This social conscience is common in major part of the region. Banning of Hindi movie in Manipur, reluctance to sing National Anthem in many parts of the NER, yearly ritual of *bandhs* on Republic Day, Independent Day etc. are vivid examples. People have to gain their livelihood, personal growth and educational opportunities by identifying themselves as Indian and on the other hand, social acceptability by their non-questioning loyalty to the custom, tradition and religion. In such a situation, superficiality becomes an obvious choice.

For a child in this region, the child's mind is the contesting ground for the four sets of knowledge: (1) traditional and religious knowledge; (2) State's prescribed knowledge; (3) non-state's prescribed knowledge; and (4) the prescribed knowledge of neo-liberal. Of course, there are overlapping areas of knowledge but what matters most are those opposing sets of knowledge. Different sets of knowledge are just like different currencies in different territories and domains. One has to buy social acceptability through an act of endorsement to a particular set of knowledge in a particular situation and for a particular location. Informally, acquired knowledge from society makes oneself at home with the society and formally acquired knowledge gives a ticket for entering into a state structure. And the two sets of knowledge are in conflict. In many ways, informal education becomes anti-formal education and *vice versa*. It is not the knowledge *per se* that makes the people a dichotomous being. It is the absence of dialogues amongst these sets of knowledge and a blanket ban of questioning any of this knowledge makes the people a dichotomous and distorted being. What shall we suppose to do in a situation like this? The need of the hour is a dialogue between these sets of knowledge. As a starting point, there must be home-to-school and school-to-home continuity. Questioning the society and questioning the state must be necessarily core agenda of the education. In short, the school must be a centre of transformation (and of Revolution!).

The present system of education expects an individual from the region to become a stand-alone person to be mainstreamed and integrated to the Indian Nation. He or she is expected to be alienated (without being independent) of complex matrix of his or her organic and indispensible relationship with his or her culture, ethnicity, inherited local economy, languages and ethnic national identity (not necessarily Indian national identity) in which his or her individuality is inevitably located. In a situation like this, how can we expect a person to remain without being a dichotomous and distorted from within? So, what ought to be the aim of education for this region? Before we try to put forward our considered views on it, let us examine the objective of education as per policies of Government of India.

India got independence in 1947 and the Constitution was enacted in 1951, but an attempt for a National System of Education system was initiated through a Commission, popularly known as Kothari Commission (1964-66). The commission had several recommendations with far reaching consequences out of which several of monumental recommendations were not considered to incorporate in the National Policy on Education (NPE) 1968. NPE

68 rhetorically mentioned Gandhiji's scheme of Basic Education reiterating that "this was a great step forward in making education directly relevant to the life of the people". The NPE 68 acknowledged that the Kothari Commission recommended "a radical reconstruction for economic and cultural development of the country, for national integration and for realizing the ideal of socialist pattern of society." It further said, "it will involve a transformation of the system to relate it more closely to the life of the people". I am assuming that the people mentioned in the document included the people of NER. Here lies the superficiality on the part of the Government of India that the education system had never attempted till date to relate closely with people of the region. Then came the National Policy on Education, 1986. While NPE 86 still refer to the NPE 68 in an attempt to maintain certain sense of continuity, we could see change of priority and social objective of the education. Instead of trying to fulfil the equal educational opportunities, the NPE 86 promoted multiple layers of education of unequal access and inequitable qualities. It introduced Non-formal Education and para-teachers for the poor and marginalised section of society defying the Constitutional mandate of equality. Thus, the NPE 86 came with policies neither good for the rich nor for the poor. It was rightly said by Acharya Ramamurti, "whatever education they receive cuts them off from their natural and social environment. They become aliens to their own community." He further questioned, "Is no education better than bad education?" In India, all the commissions' reports and their recommendations were not adequately considered diversity as an asset as well as both means and end. There lies the deficiency in dealing with an education system for a region like NER. The reluctance in policy is appropriately reciprocated by a continued expression of reluctance in being an Indian. This dimension of policy issue may be neglected further at the cost of grave consequences. Having said this much about the prevailing policy, what is the way forward? In a situation like this, can formal education be possibly a medium to initiate the historical task of re-imagining a common future without ignoring the past and present within a multi-ethnic, multi-language and plural context!

The Kothari Commission 1964-66 stated, "Social and national integration is a major problem which will have to be tackled on several fronts, including education. In our view, education can and should play a very significant role in it by introducing a Common School System (CSS) of public education; (1:35)". The New Education Policy (NPE) 1986, stated, "the concept of a National System of Education implies that, up to a given level, all students, irrespective of caste, creed, location or sex, have access to education of a comparable quality. To achieve this, the Government will initiate appropriately funded programmes. Effective measures will be taken in the direction of the Common School System recommended in the 1968 Policy." Though the National Policy of Education 1968 had overlooked the Kothari Commission's recommendation, at least a token acknowledgement had been inserted in the NPE 1986. The NPE Review Committee Report 1990, titled, "Towards an Enlightened an Humane Society" under the chairmanship of Acharya Ramamurti, popularly known as Ramamurti Commission Report recommended, "phased implementation of the Common School System within a ten year time and essential minimum legislation, particularly to dispense with early selection process, tuition fees, capitation fees etc." It further recommended, "to explore ways of including the expensive private schools into the Common School System through a combination of incentives, disincentives and legislation." Unfortunately, these recommendations were not taken seriously by the Government of India. In the Report of the Central Advisory Board of Education (CABE) Committee on Free and Compulsory Education Bill and other issues of Elementary Education 2005, Prof. Anil Sadgopal, in his written submission wrote, "the most important feature of Common School System is equitable (not uniform) quality of education for all types of schools, be they government, government aided, local body or private schools. Six essential and non-negotiable attributes of equitable quality of education need to be specified: (1) minimum physical infra-structure including library, teaching aids, playground .... including ECCE and pre-primary level; (2) professional quality of teachers and student-teachers ratio; (3) diversified and flexible curriculum to reflect the geo-cultural plurality of the country, while emphasizing certain core curriculum features of nation-wide significance; (4) pedagogy of holistic, child-friendly and liberative education; (5) apart of gender sensitivity, pedagogic and social empathy for the *dalits*, tribals, cultural and *ethnic* minorities and physically and mentally challenged children; and (6) decentralized community-controlled school system. In the report of another CABE Committee Report of Common School System and Girls' Education, 2005, in somewhat similar manner, it was defined as "Common School System means the National System of Education that is founded on the principles and values enshrined in the Constitution and provides education of a comparable quality to all children in an equitable manner irrespective of their caste, creed, language, gender, economic or ethnic background, location or disability (physical or mental), and wherein all categories of schools – i.e. government, local body or private, aided or unaided, or otherwise – will be under obligation to (a) fulfil certain minimum infrastructural (including those relating to teachers and other staff), financial, curricular, pedagogic, linguistic and socio-cultural norms; and (b) ensure free education to the children in a specified neighbourhood from an age group and/or up to a stage, as may be prescribed by the appropriate authority." From this time onward, the phrase "Common School System" was perhaps the most misunderstood and most frequently spelled phrase in the academic circle as well as administrative circle. A more refined and shorter version of definition of Common School System became available in the Report of the Common School System Commission, Government of Bihar, June 2007 as, "a system of Education providing equitable quality to all children irrespective of their caste, creed, community, language, gender, economic condition, social status and physical or mental ability." For the moment, in context of NER, if we are to build-up a system of education for the region, the CSS as it is highlighted above is the best choice to carry forward. But the CSS as it is outlined today in the policy documents need to further contextualize for the region.

For this, some premises are listed as follows:

1. Education particularly the school education is a subset of society. There must be no insulation from either side. The State must endeavour to create dialogical space in classroom. There must be negotiated continuity between home-school-society-state: neither top down nor top-up both ways to evolve a humane, democratic and egalitarian social ethos.
2. Elementary Education though it is for the children of 6-14 years as per Art. 21 A of the constitution, impacts the parents

and the communities multi-dimensionally and therefore, the concern and the scope must include parents and communities. In short, deep engagement with parents and communities must be an essential part of the education.

3. Decentralization and Community participation are neither for only implementation nor for making unilateral decision. It must be praxis for rethinking the locus of the problems and potential solutions, for re-conceptualizing the nature of governance, for re-envisioning democracy as both a way of life and a way of governance.
4. Education must be publicly supported for it is only through State's support that we can build-up a dialogical situation amongst three sets of knowledge emanated from tradition and religion, the non-state actor and the state.
5. Learning through mother tongue in a multi-lingual context must be adopted. Languages are to evolve along with social changes. A society falling short of democratic institution, culture and polity cannot afford to have adequate semantic to express the same. Within a single language too, the languages are sub-classified as per gender, social and economic class and place of origin. In short, languages are class and identity marker. The social transformation also means transforming languages.
6. Prevailing practice of partitioning knowledge in the form of subjects/discipline are to challenge. Not only partitioning of knowledge, even hegemony of some kind of knowledge too must be challenged pedagogically. So, the notion of subject, subject teachers etc. are to be done away.
7. The quest of knowledge, the joy of learning and hope for the future for my community, my state and for the whole country has to be synchronized. The nation's glory and community's glory must not be treated as anti-thesis of each other. The knowledge we imbibe must help us to transcend the prevailing narrow ethnic, chauvinistic, mono-ethnic, exclusive and communal tendency.
8. Every school must be experimental school allowing innovation to take place and making unique by linking with local situation. In short the growth of school and growth of the society must be simultaneous.

9. The proposed Common School System is not a uniform school system. What is common is equality, equity, democracy, social justice and constitutional protection.
10. The Common School System should not be imported or replicated from somewhere. It should be evolved through a deep engagement with people.

Based on the above premises, the various stages of educational process have to undergo necessary changes. In Indian context, both the Policy and Curricular framework is drawn out of Constitutional values. Out of the curriculum framework, a Curriculum is framed. Out of the curriculum, a syllabus is prepared. Out of the Syllabus, a Textbook is written. This Textbook is what tells us what to do in classroom and finally evaluation process to certify a person. This is how our education is organised. Except the curricular framework, the rest of the steps must be decentralised in the regional, state, district and block-level. This process must be one necessary condition for a workable education for the NER. The following are steps for consideration:

1. Curricular framework must be framed in the national-level with inputs from decentralised units from all-over the country. This exercise must be done as a nation-wide debate on the validity of our Constitution. Without space for understanding/reviewing the Constitution, the exercise for framing of the Curricular Framework will be a farce. A curricular framework may be given timeframe for reviewing it say five years. And this must be the only common document all-over the country.
2. Based on the curricular framework, the exercise of framing a curriculum must be decentralised. Curriculum may be designed for a geo-political units, not necessarily state-wise or district-wise. Convenience must take a backseat and people's genuine participation must be given emphasis. The exercise of curriculum development must be taken as a serious nation building exercise. That means there will be multi-curriculum for different geo-political and cultural units.
3. Preparation of syllabus must not be hijacked by national bodies. There may be a common syllabus for a specific

examination. But for at least up to secondary-level, the syllabus must reflect the diversity and genuine people's participation.

4. Textbook writing with today's IT facilities can be very creative, innovative and original. Textbook printing in large scale can be done away. In place of large scale printing, small groups of teachers, academics and parents can design textbooks or remove textbooks in the local-level. In short, every school can have different textbooks. But in any case, textbook must never be imported with a motive to earn profit by any parties.
5. *Classroom teaching*: It is here teachers' pivotal role in the education process to be re-established. The social character of the classroom must reflect sincere endeavour for a democratic social order. Every school ought to become an experimental school. Every teacher must be challenged to innovate in the process. School as a subset of society, the much needed social transformation is to be initiated within the classroom. It is here the dichotomy is to resolve.
6. *Evaluation*: This is an area which is neglected most. Evaluation to whom, by whom and for whom? The conventional evaluation system or the CCE which are practicing in the school are all student focused. The evaluation result is assumed to reflect the performance of only one party, i.e. students. It is in fact, unfair to evaluate only one party that too the party with no power of her own. Evaluation must include the evaluation of teachers, parents and society as a whole. A school is not an isolated island. So, the school's relationship with society must be carefully evaluated. The quality dimension of the education is now to be revisited.

To make the above a reality, a paradigm shift must be necessary. Some of the suggested shift can be listed as follows:

- From seeking sympathetic treatment to re-claiming empathetic relationship;
- From diversity as a problem to diversity as asset;
- From ethnic based singular approach to the multi ethnic plural approach;
- From "sending children to school" to "sending school to

home through children and sending home to school through children and *vice versa*";

- From isolating from the world of work to work as a pedagogical medium of education;
- From antagonistic relationship between informal and formal towards a continuity of dialogues between the two; and
- From a passionate defense of tradition towards an evolution of the tradition for an egalitarian society.

The list can be added more. This paradigm shift will definitely implicate an alternative model of development. A collective voice from below is to be accumulated through educational process. It is through such a system of education that a multi-ethnic democratic society can be generated in the region. This is what we call a Common School System for an alternative multi-ethnic democracy in NER.

References

Jha, M. M., Sadgopal, A., Dubey, M., (2007), *Report of the Common School System Commission*, Patna: Government of Bihar.

GOI (1986), *National Policy on Education 1986*, New Delhi: MHRD, Department of Education.

GOI (1986), *National Policy on Education 1968*, New Delhi: Ministry of Education.

NPE 86-reveiw Committee (1990), *Towards an Enlightened and Humane Society, NPE, 1986—A Review*, New Delhi: MHRD, GoI.

CABE (2005), *Report of the CABE Committee on Free and Compulsory Education Bill and other issues Related to Elementary Education*, Vols. 1-3, MHRD, GoI.

CABE (2005), *Report of the CABE Committee on Girls' Education and Common School System*, Vols. 1-3, MHRD, GoI.

NFG (2005), *3.7 Position Paper, National Focus Group on Work and Education*. New Delhi: NCERT.

NFG (2005), *2.2 Position Paper, National Focus Group on Systemic Reforms for Curriculum Change*, New Delhi: NCERT.

NFG (2005), *2.1 Position Paper, National Focus Group on Aims of Education*, New Delhi: NCERT.

Lal, Dena (2015), *Schizophrenic Alienation of N.E. India: Its Historical Roots*, http://www.e-pao.net

15

Educational System in Hill State of Sikkim

Children with Special Needs Perspective

Jharna Sharma and *Swgwmkhang Brahma*

Introduction

Better education is necessary for all to move ahead in life. It develops confidence and helps build personality of a person. School education plays a great role in everyone's life. The whole education has been divided into three divisions such as the Primary education, Secondary education and Higher Secondary education. All the divisions of education have their own importance and benefits. Primary education prepares the base which helps throughout the life, secondary education prepares the path for further study and higher secondary education prepares the ultimate path of the future and helps to lead life productively. Education is like an instrument to fight against any obstacle. Education can reduce discrimination against children with disabilities. Education, particularly inclusive education, is able to reduce discrimination through enabling children with and without disabilities to grow up together. Education gives children with disabilities skills to allow them to become positive role models and join the employment market, thereby helping to prevent poverty. Hence, education is important for all children of school going age without any discrimination based on ground such as caste, creed, sex, age, nationality, place of birth, disability etc. Excluding children and adults with disabilities from mainstream education opportunities have a negative impact. On the other hand, it would become difficult for the country and the state to achieve the Education for All or the Millennium Development Goal of Universal Completion of Primary Education without ensuring access to education for children with disabilities. Particularly, excluding children with disabilities, who needs special attentions, from educational and employment opportunities has high social and economic costs.

In India, children with disabilities in special schools fall under the responsibility of the Ministry of Social Justice and Empowerment, while children in mainstream schools come under the Department of Education in the Ministry of Human Resource Development. This division reflects the cultural perception that children with disabilities are in need of welfare rather than equality of opportunity. This particular model tends to further segregate children with disabilities, and shifts the focus from education and achieving social and economic inclusion to treatment and social isolation.

Objectives of the Study

This particular study is particularly carrying out in order to understand the following objectives: to understand the present status of education for children with special needs; to explore the response in the area in the Hill State of Sikkim; to identify the major challenges that are faced by the state in the context of education for children with special needs; and to provide suggestion in order to improve upon.

Education and Children with Special Needs

Education contributes to human capital formation and is thus a key determinant of personal well-being and welfare. Excluding children with disabilities from educational and employment opportunities has high social and economic costs. For example, adults with disabilities tend to be poorer than those without disabilities, but education weakens this association (Filme, R.D., 2008). Countries cannot achieve Education for All or the Millennium Development Goal of universal completion of primary education without ensuring access to education for children with disabilities

(UNESCO, 2009). For children with disabilities, as for all children, education is vital in itself, but also instrumental for participating in employment and other areas of social activity. Many children and adults with disabilities have historically been excluded from mainstream education opportunities. Despite improvements in recent decades, children and youth with disabilities are less likely to start school or attend school than other children. They also have lower transition rates to higher levels of education. A lack of education at an early age has a significant impact on poverty in adulthood.

Respondents with disability in the World Health Survey experience significantly lower rates of primary school completion and fewer mean years of education than respondents without disability, evidence shows young people with disabilities are less likely to be in school than their peers without disabilities (Filmer, D., 2008). This pattern is more pronounced in poorer countries (UNESCO, 2009). Primary school attendance rates between disabled and non-disabled children in India are 10 per cent (WHO, 2002). Enrolment rates also differ according to impairment type, children with physical impairment generally faring better than those with intellectual or sensory impairments. In India, a survey estimated the share of disabled children not enrolled in school at more than five times the national rate, even in the more prosperous states. In Karnataka, the best performing major state, almost one quarter of children with disabilities were out of school, and in poorer states such as Madhya Pradesh and Assam, more than half (World Bank, 2009). While the best-performing districts in India had high enrolment rates for children without disabilities — close to or above 90 per cent, school attendance rates of children with disabilities never exceeded 74 per cent in urban areas or 66 per cent in rural area. Most special education facilities are in urban areas (Porter, G.L., 2001), so, the participation of children with disabilities in rural areas could be much worse than the aggregated data imply (Singal, N., 2006).

Definitions and methods for measuring disability vary across countries based on assumptions about human difference and disability and the importance given to the different aspects of disability — impairments, activity limitations and participation restriction, related health condition, and environmental factors.

There are no universally agreed definitions for such concepts as special needs education and inclusive education, which hampers comparison of data. The category covered by the terms special needs education, special educational needs, and special education is broader than education of children with disabilities, because it includes children with other needs — for example, through disadvantages resulting from gender, ethnicity, poverty, war trauma, or orphanhood (Naidhu, A., 2008).

A stricter sense of inclusion is that all children with disabilities should be educated in regular classrooms with age-appropriate peers. This approach stresses the need for the whole school system to change. Inclusive education entails identifying and removing barriers and providing reasonable accommodation, enabling every learner to participate and achieve within mainstream settings. There are different approaches around the world to provide education for people with disabilities. The models adopted include special schools and institutions, integrated schools, and inclusive schools. Inclusive education seeks to enable schools to serve all children in their communities (Dupoux, E., Wolman, C. and Estrada, E., 2005).

The inclusion of children with disabilities in regular schools — inclusive schools — is widely regarded as desirable for equality and human rights. The United Nations Educational, Scientific and Cultural Organisation have put forward the following reasons for developing a more inclusive education system (UNESCO, 2001). *Educational:* The requirement for inclusive schools to educate all children together means that the schools have to develop ways of teaching that responds to individual differences, to the benefit of all children; *Social:* Inclusive schools can change attitudes towards those who are in some way "different" by educating all children together. This will help in creating a just society without discrimination; and *Economic:* Establishing and maintaining schools that educate all children together is likely to be less costly than setting up a complex system of different types of schools specialising in different groups of children.

Educational needs must be assessed from the perspective of what is best for the individual (Farrell, P., *et al.*, 2007) and the available financial and human resources within the country context. Many barriers may hinder children with disabilities from attending school. In some countries, education for some or all children with disabilities falls under separate ministries such as Health, Social Welfare, or Social Protection (El-Salvador, Pakistan and Bangladesh) or distinct Ministries of Special Education. In other countries (Ethiopia and Rwanda) responsibilities for the education for disabled children are shared between Ministries (Lewis, I., 2009). In India, children with disabilities in special schools fall under the responsibility of the Ministry of Social Justice and Empowerment, while children in mainstream schools come under the Department of Education in the Ministry of Human Resource Development (Naidhu, A., 2008). This division reflects the cultural perception that children with disabilities are in need of welfare rather than equality of opportunity (World Bank, 2009). This particular model tends to further segregate children with disabilities, and shifts the focus from education and achieving social and economic inclusion to treatment and social isolation. While there are many examples of initiatives to include children with disabilities in education, a lack of legislation, policy, targets and plans tends to be a major obstacle in efforts to provide Education for All (Forlin, C., *et al.*, 2008). Issues such as data collection, teacher training, access to school buildings, and the provision of additional learning materials and support are some of the hindrances for educating children with special needs, limited or inappropriate resources are regarded as a significant barrier to ensuring inclusive education for children with disabilities (Stubbs, S., 2008).

Hindrances before the Children with Special Needs

Some of the problems faced by schools that hinder the education of students with disabilities are discussed below:

Physical Barriers: Physical access to school buildings is an essential prerequisite for educating children with disabilities (Stubbs, S., 2008). Those with physical disabilities are likely to face difficulties in travelling to school if, for example, the roads and bridges are unsuitable for wheelchair use and the distances are too great (UNESCO, 2010). Even if it is possible to reach the school, there may be problems of stairs, narrow doorways, inappropriate seating, or inaccessible toilet facilities.

Curriculum and Pedagogy: Curriculum and teaching methods are rigid and there is a lack of appropriate teaching materials – for example, where information is not delivered in the most appropriate mode such as sign language and teaching materials are not available in alternative formats such as Braille — children with disabilities are at increased risk of exclusion (UNESCO, 2009). Assessment and evaluation systems are often focused on academic performance rather than individual progress and therefore can also be restrictive for children with special education needs (UNESCO, 2009). Flexible approaches in regards to pedagogy and curriculum are needed to respond to the diverse abilities and needs of all learners.

Violence, Bullying, and Abuse: Violence against students with disabilities — by teachers, other staff, and fellow students — is common in educational settings (United Nations Children's Fund, 2005). Students with disabilities often become the targets of violent acts including physical threats and abuse, verbal abuse, and social isolation. The fear of bullying can be as great an issue for children with disabilities as actual bullying (Watson, N., *et al.*, 1998). Children with disabilities may prefer to attend special schools, because of the fear of stigma or bullying in mainstream schools.

Labelling Children: Students with disability are reluctant about revealing their disability due to negative attitudes, thus missing out on needed support services (Kwon, H., 2005). With disabilities are often categorised according to their health condition to determine their eligibility for special education and other types of support services. For example, a diagnosis of dyslexia, blindness, or deafness can facilitate access to technological and communication support and specialised teaching (MacDonald, S.J., 2009). But assigning labels to children in education systems can have negative effects including stigmatization, peer rejection, lower self-esteem, lower expectations, and limited opportunities (Florian, L., *et al.*, 2006).

Inadequate training and support for teachers: Teachers may not have the time or resources to support disabled learners (Wright, S.L. and Sigafoos, J., 1997). In resource poor settings classrooms are frequently overcrowded and there is a severe shortage of well trained teachers capable of routinely handling the individual needs of children with disabilities. The majority of teachers lack sign-language skills creating barriers for Deaf pupils (Haualand, H. and Allen, C., 2009). Other supports such as classroom assistants are also lacking. For example, in India the preservice training of regular teachers includes no familiarisation with the education of children with special needs (Bines, H., *et al.*, 2007).

Attitudinal Barriers: Negative attitudes are a major obstacle to the education of disabled children (Price, P., 2003). In some cultures, people with disabilities are seen as a form of divine punishment or as carriers of bad fortune. As a result, children with disabilities who could be in school are sometimes not permitted to attend. A community based study in Rwanda found that perceptions of impairments affected whether a child with a disability attended school. Negative community attitudes were also reflected in the language used to refer to people with disabilities (Karangwa, E., Ghesquière, P., and Devlieger, P., 2007). The attitudes of teachers, school administrators, other children, and even family members affect the inclusion of children with disabilities in mainstream schools. Some school teachers, including head teachers, believe they are not obliged to teach children with disabilities (Kvam, M.H. and Braathen, S.H., 2006).

For creating universe for all and educating all children in the same environment, barriers as mentioned above needs to be addressed to ensure the inclusion of children with disabilities in education, requires both systemic and school level change (McGregor, G. and Vogelsberg, R.T., 1998).

Disability Laws/Rights and Policy

The Indian Constitution: The Constitution of India applies uniformly to every legal citizen of India, whether they are healthy or disabled. Under the constitution the disabled have been guaranteed many fundamental rights, one such right is to education. Article 21A provides that, the State shall provide free and compulsory education to all children between the age of six to fourteen years that provides quality education without discrimination based on the ground of child's economic, social and cultural background (Basu, 2015).

Right To Education Act, 2009: The Right of Children to Free and Compulsory Education (RTE) Act, 2009 has come into force (w.e.f.) 1st April, 2010. The RTE Act provides for free and compulsory education to children in the age group of 6-14 years at elementary level in a neighbourhood school. Government of India has since aligned the Sarva Shiksha Abhiyan (SSA) norms with the provisions of Right of Children to Free and Compulsory Education Act, 2009. SSA ensures that every child with special needs, irrespective of the kind, category and degree of disability, is provided meaningful and quality education. Hence, SSA has adopted a zero rejection policy. This means that no child having special needs should be deprived of the right to education and taught in an environment, which is best, suited to his/her learning needs.

The Persons with Disability (Equal Opportunity, Protection of Rights and Full Participation) Act, 1995: The persons with disability (Equal opportunity, protection of rights and full participation) Act, 1995 has come into enforcement on February 7, 1996. It is a significant step which ensures equal opportunity for the people with disability and their full participation in day to day life. The Act provides for both preventive and promotional aspects of rehabilitation like prevention, early intervention, education, employment and vocational training, reservation, research and manpower development, creation of barrier free environment, unemployment allowances, and special insurance scheme for the disabled employees and establishment of homes for persons with disability etc. Main provision of the Act is spelled below.

The PWD Act, 1995 has 8 main provisions (Fig. 15.1) and one among them is Education: elementary education is a fundamental right under the Constitution. PWD Act also enumerates various provisions to ensure right education with right format at right time for children with disabilities. It includes right of every children till the age of 18 years to get free education. They also have right to free books, scholarship, uniform and other learning materials. School should be able to provide them with the enhancing environment by creating barrier free access, appropriate transportation and restructuring or modification in the examination system to ensure optimum benefit to CWSN. Teacher training institute shall be established to develop requisite manpower etc.

The Rehabilitation Council of India Act, 1992: Persons with disability in India have been receiving rehabilitation services for more than 100 years. However, before establishment of RCI, there was hardly any planned effort made in the field for developing trained manpower. Lack of appropriate trained manpower has been one of the major constrains in expansion of rehabilitation

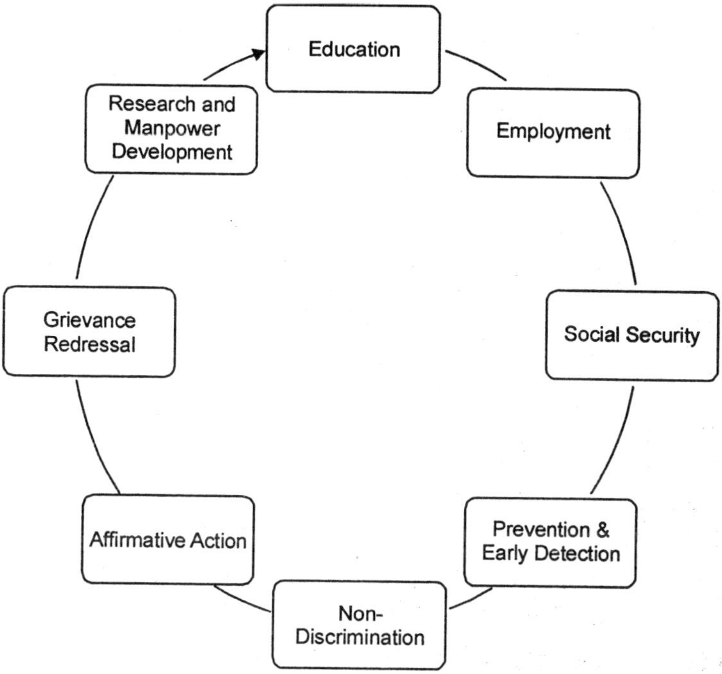

Fig. 15.1: Eight Main Provisions of P.W.D. Act, 1995
Source: Self-compiled.

service in the country. It was therefore, in 1986 decided by Government of India to set-up Rehabilitation Council of India to be responsible for the following activities: to standardize the training course for professional dealing with PWDs; development and regulation of training polices and programme; to grant recognition to the institutions running these training courses; to maintain a Central Rehabilitation Register of rehabilitation professionals; and to promote research in rehabilitation and special education.

In order to give the statutory powers to the Council for carrying out its duties effectively the Rehabilitation Council of India Act, 1992 was passed by the Parliament which came into force with effect from 22nd June, 1993. This Act provides guarantees so as to ensure the good quality of service rendered by various rehabilitation personnel. RCI is the only institute which takes care of manpower development of different categories of professionals for comprehensive rehabilitation of PWDs to meet the need of their entire life cycle, i.e. physical and medical rehabilitation, education, vocational and social rehabilitation.

Programmes and Schemes for Persons with Disabilities

There are many schemes and programme running in the country for the welfare of PWDs, but to avail any facility, concession and the benefit one should have the basic documents, i.e. disability card or identity card and the degree of disability should be at least 40 per cent in order to be eligible for any concession or benefits. However, this is not required for gaining admission in a school for formal education. The classification of various concessions being recommended is applicable to the person with permanent disabilities only.

Education Programme for Children with Special Needs: There are different provisions for education of children with disabilities. After the assessment of their disabilities by a multidisciplinary team, the child will be placed in appropriate educations setting. Children with mild and moderate disabilities of any kind may be integrated in regular school after a thorough assessment; drop-outs that have problem in availing benefits in regular schools can join open schools. Children with severe disability can attend special schools. Open and special schools also offer vocational courses for children with special needs.

(a) Inclusive Education for Disabled (IED) under Sarva Shiksha Abhiyan (SSA): The main focus of MHRD and SSA is to increase access, enrolment and retention of all children as well as improving the quality of education. The general guidelines issued by the Ministry are as follows: Every child should get free and compulsory education up till the age of 14 years; A zero rejection policy; Education to CWSN should be provided in an environment most suited to their learning needs; Flexibility in planning – to make it need based; Provision of 1200 per child for integration of CWSN per year; Encourage involvement of resource institute.

(b) Inclusive Education for the Disabled at Secondary Stage (IEDSS): This is centrally sponsored scheme under which the Centre will assist the State/UT (Union Territory) and autonomous bodies of stature in the field of education. The aims and objectives of scheme are as follows: Enable all students with disabilities completing eight

years of elementary schooling an opportunity to complete four years of secondary schooling (Classes IX to XII) in an inclusive and enabling environment; Provide education opportunities and facilities to students with disabilities in general education system at the secondary-level; Support the training of general school teacher to meet the need of children with disabilities; Provision for aids and appliances as per the need; Appointment of Special Educators and establishment of resource room in every block etc.

The scheme covers all children of age 14+ years passing out of elementary schools and studying in secondary stage in Government, local body and Government aided schools, with one or more disabilities as defined under the PWD Act, 1995 and the National Trust Act, 1999 in the age group 14 to 18 years (classes IX to XII). The scheme includes assistance for two components. (i) student oriented component, everything that ensures the CWSNs retention in the class and avoids all hindrances is covered under the component. It also provides the amount of Rs. 3000 per disabled child per annum to provide all sorts of assistance that will create an enhancing learning environment; and (ii) other component includes all those relating infrastructure, teacher training, awareness generation etc.

(c) *Special schools*: This is a programme of the Ministry of Social Justice and Empowerment. Children with severe multiple disabilities who have difficulty in coping with regular school are referred to special schools. Most of these special schools are located in urban areas and run by voluntary organisation.

(d) *National Open School (NOS)*: The NOS was established as an Autonomous Registered Society in 1989 with the mission to provide education through an open learning system at the school stage as an alternative to formal education system. It is especially suited to the need of certain categories including the disabled.

Children's Education Allowances and Scholarship: To ensure that the students with disabilities who have fair access to higher and technical education, 3 per cent seats in educational instiutions are reserved for them. Besides, the Ministry of Social Justice and Empowerment supports 500 scholarships for students for perusing their studies at the post-school-level. The objective of the scheme is to provide financial assistance to disabled students for higher and technical education. They will also be supported for acquiring special aids and appliances for studies.

Sikkim Experiences

Sikkim is one of the states amongst the twenty nine states of India. It has attained an age of around 42 years after merger with the Union of India. Sikkim is situated in the north-eastern part of the country and lies between 27° 46′ and 28° 7' north latitude and 88° and 88° 55' east longitude. Sikkim shares international border with three countries. Sikkim borders Nepal in the west, Tibet (China) to the north and east, Bhutan in the south-east and the Indian State of West Bengal to the south. Largest city and capital of Sikkim is Gangtok, the state has a population of 6,10,000 people (Census 2011). Total geographical area of Sikkim is 7096 sq. km. where East District is 954 sq. km., North District is 4226 sq. km., South District is 750 sq. km. and West District is 1166 sq. km. (*Annual Report*, 2014-15).

Sikkim has been implementing a programme then known as Integrated Education for Disabled Children (IEDC) when Sarva Shiksha Abhiyan (SSA) was incepted in 2001. Therefore, the State Project Office of SSA unanimously decided not to include any plan for the Children with Special Needs (CWSN) under SSA to avoid repetition. However, in 2007-08, a plan for Inclusive Education (IE) was included in Annual Work Plan and Budget of SSA in compliance with the directives of Ministry of Human Resource Development, Government of India. Thus, IE was started in the State of Sikkim at much later age as compared to other states. During 2008-09 only two trained manpower were employed though the advertisement was made for 4 posts. This was because of lack of trained technical manpower. Few of the caretakers were appointed in the following year, but the mass appointment were done during 2011-12. Resource Teachers and IE volunteers were appointed to implement the programme at the grassroots level with some conditions such as for the post of Resource teacher candidate with regular B. Ed. were considered with condition that they enroll and complete the course in Post-graduate post-diploma in any of the special education field within three years of appointment and for IE Volunteers they needed to undergo 6 months caregiver training programme in special education. Right after the appointment disability camps were organised with convergence with other line departments. Awareness and training of school heads, State Administrators teachers and CRC/BRC

Coordinators, motivation camp for parents was carried out. As a result, till 2014-15, they had quite a few technical persons but other important areas that need consideration to create an inclusive set-up lacked far behind like Disabled friendly toilets were constructed only in 11 schools. Other aspects of barrier free environment is neglected. Honorarium to RTs and IEVs are not encouraging which is why they switch their jobs resulting to loss of trained manpower. State does not have a single manpower that has undergone a regular course in Special Education field which is why they lack proper planning and implementation of programmes. No school is made disabled friendly and no modification in exam pattern for special needs children. Curricula and teaching methods are rigid and there is a lack of appropriate teaching materials. Till date there has been no specific modification of curriculum in the state from the perspective of CWSN (*Annual Report,* 2014-15).

Table 15.1: Literacy Rate of Sikkim

Males		*Females*		*Persons*	
2001	2011	2001	2011	2001	2011
76.04	87.30	60.41	76.43	68.81	82.20

Source: Annual Report 2014-15, State Project Office (SSA), HRDD, Government of Sikkim, Gangtok.

Table 15.1 shows the increasing trend of literacy rate of Sikkim, where the female literacy rate has increased faster than male literacy rate, even faster than the state literacy rate.

Table 15.2: District-wise Enrolment Class Pre to XII 2013 Session

Sl. No.	*Classes*	*East*	*West*	*North*	*South*	*Total*
1.	Pre-primary	288	725	137	815	1965
2.	I-V	19,046	12,326	3,401	12,605	47,378
3.	VI-VIII	15,058	9,248	2,309	10,095	36,710
4.	IX-X	8,277	4,807	1,231	4,826	19,141
5.	XI-XII	5,850	3,359	831	2,657	12,697
6.	I-XII	48,231	29,740	7,772	30,183	1,15,926
7.	Pre-primary-XII	48,519	30,465	7,909	30,998	1,17,891

Source: PME Section/HRDD.

Table 15.2 shows that in 2013 (State Government Institutions only), from pre-primary to XII 1,17,891 are enrolled in schools, 1,965 are in pre-primary, 47,378 are in I-V, 36,710 are in VI-VIII, 19,141 are in IX-X, 12,697 are in XI-XII and 1,15,926 are in I-XII. Out of 1,17,891, 48,519 are from East, 30,465 are from West, 7,909 are from North, and 30,998 are from South.

Table 15.3: District-wise Enrolment Class Pre to XII 2014 Session

Sl. No.	Classes	East	West	North	South	Total
1.	Pre-primary	1,275	987	257	1,165	3,684
2.	I-V	16,752	10,613	2,943	11,121	41,429
3.	VI-VIII	14,427	9,043	2,173	9,850	35,493
4.	IX-X	9,386	5,562	1,323	5,577	21,848
5.	XI-XII	6,671	3,546	900	3,162	14,279
6.	I-XII	47,236	28,764	7,339	29,710	1,13,049
7.	Pre-primary-XII	48,511	29,751	7,596	30,875	1,16,733

Source: PME Section/HRDD.

Table 15.3 shows that in 2014 (State Government Institutions only), from pre-primary to XII, 1,16,733 are enrolled in schools, 3,684 are in pre-primary, 41,429 are in I-V, 35,493 are in VI-VIII, 21,848 are in IX-X, 14,279 are in XI-XII and 1,13,049 are in I-XII. Out of 1,16,733, 48,511 are from East, 29,751 are from West, 7,596 are from North, and 30,875 are from South.

Table 15.4: District-wise Enrolment Class Pre to XII 2015 Session

Sl. No.	Classes	East	West	North	South	Total
1.	Pre-primary	1,256	871	335	744	3,206
2.	I-V	14,040	8,514	2,348	9,224	34,126
3.	VI-VIII	14,251	9,231	2,186	9,380	35,048
4.	IX-X	9,850	5,551	1,384	6,315	23,100
5.	XI-XII	6,370	3,729	938	3,446	14,483
6.	I-XII	44,511	27,025	6,856	28,365	1,06,757
7.	Pre-primary-XII	45,767	27,896	7,191	29,109	1,09,963

Source: PME Section/HRDD.

Table 15.4 shows that in 2015 (State Government Institutions only), from pre-primary to XII, 109,963 are enrolled in schools, 3,206 are in pre-primary, 34,126 are in I-V, 35,048 are in VI-VIII,

23,100 are in IX-X, 14,483 are in XI-XII and 1,06,757 are in I-XII. Out of 1,09,963, 45,767 are from East, 27,896 are from West, 7,191 are from North, and 29,109 are from South.

Tables 15.2, 15.3 and 15.4 makes clear that the enrolment of the students in the schools from pre-primary to XII is reducing yearly, in the year 2013 there were 1,17,891 students, in 2014 there were 1,16,733 and in the year 2015 there were 1,09,963 students. Somewhere there seems to be lack of encouragement. Most of the couples these days prefer single child and they send them to private schools as they can afford it and the facilities in terms of co-curriculum activities are higher in private schools.

Table 15.5: Category-wise CWSN 2014-15 Enrolled at Elementary Level

Sl. No.	Categories	No. of CWSN enrolled in Schools				
		Total	North	East	West	South
1.	LV (Low Vision)	346	31	197	63	55
2.	TB (Total Blind)	37	00	00	00	37
3.	HI (Hearing Impairment)	139	18	62	30	29
4.	SI (Speech Impairment)	248	23	93	68	64
5.	OI (Orthopedic Impairment)	179	16	63	47	53
6.	CP (Cerebral Palsy)	24	03	12	04	05
7.	MR (Mental Retardation)	93	12	26	19	36
8.	LD (Learning Disability)	206	03	36	132	35
9.	MD (Multiple Disability)	66	07	31	13	15
10.	ASD (Autistic Spectrum Disorder)	12	01	03	05	03
	Total	**1,350**	**114**	**523**	**381**	**332**

Source: DISE 2014-15 & DESME, available at Source: Annual Report 2014-15, State Project Office (SSA), HRDD, Government of Sikkim, Gangtok.

Table 15.5 shows that there are 1,350 CWSN enrolled in elementary school, where 346 are LV, 37 are TB, 139 are HI, 248 are SI, 179 are OI, 24 are CP, 93 are MR, 206 are LD, 66 are MD, and 12 are ASD.

Table 15.6 shows that there are only 86 CWSN enrolled in the secondary level whereas the total enrollment of students in secondary-level is 37,583 (as per 2015 data, Table 16.4) which signifies that there are only 0.2 per cent CWSN in secondary level. On the other hand, in elementary level there are 72,380 students enrolled but out of that only 1,350 are CWSN, i.e. 1.8 per cent is CWSN. Now, the figure shows the disparities. It is clear from the

Table 15.6: CWSN Enrolled at Secondary Level

Sl. No.	Categories of Disabled Children	As per UDISE 2014-15
1.	Blindness (TB)	08
2.	Low Vision (LV)	20
3.	Hearing Impairment (HI)	08
4.	Speech Impairment (SI)	14
5.	Loco Motor Impairment (LI/OI)	18
6.	Mental Retardation (MR)	05
7.	Learning Disability (LD)	08
8.	Cerebral Palsy (CP)	01
9.	Austin	01
10.	Multiple Disability (MD)	03
	Total	**86**

Source: UDISE, 2014-15, State Project Office (IEDSS).

enrolment rate that a lot of CWSN does not get a chance to attain school as the national average says that State of Sikkim has higher prevalence of disability, i.e. more than 2.5 per cent (Census, 2011), but when it comes to educating them only 1.3 per cent gets a chance to attend school. The figures are more discouraging when it comes to secondary education, it becomes clear that when CWSN gets promoted from elementary to secondary level, the number of the students get reduced, i.e. 1,350 to 86 or 1.8 per cent to 0.2 per cent. There are several reasons for which the number of CWSN is not attending schools and those who are in school system drop-out in secondary-level. The reasons have to be addressed by the State immediately. Otherwise, the State will face a lot of problems in near future.

The Government of Sikkim has implemented the plans and the policies of the Government of India in terms of education of Children with Special Needs. For example: the schemes like Inclusive Education under SSA and IEDSS under the RMSA are functioning. Apart from that there are three Special Schools which function under Department of Social Justice and Empowerment. As far as the state is concerned there are no educational policies and facilities specially designed for CWSN. Whatever little work in terms of inclusion of CWSN in the mainstream that is happening in the State is only through Government of India (GoI) schemes. Some of the major challenges that are faced by the State are as follows: no state policies or programmes of Government of Sikkim, lacks framework for CWSN and no section in the Human Resource

Development Department that looks after Disabled Education, lack of trained manpower/special educators heading the projects, attitudinal and environmental barriers, low awareness, curriculum is not as per the need of CWSN and curriculum gets tougher as they promoted to higher classes, negative attitude; infrastructure barriers; schools are too far to attend, no provision of government to appoint special educator on regular basis, lack of motivation among the employees; regular teachers not ready to accept CWSN in the class, and lack of technical person implementing the programmes in concerned department.

Conclusion

The study shows that education contributes to human capital formation, which is a key determinant of personal well-being and welfare, where excluding children with disabilities from educational and employment opportunities have high social and economic costs. Particularly, for children with disabilities, including all children, education is vital in itself, but also instrumental for participating in employment and other areas of social activity. But, many children and adults with disabilities have historically been excluded from mainstream educational opportunities. In India, it has been noticed that children with disabilities comes in special schools and it falls under the responsibility of the Ministry of Social Justice and Empowerment. On the other hand, regular children come in mainstream schools and it come under the Department of Education in the Ministry of Human Resource Development. This shows the division of education and this division reflects the cultural perception that children with disabilities are in need of welfare rather than equality of opportunity. But this particular model tends to further segregate children with disabilities, and shifts the focus from education and achieving social and economic inclusion to treatment and social isolation. Without dividing the education, there is a need to go for inclusive educational system into the mainstream education system in order to bring equality and human rights where there would be developed ways of teaching that responds to individual differences, to the benefit of all children; change of attitudes towards those who are in some way different by educating all children together and it would help in creating a just society without discrimination; less costly than setting up a complex system of different types of schools specializing in different groups of children.

It is not easy things to bring them into mainstream schools since there are some hindrances before the children with special needs such as – physical barriers, rigid curriculum and teaching methods, lack of appropriate teaching materials, violence against students with disabilities by teachers, other staff, and fellow students. Students with disabilities often become the targets of violent acts including physical threats and abuse, verbal abuse, and social isolation, the fear of bullying can be as great an issue for children with disabilities as actual bullying; students with disability are reluctant about revealing their disability due to negative attitudes, inadequate training and support for teachers; attitudinal barriers etc.

The study in Sikkim shows that there are many obstacles in relation to the education of children with special needs, e.g. lack of trained manpower/special educators, attitudinal barriers; environmental barriers; low awareness; no proper state policies; lack of technical person implementing the programmes in concerned department etc. To educate children including children with special needs, the above discussed barriers needs to be addressed to ensure and create inclusive setting for all. To counter the entire problem as mentioned above State needs to come up with their own policy in regards to education of CWSN instead of relying on GoI schemes. Government of Sikkim should come-up with establishment of Disability Cell under HRDD that will look after all the matter related to CWSN. Sikkim needs to have properly trained manpower/special educators, who are able to give proper attention to the children with special needs, awareness programme and proper state policies in relation to the education of the marginal children including children with special needs; curriculum adaptation as per the need of CWSN technical person to implement the programmes in concerned department etc. Along with that the state needs to solve the attitudinal and environmental barriers. If State's response is positive then hopefully we can see the enrolment rate of CWSN going higher in near future, thereby giving them the most powerful gift of education which will give children with disabilities skills to allow them to become positive role models and join the employment market, thereby helping to live a dignified life.

References

Basu, Durga Das (2015): *Introduction to the Constitution of India* (Gurgaon: Lexis Nexis).

Bines, H., Lei, P., (ed.) (2007): *Education's missing millions: including disabled children in education through EFA FTI processes and national sector plans.* Milton Keynes, World Vision UK.

Dupoux, E., Wolman, C., Estrada, E. (2005): "Teachers' attitudes toward integration of students with disabilities in Haiti and the United States", *International Journal of Disability Development and Education*, 52: 43-58.

Farrell, P., *et al.* (2007): "SEN inclusion and pupil achievement in English schools", *Journal of Research in Special Educational Needs*, 7: 172-178.

Filmer, D. (2005): *Disability, poverty and schooling in developing countries: results from 11 household surveys* (Washington: World Bank).

Florian, L., *et al.* (2006): "Cross-cultural perspectives on the classification of children with disabilities": Part 1 "Issues in the classification of children with disabilities", *The Journal of Special Education*, 40: 36-45.

Forlin, C., Lian, M.G.J. (ed.) (2008): Reform, inclusion and teacher education: toward a new era of special education in the Asia Pacific Region (London: Routledge Publications).

Government of India (2011): *Census of India.*

Government of Sikkim (2014-15): *Annual Report 2014-15*, State Project Office (SSA), HRDD (Gangtok: Government of Sikkim).

Haualand, H., Allen, C. (2009): *Deaf People and Human Rights* (Helsinki, World Federation of the Deaf and Swedish National Association of the Deaf).

Karangwa, E., Ghesquière, P. and Devlieger, P. (2007): "The grassroots community in the vanguard of inclusion: the Rwandan perspective", *International Journal of Inclusive Education*, 11: 607-626.

Karangwa, E. (2006): Grassroots community-based inclusive education: exploring educational prospects for young people with disabilities in the post-conflict Rwandan communities (Louvain: Centre for Disability, Special Needs Education and Child Care).

Kvam, M.H. and Braathen, S.H. (2006): *Violence and Abuse against Women with Disabilities in Malawi* (Oslo, SINTEF).

Kwon, H. (2005): "Inclusion in South Korea: the current situation and future directions", *International Journal of Disability Development and Education*, 52: 59-68.

Lewis, I. (2009): *Education for Disabled People in Ethiopia and Rwanda* (Manchester, Enabling Education Network).

MacDonald, S.J. (2009): *Toward a Sociology of Dyslexia: Exploring links between Dyslexia, Disability and Social Class* (Saarbruken: VDM Publishing House).

McGregor, G., Vogelsberg, R.T. (1998): *Inclusive Schooling Practices: Pedagogical and Research Foundations.* A synthesis of the literature that informs best practices about inclusive schooling (Baltimore: Paul H. Brookes).

Naidhu, A. (2008): "Collaboration in the era of inclusion" in Forlin C, Lian M-GJ, (ed.) *Reform, Inclusion and Teacher Education: toward a new era of special education in the Asia Pacific Region* (London: Routledge Publications).

Porter, G.L. (2001): Disability and inclusive education (Paper prepared for the Inter American Development Bank Seminar, Inclusion and Disability, Santiago).

Price, P. (2003): "Education for All (EFA): an elusive goal for children with disabilities in developing countries in the Asian Pacific Region", *Asia Pacific Disability Rehabilitation Journal*, 14: 3-9.

Right to Education Act, 2009.

Singal, N. (2006): "Inclusive education in India: international concept, national interpretation", *International Journal of Disability Development and Education*, 53: 351-369.

Stubbs, S. (2008): *Inclusive Education: Where there are few Resources*. (Oslo: Atlas Alliance).

The Persons with Disability (Equal Opportunity, Protection of Rights and Full Participation) Act, 1995.

The PWD Act, 1995.

The Rehabilitation Council of India Act, 1992.

UNCF (2005): Summary report. Violence against children. UN Secretary-General's report on violence against children. Thematic group on violence against children. Findings and recommendations (New York: United Nations Children's Fund).

UNESCO (2001): *Understanding and responding to children's needs in inclusive classrooms* (Paris: United Nations Educational, Scientific and Cultural Organization).

UNESCO (2009): *Education for All Global Monitoring Report* (Paris: United Nations Educational, Scientific and Cultural Organization).

UNESCO (2009): *Policy Guidelines on Inclusion in Education* (Paris: United Nations Educational, Scientific and Cultural Organization).

UNESCO (2010): *Reaching the Marginalised EFA Global Monitoring Report 2010* (Paris: United Nations Educational, Scientific and Cultural Organization).

Watson, N., *et al.* (1998): *Life as a Disabled Child: Research Report* (Edinburgh: University of Edinburgh).

WHO (2002–2004): *World Health Survey* (Geneva: World Health Organization).

World Bank (2009): *People with Disabilities in India: from commitments to outcomes* (Washington: Human Development Unit, South Asia Region, World Bank).

Wright, S.L., Sigafoos, J. (1997): "Teachers and students without disabilities comment on the placement of students with special needs in regular classrooms at an Australian primary school", *Australasian Journal of Special Education*, 21:67-80.

16

Educational Status Among the Tea Garden Workers

A Case Study of Cachar District of Assam

Pradip Kurmi and *Sumanash Dutta*

1. Introduction

Marginalisation is a process where a group of people is excluded or ignored from their desired needs from the rest of the society. It is a socio-economic and political phenomenon whereby a section of people or a particular community is denied involvement in economic, social, political activities. They are denied to enjoy the basic needs of life, fundamental rights, right to education, right to participate, right to equal employment etc. At this level, member of such group of people may lack access to formal education, gender equity or denied access to participate in decision-making process. Such denials create conflicts between groups of people and divide the society into marginalised and dominant people, exploited class and exploiter class. It is rightly explained by the concept of Karl Marx of Haves and Have not's. Education of marginalised people stands for where a section of people is deprived of enjoying the basic facilities to take necessary education. A unique example of this being the case of the tea garden labourers of Assam. They are the marginalised section of people who are not only exploited by the enterprise, but also allegedly deprived by the government.

The establishments of tea industry of Assam necessitate recruitment of huge number of labour force. The tea companies were in great need of utilizing labour force for the growth of tea industries, which they could not manage locally. This necessitated importation of labour from different parts of India and as such these labourers were trapped by company's "thickaders" who promised of good earnings and amazing life for them in the tea gardens. The success of tea plantation experiment in upper Assam encouraged the British authorities to develop more tea business in other districts of Assam. Barak Valley was also viewed as important for the British in the sense of commerce as because the climatic condition and soil of Barak Valley was also suitable for tea plantation like other tea producing parts of Assam. Captain Thomas Fisher, the first superintendent of Cachar (the present Barak Valley) began to plan to develop plantation in the area like the other parts of Assam. The first tea plantation of Cachar district started at Barshangan (near the present Kathal tea garden) in 1856 by G. Williamson, who had a large number and flourishing tea plantation estates in upper Assam. The arrival of tea garden labourers into this valley was a historical and tragic incident, for they are treacherously brought to work in tea plantation. The tea gardens labourers were brought to Karimganj and Silchar (the Headquarters of Cachar) from Narayanganj, Calcutta (the present Kolkata) through Goalundo ghat – a place near the confluence of Padma and the Brahmaputra rivers. At present there are 66 tea gardens in Cachar district having 33,161 number of labourers employed in these tea gardens out of which, 17,661 are male labourers and 15,500 are female labourers. The existing literature suggests that the economic life of the tea garden labourers is full of miseries and deprivations. They are deprived in almost all the basic areas of needs like income, education and health, allegedly both the company as well as the government being the perpetrators. They have almost no other sources of income apart from the daily wages they earn from the tea gardens.The labour wage rate is also quite low in comparison with the wages of their counterparts who are engaged in other sectors.

Definite success of a community and State depend upon their educational and intellectual attainments. But tea garden labourers are deprived of Education by and large. It seems to be a curse for this great community of Assam. The right to education is universal and does not allow for any form of exclusion or discrimination. The Right of the Children to Free and Compulsory Education or Right to Education Act was passed by the Indian Parliament on

4th August, 2009 to execute the Article 21(A) which was inserted after 86th Amendment of the Constitution. Article 21(A) states, "The state shall provide free and compulsory education to all children of the age group 6-14 years. According to RTE Act, 2009, "Every child of the age of 6 to 14 years shall have a right to free and compulsory education in a neighbourhood school till completion of elementary education. Though the Tea Garden labourer of Assam play a remarkable role in shaping the socio-economic structure of Assam, they are still far behind in education. The tea garden labourers are much reluctant of sending their children to even primary school. Children of Plantation labourers either stay at home for looking after their younger siblings or engage themselves as casual labour in plucking, weeding, hoeing and nursery work in the tea gardens. The lack of educational facility for various reasons kept them in Dark Age as education is a powerful instrument through which one can solve all sorts of problems. Lack of basic need facilities in the tea gardens deters their all-round development and prosperity. The situation is much pathetic in case of women labourers of the tea garden. The plights of tea garden lobourers provide an ample scope for researchers to carry out research to find out the actual situation of tea garden labourers in Cachar district.

2. Objective of the Study

In this backdrop, the present research is carried out with the following objectives:

(i) To examine the educational status of tea garden labourers in the tea gardens of Cachar district.
(ii) To highlight the available educational institutional facilities in the tea gardens of Cachar district.
(iii) To examine the factors responsible for the present level of education in the tea gardens of Cachar district.

3. Methodology

The study is based on primary data. The geographical area of the study is Cachar district of Assam. For the purpose, the researchers have selected ten (10) tea gardens in Cachar and from each tea garden fifteen households are selected randomly. Hence in total, the sample comprises of 150 household of tea garden labourers of Cachar district. Data from these selected sample households are collected with the help of a well structured schedule through personal interview method. The schedule contains all the relevant information related to education that may serve the purpose of the present study.

4. Data Analysis, Results and Interpretation of Results

In this section, descriptive statistics of important sample household characteristics are presented in Table 16.1 along with the discussion on the statistics. The systematic analysis will help to meet the objectives of the study.

Table 16.1: Demographic Characteristics of Tea Garden Labourers of Cachar District

Variables	*Mean*	*Standard Deviation*
Level of Education	3.73	1.95
Family Size	5.94	2.76
Land holdings	0.655	1.56

Data Source: Field survey.

Table 16.1 reflects the demographic characteristics of tea garden labourers of Cachar district. Table 16.1 reflects that the level of education is very low among the tea garden workers of Cachar district. Average level of education among the tea garden workers is only 3.73 years while standard deviation is 1.94. Again on the other hand average family size of the tea garden workers is 5.94 which are quite high with standard deviation 2.75 which points towards significant degree of disparity in the family size variable. Family size has supposedly direct impact on the level of education. The larger the family size, the higher will be the possibility of members having low level of education. Table 16.1 also shows that average size of landholdings of the households of tea garden labourers is 0.655 *bigha* and the standard deviation of this variable is 1.56 which together corroborate the fact that the families are having very small size of land under their possession.

Table 16.2: Household Economic Characteristics of Tea Garden Labourers of Cachar District

Variables	*Mean*	*Standard Deviation*
Number of Earning Members	1.33	0.54
Family Income From T.G. (in Rs.)/year	37460	72742
Family Income From Other sources (in Rs.)/year	12463	1017.6
Family debt (in Rs.)	1371.27	2275.18
Savings (in Rs.)	600	400

Data Source: Field Survey.

Table 16.2. reveals that the average number of earning members in tea garden households is 1.33 with deviation 0.54. It is found in the survey that on the one hand size of the family is very large but the earning members in the family, on the other hand, is very few. In respect of the family income earned from tea garden and other sources, the mean family income per year from tea garden and from the other sources is Rs. 37,460 and Rs.12,463 respectively.

Again the observed extent of family debt is found to be very high and savings very low. Average family debt per year is of Rs.1371.27 with standard deviation 2275.18. On the other hand average savings is only Rs. 600 with standard deviation 400. From these figures, it can be stated here that the economic condition of tea garden labourers in Cachar district is very poor. They have negligible opportunity to venture outside the garden jurisdiction to earn more income. In that sense, they are living the life of a bonded labourer. The labour wage rate is also quite low in comparison with that of their counterparts who are engaged in other sectors of the economy. Though the garden labourers have been contributing to the production system of the Tea gardens since long, their economic conditions presumably remains unchanged over time. Economic condition of a family has impact on the education of their children. As the family is very poor, their children get little scope for higher education.

Table 16.3 shows the number of educational institutions within 5 (five) k.m. range of the household. Average number of L.P. school in tea gardens, within the specified range of Cachar district is only 2.90 while average number of M.E. school is 1.22, average number of high school is 0.73 and average number of colleges is 0.02. From Table 16.3, it appears that there are virtually 3 L.P. Schools, 1 M.E.

Table 16.3: Availability of Educational Institutions in Tea Gardens of Cachar (Schools Within 5 k.m. from Household)

Variables	Mean	Standard Deviation
Number of LP Schools	2.90	1.33
Number of M.E Schools	1.22	0.72
Number of High Schools	0.73	0.45
Number of Colleges	0.02	0.14

Data Source: Field Survey.

School and no High School and College within the range of a sample household. In order to get admission into High school and Colleges the children of tea garden labourers have to travel a distance of more than 5 (Five) k.m. from their household. This reflects the deprivation level among the tea gardens in respect to availability of educational institution in their habitation areas.

Table 16.4: Educational status of workers of Tea Gardens in Cachar District

Variables	Total Number of Respondents (Affirmative Responses)	%
Willinness to send daughter for higher studies	50	33.3
Preference for daughter's Marriage Over Education	106	70.67
Any Drop-out below M.E School	116	77.33

Data Source: Field Survey.

Table 16.4 shows that only 33.3 per cent of the respondents are willing to send their daughter for higher studies in the sample of tea garden households of Cachar district. In a response from respondents regarding their choice between education and marriage for their daughter, 70.67 per cent respondents gives more preference for marriage than education. Further, the table also shows that 77.3 per cent respondents have dropped out child (children) in their households who could not complete M.E. level of schooling.

Table 16.5 reveals that in 2009 pass per cent of H.S.L.C. Examination in Assam is 62.39 whereas in Cachar it is 64.84, but in Tea garden, it is only 36.63. Such performance in H.S.L.C. Examinations shows poor educational status in Tea garden areas. Table 16.5 also reflects the performance in H.S.L.C. Examinations

Table 16.5: Performance of H.S.L.C. Examination in Assam, Cachar and Tea Garden Areas (*In* %)

Year	*Assam*	*Cachar*	*Tea Garden Areas*
2009	62.39	64.84	36.63
2010	64.69	65.17	38.07
2011	71.08	65.17	53.50
2012	69.63	54.72	44.78
2013	70.71	58.25	50.76

Source: *Result Hand Book of H.S.L.C. Examination* 2009, 2010, 2011, 2012, and 2013.

in 2010, 2011, 2012, 2013. In 2010, 2011, 2012, 2013 pass percentage in H.S.L.C. Examinations are 64.69, 71.08, 69.63 and 70.71 respectively in Assam and 65.12, 65.17, 54.72, 58.25 in Cachar. The pass percentage of H.S.L.C. Examinations in 2010, 2011, 2012, and 2013 are 38.07, 53.50, 44.78 and 50.76 in tea garden areas respectively. One of the main reasons behind poor performance is that children are found to do very strenuous work under very severe climatic condition. They are also made to work in the factories, against the established law. Only a few workers having rather sound financial condition send their children to L.P. or M.E. school and if possible outside the garden for higher studies. It is noticed that no effort has been made on behalf of the management for imparting education to the children of the Tea garden labourers.

5. Conclusions, Policy Recommendation and Suggestion

The major thrust of the study was directed towards investigating the level of education in the tea garden areas in Cachar district. On the basis of the present study following are some conclusions, policy recommendation and suggestion made to improve the level of education among the tea garden labourers in Cachar district:

(i) The level of family size has an impact on the level of education. In Tea gardens of Cachar, it is found that size of the family is larger and that apparently have a negative impact on their level of education.

(ii) Poor economic condition in tea gardens of Cachar is detrimental to educational attainments of household members of tea garden community. The level of household income is found very low. Level of household income always has positive influence on the attainment of children education, as found in literature.

(iii) Distance of educational institution has also an impact on the attainment of the level of education in Cachar district. But it is found in the research that there are very poor educational facilities available in tea garden areas of Cachar district. There is negligible number of high school available in tea garden areas of Cachar.

Recommendations for Improvement

The following recommendations are made on priority basis to improve the level of education of the labourers of the tea gardens in Cachar district:

(i) Various self-employment generation and poverty alleviation programmes like Mahatma Gandhi National Rural Employment Guarantee Scheme (MGNREGS), Sampoorna Gramin Rojgar Yojana (SGRY), Swarna Jayanti Svarojgar Yojana (SJSY) is in force in Cachar district introduced by the Government of India. But the coverage of the government programmes is very dismal. Step should be taken for proper implementation of these programmes and inclusion of tea garden communities in those programmes to improve the economic condition of tea garden populations.

(ii) Awareness campaign should be organised on the various government programmes through wide publicity in tea garden areas to improve the awareness level of the tea garden communities about these programmes.

(iii) Government should take necessary step to establish higher education institutions in tea garden areas. Step should be taken so that in every tea garden there shall be at least one high school.

(iv) Existing literature has upheld the role of mother in educational attainment of her children. Necessary steps should be taken to raise the level of mother's education in tea garden areas. Though instantly it is not possible to increase the mother's level of education so stress should be given on girl's education.

References

Dasgupta, Malay (2011): "Impact of early marriage on fertility among S.C., S.T. and Tea tribe communities of Dibrugarh District, Assam India: An analysis through logistic regression" in *International Journal of Educational Planning and Administration*, ISSN_ 2249-3093, Volume I, Number 3, pp. 211-215.

Hazarik, Kakali (2012): "Tea tribes are lagging behind in the process of urbanization: A study on selected tea gardens of Jorhat district, Assam" in *International Journal of Trends in Economics, Management and Technology*, Volume I, Issue 6, December, pp. 2-6.

Medhi, G.K., Hazarika, N.C., Shah, B. and Mahanta, J. (2006): "Study of Health Problems and Nutritional Status of the Tea Garden Population" in Assam in *Indian Journal of Medical Science*, Vol. 60, No. 12, December 2008, pp. 498-505.

Moestu, H. and Huttly, S. (2008): "Adult education and child nutrition: the role of family and community" by *Journal of Epidemiology and Community Health BMJ*, Vol. 62, No. 2, pp. 153-159.

Palmer, Robin (1986): "Working condition and worker response in Nyasaland Tea Estate, 1930-1953" by *Journal of African History*, Cambridge University Press, Volume 27, No. I, pp. 105-126.

Patanwar, Pratibha and Sharma, K.K.N. (2013): "Nutritional Status of Kurmi Adolescent Girls of Raipur City, Chhattisgarh, India" by *International Journal of Science and Research Publications*, Volume 13, Issue 11.

Varma, Nitin (2005): "Coolie Act and the Acting Coolies: Coolie Planter and State in the Late Nineteenth and Early Twentieth Century Colonial Tea Plantation of Assam" by *Social Scientist*, Volume 33, Number 5-6.

17

Implementation of Right To Education in Assam

A Study

Tarun Dutta

Though the Right To Education (RTE) Act, 2009 came into force in 2010 itself, the scenario in Assam is not very encouraging even six years after its enactment. The State Government took its time to develop the State rules and almost two years were spent in putting the systems in place. A few studies done by ActionAid, Pratham and RTE Forum brought out many worrisome shortcomings in ensuring RTE in the schools.

While the State had the advantage of already implementing programmes like District Primary Education Programme (DPEP) and schemes like Sarva Shiksha Abhiyan (SSA) and initiating some innovative teaching learning practices in certain schools and clusters, due to many systemic flaws and shortsighted policies as well corrupt practices by certain officials, the school education scenario in Assam is quite alarming today. Many children virtually remain out of school and many schools are almost dysfunctional while more and more parents prefer to send their children to private schools. At times one gets the impression that the stakeholders are either only paying lip service to the RTE Act or, worse still, are not even aware of the real spirit of this historic piece of legislation granting elementary education as a free and compulsory right to all children of age between 6 years to 14 years in India.

The last few decades saw much action in educational reforms in the country. Post Jomtien and Dakar conferences, with India committing itself to the Millennium Development Goals — universalization of Elementary Education became a major focus area.

If the Nineties was the decade of various experimental projects like Lok Jhumbish, Andhra Pradesh Primary Education Project (APPEP), Bihar Education Project (BEP), Uttar Pradesh Basic Education Project (UPBEP), District Primary Education Project etc., which targeted districts/regions identified as having low female literacy, the next decade went for the massive all encompassing effort, namely Sarva Shiksha Abhiyan. The goals were more or less the same — to provide quality primary education (up to class V in earlier cases, while in SSA it was up to class VIII) to all the children, especially those coming from various disadvantaged groups.

In Assam, too, SSA was launched in 2001 along with rest of the country and the State mission which was coordinating the DPEP in nine districts of the state took over the SSA Mission.

The SSA completed ten years of its project period in 2011 and now SSA mission has taken over as the nodal agency for implementation of RTE Act. Meanwhile, a new Rashtriya Madhyamik Shiksha Abhiyan (RMSA), focusing on secondary education has also been launched.

To take stock of how far the SSA in Assam has progressed in almost two decades in the key areas of access, retention and quality improvement, we with support from ActionAid, took up a study in 2011-12 focusing primarily on marginalised groups in difficult areas. The districts of Nalbari, Dhemaji, Morigaon and Baksa were selected with special reference to communities like Mishing, Tiwa, Hazong, Bodo, *Adivasis*, both indigenous and immigrant Muslim, Bengali migrants, indigenous fishermen etc. and groups like marginalised peasants, tea garden workers, manual wage earners and migrant labourers. We also made a point of visiting areas affected by flood, erosion, sand deposition and interacting with the affected people.

The study of the present situation and the challenges faced by the marginalised groups provided us with quite significant insights. The major one being that there are different types of marginalisation or deprivation. If some communities have remained marginalised for ages, there are others who suddenly find themselves in such unenviable situation due to factors beyond their control — both natural and man-made.

We also observed that while the villages and remote habitations were getting exposed to many urbanising trends, the small towns were rapidly acquiring all the urban characteristics. At the same time, natural phenomena (paradoxically sometimes result of various man-made "developmental" projects or efforts) like flood, erosion, sand deposition etc. too causes immense change to the lives of those affected. And more alarmingly both the impact as well as frequency of such "disasters" seem to have increased quite a lot in last 2-3 decades, leading to large scale and acute marginalisation in the State. We also observed that it was the traditionally marginalised communities like STs, SCs and minorities, who are more vulnerable to the latter types of phenomena quite often.

Rapid change in ecology can have serious implications for the livelihoods and the lifestyles of the inhabitants in the process also impacting schooling of their children. Changed occupations and lifestyles demand a new set of skills and values. The education system has to be fully geared to provide that. Unfortunately, we felt, SSA — or for that matter the State Education department, was pathetically unequipped for, as well as, insensitive to such an alarming scenario.

The Right of Children to Free and Compulsory Education (RTE) Act, 2009 came into force five years back on 1st April, 2010. The Act derives from the 86th Constitutional Amendment Act, 2002 and is an outcome of a hundred years of struggle with a vision of universalisation of elementary education that the leaders of the freedom movement and the founding fathers of the nation had. The Act entitles each child aged 6 to 14 years to free and compulsory education as a fundamental right. A historic judgement of the Supreme Court of India concluded that this right derives from the very spirit and principles of the country's constitution. Thus, right to education, today is a legally ensured right.

In our survey to assess how the Right To Education is being ensured in Assam, we had selected the districts of Nalbari, Dhemaji, Morigaon and Baksa with special reference to indigenous and migrant as well as marginalised communities. We found worrisome shortcomings in ensuring RTE in the schools, and the problem stemmed from the shortcomings and weaknesses of the Sarva Shiksha Abhiyan (SSA) itself, the delivery mechanism to guarantee right to education.

It emerged from our discussions with various stakeholders in the field that the interventions like SSA, though started with ambitious aims and objectives, could not achieve much of them due to flaws both at policy and implementation level. Lack of coordination at policy-level, centralized planning, dynamics of political interference, lack of accountability and at times very grave corruption at various levels are some of the key malaise which often distorted the all noble aims and goals of SSA.

Very often we heard about the lack of transparency in the decision-making process of SSA. Many complained about the decision-making process becoming kind of a black box. There have been many changes in the delivery mechanism since the days of DPEP and early SSA in recent times. There is much more multiplicity of agencies involved in the implementation now. The above situation, leads to lack of accountability as no one is responsible. The various government agencies involved in the delivery of education have their own rules, norms and criteria leading often to situations where left hand did not know what the right was doing.

Too much of centralization has become a bane for SSA. The whole system was planned from the headquarters and there is very little local participation in the planning process. Many teachers, we found, were quite disillusioned and at times felt exploited by senior decision-makers. Sometimes, they had to bear the brunt of becoming guinea pigs of various experiments designed from the top.

Various government policies such as providing free textbooks under RTE Act, addition of class V to primary section, no detention policy etc. has also led to chaotic situations in many cases. For example, due to no detention policy, students may practically enter high school without really mastering basic competencies in either language or mathematics, creating frustrating situations for high school teachers.

The primary base of education is weakening day by day, now creating a very challenging situation for the secondary stage. The lack of specialist subject teacher at the elementary level later creates difficulties as the new curriculum and textbooks require much more specialised knowledge on part of the teachers. In such a scenario parents having to send their children either to private schools or provide private tuitions is becoming a reality.

A major handicap of the system, we found, is the lack of teachers for science and mathematics as current syllabus for these subjects is of much higher order which can be taught only by those specialising in these subjects. Though there have been trainings organised by SSA for equipping the teacher, often teachers do not take them seriously for various reasons—many feel they are neither relevant nor practical. There were complaints that often the trainings were either repetitive or perfunctory.

Changing courses and curricula are also affecting the education scenario. The curriculum and method of teaching is frequently changed. Interestingly, we were told, textbooks in State schools have changed four times in last sixteen years. Adding to class V, the introductions to subjects like English, Hindi etc. is also creating problems in schools, because most of the teachers find the additional subjects difficult. Same is the case with the mathematics of the class V level.

There have been problems in the distribution of free textbooks under RTE. In most of the cases textbooks reached very late, sometimes they were much less than required. There has been also allegations that in the name of free textbooks, the authorities suddenly introduced CBSE books which have been merely translated without any adaptation or localisation.

Right to Education in Assam will remain a fundamental right on only paper so long as its delivery mechanism — the Sarva Shiksha Abhiyan (SSA) remains inadequate and faulty. With the major challenges before school education in the State, the demand is for up-to-date curriculum and quality textbooks, effective classroom teaching, marks-based evaluation and other facilities to enable pass-outs to compete in the job market.

Our study made us feel that SSA has failed to reach the most interior areas in Assam and connect with the most vulnerable groups even in terms of access, not to mention of retention and quality improvement. One felt that SSA somehow reaches usually those places which are reachable while the unreachable often remain still underdeveloped. It was unfortunate to find that there were still places where the system failed even in providing access of government schools for children of many marginalised communities, even after ten years of launching of SSA.

Lack of sufficient teachers is a major factor affecting education in the State. The number of single teacher schools with high enrolment is most alarming. In many cases even the schools earlier having sufficient teachers have been rendered dysfunctional due to not filling up the vacancies. Though we learnt that further appointment of teachers remained banned by High Court order since 2001, it was really surprising to find the government not taking adequate steps to convince the honourable court about the absolute necessity of starting the recruitment process in the long ten years.

This single factor of not having adequate teachers has negated most of the positive interventions of DPEP or SSA in the education sector. For example all measures for quality improvement as well as access and retention such as trainings, monthly meetings, Cluster Resource Centres (CRCs), Mid-Day-Meal (MDM) etc. fail in such single teacher schools. A CRC coordinator from a single teacher school cannot do much justice to children to his school, let alone provide academic support to other schools in his cluster.

As for Mid-Day Meal, the scheme is not having its desired impact — rather, it has become counter-productive in many cases with allegations and counter-allegations about large-scale corruption, rice not reaching schools in time or being of inferior quality or no money provided for its cooking.

We got the impression that though SSA has significant achievements in terms of hardware, providing infrastructure and facilities to schools, but the same cannot be said about the software such as availability of sufficient qualified and motivated teachers.

Many complained that even support visits from SSA authorities happen only in places where vehicles can go. Even schools/ habitations 2-3 kms away from motorable roads remained unvisited, and hence neglected, for years. This seems to be the tragic story of development in Assam in last ten years.

There have been some other alarming trends affecting the educational scenario in recent past. First among them is the steep fall in enrolment in many government schools. Linked with this is the mushrooming of private schools, including in Assamese medium, even in rural areas. Many parents probably, rightly or wrongly, feel that the private schools equipped their children better for the competitive market.

This has led to other alarming tendencies. In certain cases, the unpleasant truth that came out was — it is only the very poor who still send their children to the government schools, having no other options.

However, there were also many counter examples to the popular myth that government schools in the urban setting are losing out to the private schools. There were a number of government schools in urban areas which were having very high enrolment and functioning well.

There have been some achievements by the SSA too. The civil works has been a strong component of SSA, evidence of which could be seen in most of the districts studied. There were also schemes like Education Guarantee Scheme (EGS), bridge courses, Kasturba Gandhi Balika Vidyalaya (KGBV), community volunteer scheme etc. The EGS centres, especially, has been one of the popular and successful interventions for marginalised groups. However here too, there has been much bungling by decision-makers which may have very serious repercussions in the coming days.

We got the impression that even those involved in the delivery mechanism at various levels, feel quite overburdened and at times, exploited victims of a heartless system. They are expected to work outside normal office hours even at night or in holidays. But there is no compensation in terms of remuneration or other allowances. In case of the contractual employees there is neither provision for health nor retirement benefits. In fact, they do not have even job security.

The biggest weakness of the education system in Assam is that it is very slow to react to changing situations and demands. Responses at every level always come very late, sometimes never, and at times in an inappropriate manner. The schools, too, suffer from lack of a rapid response mechanism. In private schools, if there is some drawback, the management can respond immediately, while in the government system the long chain from head teacher through BEEO up to DEEO office will take despairingly long time to respond.

(The author duly acknowledge ActionAid, NERO for financial support to carry out the project and Mr. Mukut Lochan Kalita who was the consultant of the project.)

References

Aggarwal, J.C., 1993. *Development and Planning of Modern Education*, Delhi: Vikas Publishing House Pvt. Ltd.

Aggarwal, J.C., 1990. *Educational Reforms in India World Perspective*, Doaba House, Delhi.

Best, J.W. and Kahn, 2007. *Research in Education*, New Delhi: Prentice Hall of India Pvt. Ltd.

Bhaskara, R.D. (Ed.), 1998. *Community and School Nutrition Education*, New Delhi: Discovery Publishing House.

Bhaskara, R.D. (Ed.), 2001. *Education for the 21st Century*, New Delhi, Discovery Publishing House.

Bhaskara, R.D., 1998. *Reforming School Education*, New Delhi: Discovery Publishing House.

Dayal, B., 2005. *Development of Educational System in India*, New Delhi: Dominant Publishers and Distributors.

Dutta, T., Kalita, M., 2015. *Education of Marginalised Communities of Assam—An Evaluation on the Impact of Sarba Shiksha Abhiyan*, ActionAid, Guwahati.

Kamei, G. (2009) Education in North-East India: Problems of Democratization. Horam, M. (Ed.). *The Rising Manipur Including other North-Eastern States*. New Delhi: Manas Publication.

Shishak, T.A. (1992) *North-Eastern Tribals and Language Issues*. The Tangkhul Theological Association. Ukhrul, Manipur.

Sidhu, K.S., 1990. *Methodology of Educational Research*, Delhi: Sterling Publishers Pvt. Ltd.

Singh, L. L. (2000) Universalisation of Elementary Education in the Hill Areas of Manipur. Horam, M. (Ed). *The Rising Manipur Including other North Eastern States*. New Delhi: Manas Publication.

Singh, N.S. (2011) State of Education in Manipur. *Economic and Political Weekly*, Mumbai. June 4, 2011. Vol. XLVI, No. 23.

Singh, R.M. (2006) *Tribal Development in 21st Century*. New Delhi: Mittal Publications.

Venkateswara, R.V., Vijaya, L.V., Vamsi, K.V., Bhaskara, R.D., 2004. *Education For All*, New Delhi: Sonali Publications.

18

Manipuri Medium Secondary Schools in Assam

M. Ningamba Singha and *M. Ninghaiba Singha*

The Article 350A of the Constitution of India provides the Media of Instruction for Linguistic Minorities in their mother tongue at Primary Stage of education. After that, the All India Council for Education adopted a policy "Three Language Formula" (TLF) in 1956. The National Policy on Education of 1968 spoke about the regional languages and the TLF. The National Policy on Education, 1968 recommended the inclusion of the TLF "which includes the study of a Modern Indian language at the Secondary stage. This was reiterated in the Education Policy, 1986 and was adopted as the Programme of Action by the Parliament in 1992. These are major attempts to arrive at a language policy for education in India."

To avail the facilities of Article 350A, TLF and other Educational Language Policies etc., the Manipuris in Assam started their demand from early 1950s onwards. As a result of their demand, Manipuri Medium was started at L.P. Schools in 1956, then M. E. Schools in 1965 and up to H.S.L.C. Schools on the basis of experimental basis in 1979 and finally in the year 1984 under the Board of Secondary Education, Assam (SEBA) in Assam. Presently, the status of increasing the establishment of Manipuri Medium Secondary Schools in Assam is very slow, though the State Government followed various Education Policies of India. But the passed percentages of students from the Manipuri Medium Secondary Schools are increasing and their performances are also remarkable. Though, the performances of students in Manipuri

Medium Secondary Schools are increased, the number of enrolment in these Schools are decreased day-by-day in Assam. Thus, the chapter tries to analyse the Manipuri Medium Secondary Schools in Assam with facts and figures.

Language Education in India

Language being the most important medium of communication and education, its development occupies an important place in the National Policy on Education and Programme of Action. Therefore, promotion and development of Hindi and other 21 languages listed in the Schedule VIII of the Constitution including Sanskrit and Urdu have received due attention. In fulfilling the Constitutional responsibility, the Department of Higher Education is assisted by autonomous organisation and subordinate offices.

The States Reorganization Commission had asked the Union Government to elucidate a policy outline for education in mother tongue at the Secondary stage. The All India Council for Education recommended the adoption of the Three Language Formula (TLF) in September 1956. The endorsement for this formula came from various directions. It was adopted by the Chief Ministers' conference. The National Policy on Education of 1968 spoke about the regional languages and the Three Language Formula. The 1986 Policy reiterated the earlier stand. The National Policy on Education, 1968 recommended the inclusion of the TLF "which includes the study of a modern Indian language, preferably one of the Southern languages, apart from Hindi and English in the Hindi speaking states, and of Hindi along with the regional language and English in the non-Hindi speaking states", at the Secondary stage. This was reiterated in the Education Policy, 1986 and was adopted as the Programme of Action by the Parliament in 1992. These are major attempts to arrive at a language policy for education.

Since education is in the concurrent list of the Seventh Schedule of the Constitution, the language policy formulation for education and its implementation is left to the State Governments under the Constitutional safeguards, recommending the broad guidelines cited above. However, the TLF did not come into practice in all the states consistently. Also, whatever was termed and practiced as TLF was not uniform in all the states that accepted it as a norm.

Manipuri Medium Secondary Schools in Assam

It has already mentioned that to avail the facilities of Article 350A, TLF and other Educational Language Policies etc., the Manipuris in Assam started their demand for introduction of Manipuri Medium in the State from early 1950s onwards. As a result of their demand Manipuri Language was introduced as a Medium of Instruction at L.P. School Stage in 1956, then M. E. School Stage in 1965 and up to H.S.L.C. School Stage on the basis of experimental basis in 1979 and finally in the year 1984 under the Board of Secondary Education, Assam (SEBA) in Assam. The demand for introduction of Manipuri Medium in the H.S.L.C. Stage of Education in Assam was started from 1963 onwards and continued up to 1979. There is no Constitutional recognition of the right to have instruction in Mother tongue at H.S.L.C. Stage for Linguistic Minorities. The Government treats differently from education of the Primary Stage to H.S.L.C. Stage of Education.

But movement for introduction of Manipuri Medium at the Secondary Schools began to get its momentum during the early part of 1972. Meanwhile by this time, W. Subhankar Singha became M.L.A. from Lakhipur Constituency in Assam Legislative Assembly Election. In March, 1972, a group of Social workers under the leadership of Erungbam Chandra Singha, President Assam Manipuri Sahitya Parishad, Cachar Branch, Sri Yumnam Nanda Kumar Singha, Lakhipur and W. Subhankar Singha, M.L.A. went to Shillong to meet Sri Sharat Chandra Sinha, Chief Minister of Assam at Shillong at his Bunglow for the purpose of introduction of Manipuri Medium at H.S.L.C. Stage of Education in Assam. After thorough discussion with Chief Minister, he assured that he will try his level best to solve the matter. This verbal message of Chief Minister for the introduction of Manipuri Medium at High School was given by W. Subhakar Singha at a meeting of the all the Headmaster of High Schools of Manipuri prevailing areas held at the residence of E. Chandra Singha, President, Assam Manipuri Sahitya Parishad, Jaffirbond. Though there was no any notification or order from the Government side to introduce Manipuri Medium at the High Schools Stage of Education in Assam. By their own efforts, the Manipuris of Assam established High Schools in Manipuri inhabited areas of Barak Valley and introduced Manipuri Medium in those High Schools.

By that time the Bodos, a Linguistically Minorities Community in Assam also placed their demands to the Government of Assam for introduction of Bodo Language as a Medium of Instruction at Secondary Schools in Assam. The demand of the Bodos got a momentum from the Government of Assam due to Bodo MLAs not less than 10 had submitted an ultimatum to the Chief Minister of Assam, who conceded the demands of Bodo MLAs for introduction of Bodo Medium at Secondary level in 1975. Seeing momentum of the Bodo language movement, Government of Assam has taken a Cabinet decision order for introduction of Bodo as a Medium of Instruction in Assam in 1975. Thus, Bodo language was introduced as a Medium of Instruction at Secondary level in Assam in the year 1976. Meanwhile in Manipur State also Manipuri medium was recognized in the year 1976, according to the Secondary Board of Education, Manipur Notification No. CS/7dt. Imphal 26th October, 1976, Manipuri language was recognized as a Medium of Instruction in the H.S.L.C. level in Manipur.

According to the decision of the Chief Minister in the month of September 26, 1977, a Commission was formed to look into present status of those Manipuri Medium High Schools established during 1970s in Assam. Only a one man consisting Commission of SEBA by Sri J. Bharali, Academic Officer, SEBA visited and inspected the different areas of Cachar district. On 27 September, 1977, he inspected Manipuri Medium High Schools of Lakhipur and Sonai areas and he also inspected Manipuri Medium High Schools of Hailakandi Sub-Division on 28-09-1977. In the Report of Sri J. Bharali submitted to SEBA, he highlighted the findings of Manipuri Medium existence in the High Schools of Manipuri inhabited areas of Assam.

On the basis of Report submitted by Sri J. Bhorali several meetings were held between the leaders of MSP, Cachar Branch, W. Subhankar Singha, M.L.A. and officials of SEBA to discuss about the matter. Meanwhile, according to a meeting held at Kashipur, Silchar in the month of April, 1978 two Parishads, i.e. Manipuri Sahitya Parishad, Cachar Branch and Assam Manipuri Sahitya Parishad became united under the nomenclature Manipuri Sahitya Parishad, Assam. At last on 8th June, 1978, an agreement was signed between Shri E. Chandra Singha, President, Manipuri Sahitya Parishad, Assam and Shri D. Gogoi, Chairman, Board of Secondary Education, Gauhati under the Vide memo SEBA/CA/

4515-4516 dt. 8th June, 1978. Under this agreement Manipuri language was recognized to introduce as a medium of instruction in those 26 English Medium High Schools established in Cachar District during the 1960s.

After the conversion of those 26 English medium High Schools to Manipuri medium in the year 1978, finally on 28th July, 1978 according to Government Notification of SEBA under No. SEBA/AB-IM/I/MAN/8687 gave permission for Manipuri Medium at the H.S.L.C. Exam in Assam on experimental basis for Five years and subsequently extended for further period of 2 years, i.e. up to 1985 H.S.L.C. Exam. According to this notification total numbers of 1046 Students from 26 High Schools of Cachar District were allowed to give their H.S.L.C. Exam, 1979 in Manipuri Medium.

After the fall of Janata Government in the month of September, 1979, Congress Government headed by Sri Jogendra Nath Hajarika formed Government on 9th September, 1979. During his tenure, demand for the recognition of Manipuri medium on permanent basis at the H.S.L.C. in Assam began to get momentum. On 17th November, 1979, a meeting on the demand of the All Assam Manipuri Bhasha Parishad (AAMBP) held at Janata Bhavan in the Cabinet Conference Hall with Sri Premadhar Bora, Education Minister in the chair along with the deputationists comprise of Shri W. Subhankar Singha, Ex- MLA, President, AAMBP, Shri Kazi Kutubuddin Ahamed, MLA, Sri Gauri Sankar Roy, MLA, and Shri R. K. Konung Sana, Principal, Dullabchara Higher Secondary School, Dullabchara. In the meeting, Joint Secretary, Education Department, Managing Director, Assam State Text book production and publication Ltd., Additional DPI, Academic Officer of SEBA, Academic Officer of Textbook Co-ordination and Assistant Director educational planning were also present. After long discussion about the matter, the Government officials also opined about their willingness to solve the matter. Accordingly, Govenment machinery processed the matter of Manipuri medium expeditiously. But the Government collapsed by last part of the December 1979. No memorandums were submitted to the Government during the period from December 1980 to March 1982.

Regarding the issue for introduction of Manipuri Medium at Secondary School in Assam on 5th August, 1983, a memorandum was submitted by MSP, Assam to Sri Hiteswar Saikia, Hon'ble Chief Minister of Assam on his visit to Silchar. Subsequently series of memorandums on the issue were submitted to the Government of Assam. On 9th December, 1983 again a meeting was held at Janata Bhavan, Gauhati between W. Subhankar Singha, Ex-MLA, the President, AAMBP and Government officials on the issue. In the meeting W. Subhankar Singha placed before the Government officials about the long standing demands of the AAMBP for the introduction of Manipuri Medium at High School Stage on permanent basis, the availability of Textbook and competent teachers and results in H.S.L.C. Exam etc. and necessity for Manipuri medium was thoroughly discussed in the meeting. In the meeting a suitable decision for Manipuri media at High School level of Education was taken. Accordingly, the Commissioner and Secretary was advised by the Minister of Education to frame a cabinet memorandum on Manipuri medium at High School stage of Education. In the Draft memorandum of Commissioner and Secretary to the Government of Assam states that Manipuri medium has already introduced as a medium of instruction and Exam at middle English stage in Assam erstwhile Cachar district in particular. With a view to switching over Manipuri students using English Textbooks at High School stages imparted education in Manipuri have been permitted by SEBA for a period of 5 years commencing from 1979 to answer question in Manipuri in all the subjects except English vide its No. SEBA/LM/MAN/8687 dated 23-07-78 and subsequently permission extended for a further period of 2 and years, i.e. HSLC Exam 1985. Affirmation in that respect has further been re-asserted by SEBA in its No. SEBA/AB/LM/1/78/8664 dated 17-07-82. The matter has been being processed since long that many a time and examined at Government level. Finally, a discussion was held on the matter by the Education Minister in his chamber by the last part of December 1983 attended by all the concerned departmental officials including SEBA's Secretary. They took a suitable decision. But according to Government Notification No. EMI-183/62/60 dated 23-04-65 and EMI-184/75/17 dated 17-10-75, the language that can be introduced as medium of instruction at Secondary stage, "will be Modern Indian Language, mentioned in the Eighth Schedule of the Constitution of India as well as English. An exception may be made in case of Hills Districts." It may be mentioned that the introduction of Bodo as Medium of instruction at High School stage of Education in lower part of Bramhaputra Valley has been entirely contrary to this rule.

As such there is no technical bar for the introduction of Manipuri medium like Bodo medium as a medium of instruction at High School level in Assam. English Medium so long prevalent converted to Manipuri Medium. The draft cabinet memorandum was approved by Education Minister and sent it to the Chief Minister for his consent for placing the memorandum before the Cabinet. Hence, Cabinet memorandum was submitted if the Manipuri language like Bodo in addition to the languages mentioned in the Eighth Schedule of the Constitution of India could be introduced as medium of instruction at High School stage in Assam, both Cachar and Karimganj Districts in particular.

Accordingly, the Minister at a Cabinet meeting by the first week of January, 1984 with Shri Hiteswar Saikia, Chief Minister in the chair resolved that Manipuri be introduced as a Medium of Instruction at High School level of Education. Thus, finally in the year 1984 during Chief Ministership of Sri Hiteswar Saikia, Manipuri Language has been introduced permanently as a Medium of Instruction at High School Stage of Education in Assam according to order No. EMI-150/79/112. "The Governor of Assam is pleased to approve the introduction of Manipuri Language as a Medium of Instruction at the High School Stage of Education." Thus, as a result of the effort of individuals and different Non-Governmental Manipuri Organisations of Assam, Manipuri medium was introduced as a medium of instruction up to High School level in Assam. As far back up to 1980 there were total 200 Manipuri Medium L.P. Schools, 36 Manipuri Medium M.E. Schools and 26 Manipuri Medium High Schools in Assam.

The Scenario of Manipuri Medium Secondary Schools in Assam

The scenario of Manipuri Medium Secondary Schools in Assam can be seen in the following tables. The figures in respect of number of students appeared in Bodo and Manipuri Medium in respect to HSLC Exam since from their introduction as a Medium of Instruction in Assam as per SEBA's information can be seen in Table 18.1.

From Table 18.1 we can see that since from the commencement of Manipuri Medium in the year 1979, the number of students answering in Manipuri Medium is very encouraging and compared favourably with Bodo Medium. Presently, there are total 32

Table 18.1: Comparative Year-wise Numbers of Students Appeared in the HSLC Examination in Bodo and Manipuri Medium in Assam

Year	Bodo Medium	Manipuri (MIL)	Manipuri Medium
1976	610	537	N/A
1977	659	697	N/A
1978	867	867	N/A
1979	1196	1196	1043
1980	–	N/A	1903
1981	2160	N/A	–

Source: Wangkhem Subhankar Singha, p. 35.

numbers of Manipuri Medium High Schools in Assam. Table 18.2 shows the district-wise number of Manipuri Medium High Schools in Assam.

Table 18.2: District-wise Manipuri Medium Secondary Schools/High Schools in Assam

Sl. No.	District/State	Medium	High Schools
1.	Cachar	Manipuri	26
2.	Hailakandi	Manipuri	5
3.	Karimganj	Manipuri	1
4.	Assam	Manipuri	32

Source: Field Survey from 06-08-012 to 08-08-2012.

Tables 18.3 to 18.6 show Manipuri Medium Secondary Schools and their performance in last H.S.L.C. Examination 2012 in Assam.

Issues Summarized

In spite of fact that today in India and Assam too, the number of Schools in general and particularly different Medium of Instructions are increased day by day. The number of enrolment of students in different Medium of Schools in general and particularly Manipuri Medium in Assam are decreased day by day and this condition of enrolment of the students in Manipuri Medium from Primary to Secondary Schools became miserable. And a number of enrolment of the students in Manipuri Medium Schools in Assam are flexible, as we see from the field survey report from the different Manipuri Medium High Schools situated in Assam. Though, the performance of the Manipuri Medium High

Table 18.3: Year-wise Performance Report of the Candidates in the H.S.L.C. Examination, 2012 in Assam

Year	Candidate passed in Division					
	Appeared	1st Div.	2nd Div.	3rd Div.	Total Pass	Over all percentage
2002	1,77,075	9,801	18,614	43,959	72,374	40.87
2003	1,75,183	9,596	17,786	49,892	77,274	44.11
2004	1,84,771	11,843	21,359	58,809	92,011	49.79
2005	2,07,083	12,635	24,500	72,782	1,09,917	53.79
2006	1,99,786	13,352	25,815	67,816	1,06,983	53.54
2007	2,03,829	12,594	24,216	75,146	1,11,956	54.93
2008	2,39,606	17,084	29,714	93,820	1,40,618	58.68
2009	2,34,741	17,137	29,709	97,645	1,44,491	61.55
2010	2,70,930	19,034	31,720	1,20,522	1,71,276	63.21
2011	2,73,701	19,084	50,853	1,22,702	1,92,639	70.38
2012	2,78,704	26,203	68,180	99,684	1,94,067	69.63

Source: Result Book, H.S.L.C. Examination 2012, SEBA, Assam.

Table 18.4: District-wise performance Report in the H.S.L.C. Examination, 2012 in Assam

Districts	Appeared	1st Div.	2nd Div.	3rd Div.	Total	Pass Percentage
Cachar	13,957	927	2,101	4,609	7,637	54.72
Hailakandi	4,471	357	855	1,656	2,868	64.15

Source: Result Book, H.S.L.C. Examination 2012, SEBA, Assam.

Schools situated in different districts of Assam in H.S.L.C. Examination, 2012 are increased as compared to performance of the candidate in the H.S.L.C. Examination, 2002 and process of the performance of result are increased from last numbers of year examinations. But the parents of the Manipuri community now a day does not want to send their children to these schools. The problems are same in the case of other different Medium schools not only in Assam, but also all-over India. This problem is mainly due to dominance of English language and its Medium Schools are increased day by day and the parents as well as students of all communities preferred to English for their study purpose. And they think that by learning English Medium their children can able to compete with other different Medium children. It is their belief and now the process has become tradition and followed by maximum number of parents without measuring the capability

Table 18.5: Manipuri Medium School-wise Performance Report in the H.S.L.C. Examination, 2012 in Assam

Sl. No.	*Name of the School*	*District*	*Medium*	*Appeared*	*Candidate Passed Division*			*Total*	*% of Pass*
					1st Div	*2nd Div*	*3rd Div*		
1.	Balaram High School	Cachar	Manipuri	30	01	12	15	28	93.33
2.	Barkhola High School	Cachar	Manipuri	08	00	01	05	06	75.00
3.	Bantarapur High School	Cachar	Manipuri	25	03	07	10	20	80.00
4.	Baskandi High School	Cachar	Manipuri	35	05	18	12	35	100
5.	Earl High School	Cachar	Manipuri	50	02	08	20	30	60.00
6.	Govindanagar High School	Cachar	Manipuri	34	01	03	03	07	23.33
7.	Ibemhal High School	Cachar	Manipuri	15	04	07	03	14	93.33
8.	Jagaimathura High School	Cachar	Manipuri	76	01	13	44	58	76.31
9.	Jarma Singha High School	Cachar	Manipuri	05	—	—	01	01	20.00
10.	Kameswar High School	Cachar	Manipuri	01	00	00	01	01	100
11.	Kamaleswari High School	Cachar	Manipuri	10	00	02	06	08	80.00
12.	Khoraikandi Public High School	Cachar	Manipuri	24	03	08	12	23	95.83
13.	Khunow High School	Cachar	Manipuri	27	03	08	10	21	77.77
14.	K.I.M. Hajari High School	Cachar	Manipuri	13	02	04	04	10	76.92
15.	Lalang Manipuri High School	Cachar	Manipuri	65	00	20	30	50	76.92
16.	Lamagram High School	Cachar	Manipuri	12	01	05	03	09	75.00
17.	Maspara High School	Cachar	Manipuri	07	00	02	03	05	71.42
18.	Thambau High School	Cachar	Manipuri	10	01	01	04	06	60.00
19.	Salipur High School	Cachar	Manipuri	10	00	06	03	09	90.00
20.	Sapormoina High School	Cachar	Manipuri	13	02	04	04	10	76.92
21.	Sibpur High School	Cachar	Manipuri	25	02	07	09	18	72.00
22.	Sribar High School	Cachar	Manipur	11	02	04	02	08	72.72
23.	Singerbond High School	Cachar	Manipuri	26	03	07	13	23	88.46
24.	Sonai Juboti High School	Cachar	Manipuri	55	05	27	13	45	81.81
25.	Virtikendrajit High School	Cachar	Manipuri	07	01	03	02	06	85.71
26.	Y.S. Memorial High School	Cachar	Manipuri	10	00	02	04	06	60.00
27.	Indramani Public High School	Hailakandi	Manipuri	24	02	10	05	17	70.83
28.	Model High School	Hailakandi	Manipuri	13	01	03	05	09	69.23
29.	Purbokitarbond High School	Hailakandi	Manipuri	08	02	03	02	07	87.50
30.	Nimaichandpur High School	Hailakandi	Manipuri	01	00	00	01	01	100
31.	Sanarei Mitei High School	Hailakandi	Manipuri	43	9	19	15	43	100
32.	Manipuri High School	Karimganj	Manipuri	00	00	00	00	00	00

Source: Field Survey from 09-08-2012 to 13-08-2012.

label of their children's knowledge, they send their children and now-a-days, they are following this tradition blindly in the State.

This problem or matter should be taken by us in very strong hold, to safe our language in the field of education. If our negligence about this problem then, in last few decades our students are unable to learn and speak in their mother tongue. If we continuing with this problem then one day our language will totally extinct from

Table 18.6: Comparative Year-wise Study of the performance of Manipuri Medium Schools in H.S.L.C. Examination, 2002 and 2012 in Hailakandi District, Assam

Sl. No.	Performance of the Manipuri Medium Schools in H.S.L.C Exams			H.S.L.C, 2002		H.S.L.C, 2012		Pass Percentage	
	Name of the School	District	Medium	Appeared	Passed	Appeared	Passed	Pass% of 2002	Pass% of 2012
1.	Indramani Public High School	Hailakandi	Manipuri	67	18	24	17	26.86	70.83
2.	Model High School	Hailakandi	Manipuri	17	10	13	09	58.82	69.23
3.	Nimaichandpur High School	Hailakandi	Manipuri	10	05	01	01	50.00	100
4.	Purbokitarbond High School	Hailakandi	Manipuri	13	06	08	07	46.15	87.5
5.	Sanarei Mitei High School	Hailakandi	Manipuri	36	19	43	43	52.77	100

Source: Field Survey from 15/08/2012 to 17/08/2012.

the world of Human Civilization. By continuing the process of learning English Medium then we can not give the complete security about our life and with this process, one day we will automatically forget about our own language as well as culture.

Education is a requirement for the progress and development of Human beings. The main thrust of educational activities should be promotion of the quantity, quality and excellence, all these at a time. Presently, the status of increasing Manipuri Medium from Primary to Secondary level schools in Assam is in a very slow process, though the State Government followed various Education Policies of India. But the passed percentage of candidates in the Manipuri medium High schools has increased and their performance is also increased since its inception as a Medium of Instruction in the State. As we see from the above the comparative year-wise data of H.S.L.C. Examination 2002 and 2012 mentioned in Table 18.6 collected from the field survey in Hailakandi district of Assam. Though, the performances of candidates in Manipuri Medium Secondary/High schools has increased, the number of enrolment in these schools has decreased day by day in Assam.

REFERENCES

B. Mallikarjun, Ph.D. (2004.) "Language Rights and Education in India" from *Language in India,* Volume 4: 1 February, 2004.

Devi, M. Shanti (2001). *Development of Education in Manipur*, New Delhi: Rajesh Publications, p. 26.

Education in India from Wikipedia, the free encyclopaldia, Accessed on 10/06/2014.

Lyndem, Biloris and Dc, Utpal Kumar, (Eds.) (2004). *Education in North East India*. New Delhi: Concept Publishing Company, p. 97.

Memorandum submitted to Shri Hiteswar Saikia, Chief Minister of Assam at Silchar by the Manipuri Sahitya Parishad, Assam on 5th August, 1983.

Nancyh, Hornberger, Language Policy, Language Education, Language Rights: Indigenous, Immigrant, and International Perspectives. *Language in Society*, 27: 439–458. Printed in the United States of America.

NCERT, 7th All India Education Survey (2002) *Media of Instruction and Languages Thought*, New Delhi, Accessed on 15/07/2012 from www.ncert.nic.in.

Singha, Wangkhem Subhankar (2005) *Manipuri Media Affairs at Primary and High School Stages of Education*, Souvenir. SJCCS, Manipuri M.E. School, Silchar, p. 30.

Vanishree, V.M., MAPL and ELT (2011, February 2) "Provision for Linguistic Diversity and Linguistic Minorities in India." Masters Dissertation. Retrieved on 15 June, 2012, from *Language in India*, Website: http://www.languageinindia.

19

Psychological Hazards of Early Childhood: Bullying

Lipika Barman and *Suneeta K. Ganguly*

Introduction

Bullying is defined as mean, hurtful behaviour that occurs repeatedly in a relationship with an imbalance of power or strength. Bullying is defined as an act of aggression directed toward others. (Ledley, Storch, Coles, Heimberg, Moser and Bravata, 2006). It is a form of emotional and physical abuse that has three defining characteristics:

1. DELIBERATE—a bully's intention to hurt someone.
2. REPEATED—a bully target the same victim again and again.
3. POWER IMBALANCE—a bully chooses victims he or she perceives as vulnerable.

Types of Bullying

1. Physical bullying involves hitting, pushing, tripping and other kinds of force.
2. Verbal bullying involves hurtful comments, name calling, teasing.
3. Social bullying involves using relationship to hurt someone.

Bullying does not develop suddenly and mysteriously and

appear like a full blown among children. Children as young as age 3 can do participate in bullying. We often see the emergence of bullying in early childhood settings, such as daycare, pre-school, home care groups and kindergarten classrooms. Early childhood settings provide an oppourtunity for educators to effectively prevent and stop the emergence of bullying behaviour and to foster the development of positive social interaction.

Bullying is significant to consider the prevalence of bullying within pre-school and the primary school years because this is a time when children's social competence begins to soar, affecting their abilities to experience an array of emotions (Belacchi and Farina, 2010).

Teachers in early childhood settings often overlook bullying, for a variety of reasons. They may think that young children are too naïve and innocent to bully and that they are incapable of deliberate behaviours that are intended to harm other children. They may dismiss or ignore unacceptable behaviours, saying "Kids will be kids" or labelling particular children as "challenging." Teachers may also fail to see the bullying because there is inadequate supervision or because it happens when adults are not watching. They may fail to understand that early or "pre-bullying" behaviours will turn into bullying.

Imagine your children playing during centre time, when you hear some of them saying, "I do not like the way you look" or "I do not like your outfit—it looks dumb." Statements like these may be related to the acts of bullying.

Need and Significance of the Study

Transitional period is one of the times where changes take place abruptly. We all know that change is the salt of life, but such changes all of a sudden cannot be accepted by every individual. Every human needs time, skill and effort to accept these changes. So, when we consider early childhood, a period from babyhood to adolescence, there starts coming one of the upcoming psychological hazard, i.e. BULLYING. As we know that problems are the entertaining channels of our life, we need to attend such channels with proper selection, alertness and consciousness. Every stage has problems, but we need to attend it carefully with proper guidance and concentration from parents and teachers. Bullying is one of the most important stumbling block of early childhood of today's generation. This has led to an innumerable social, emotional, cognitive and psychological problem of the child.

So, here we would like to highlight various issues and events faced by children of both genders related to bullying and try to solve problems related to it.

Objectives

1. To explore bullying in early childhood stage.
2. To find out the main reasons of bullying.
3. To find out the educators' role to find out a bully.

Which Behaviours should Early Childhood Educators Pay Attention to?

1. Shouting "Mine!" while grabbing a toy is a typical behaviour of young children that is not usually considered bullying. However, if educators allow this behaviour to be directed repeatedly and intentionally toward a targèted child without intervention, it can lead to verbal and physical forms of bullying.

2. Young children like to whisper secrets and call each other silly names. But when whispering spreads rumours or private information, when silly names become hurtful name-calling, and when one child repeatedly becomes the target, these childhood games should be considered bullying.

3. Children's make-believe play provides opportunities for some children to manipulate and assert power over their playmates. Children who take charge of assigning the roles of mother, father, baby, and dog in a make-believe family are not yet bullying. But when these children consistently assign one child to play the less desirable roles (*e.g.*, the dog, the baby, or the bad guy), do not permit playmates to switch roles, and even control the child's actions (demanding that the child bark, cry, or go to jail), they are deliberately and repeatedly using their power to take advantage of a vulnerable child—a key component of bullying.

4. Children who say, "You cannot play with me", may not yet be deliberately excluding selected classmates, but this behaviour can easily develop into relational bullying and escalate into the more sophisticated forms of social exclusion used by older children

(*e.g.*, "You can not be my friend if you' are not friends with her"). Even five year olds have been observed manipulating their classmates to single out and exclude a vulnerable peer.

With an understanding of the variety of ways that young children engage in different forms of bullying, early childhood educators can be prepared to address bullying through prevention, intervention, and follow-up.

Vicky's Story 2

Five year-old Vicky waited for all her friends to get their lunches and sit at the table. Then she asked them to raise their hands if they liked chocolate. She raised her hand, and everyone followed. Next she said, "Raise your hand if you like spaghetti." She raised her hand, and once again so did everyone else. Finally, she said, "Raise your hand if you like Carmen." She did not raise her hand, and neither did any of the other girls at the table. Carmen, who was seated near the end, began to cry. (CARMEN- A MALE GIVEN NAME).

Bullies are Made ...Not Born...and This Begins at a Very Early Age.......

Important Points to Remember

1. Bullying among young children may look different from bullying among older children.
2. Hurtful pre-bullying behaviours may lead to bullying when they become repetitive and intentional and involve an abuse of power.
3. Early intervention can prevent pre-bullying behaviours from developing into bullying.
4. Stopping bullying immediately can prevent it from escalating and spreading.

The Good News is that Bully is Preventable

How do we stop Bullying?

While school-age bullying receives significant attention, very little is paid to the connection between early childhood and later bullying. Bullies are made, not born, and this begins at a very early age. Early childhood presents an unparalleled opportunity to prevent bullying by addressing behaviour and aggression in early childhood before it becomes organized and intentional. Promoting "pro-social" behaviours such as empathy and kindness during this critical period helps build skills that prevent later bullying behaviours, as well as the risk of being bullied. Research also shows that the prevention of bullying and its consequences can be enhanced by focusing on risk groups in early life.

The Child Trends report and this policy brief do not focus on early childhood "bullying." Instead, the focus is on aggressive or mean behaviour and how it can develop into bullying in the future. Actual bullying in schools is legally defined by four characteristics:

1. Harm is intended;
2. It is repeated or has the potential of being repeated;
3. It represents a power imbalance between the victim and aggressor; and
4. Bullying can be physical, verbal or involve social isolation.

The rationalization for bullying sometimes includes differences of social class, race, religion, gender, sexual orientation, appearance, personality, reputation, strength, size or ability. In contrast, aggressive or mean behaviour in an early childhood setting is usually about getting something children want or protecting what they consider theirs, like a certain toy or friend. This behaviour is especially true for children under age 4- 7. They may grab a toy away from another child, but harm is not intended. It is important not to confuse typical social and emotional behaviour of young children with warning signs that the child is at risk of developing bullying behaviour later in life.

For example, the aggression associated with temper tantrums by two-year-olds is a well-known developmental phase. However, aggression is expected to decrease along a developmental trajectory, as social and emotional skills help children increasingly control their emotions as they grow.

It is important for parents and early educators to pay attention to persistent aggressive and mean behaviours in very young children. These can happen in early childhood settings such as child care, pre-school, playgroups, kindergarten classrooms and on playgrounds. Kinds of behaviour to watch for is excluding a peer from a group or activity, making mean faces, pushing, or regularly grabbing objects. In older children (4 to 6), aggressive behaviour begins to develop into actions that can intimidate other children. If an aggressive child targets another child and makes he or she give up a toy, without intervention, the aggressive child will likely target that child again. If this behaviour happens repeatedly, it goes beyond just getting something the aggressor wants and becomes largely about controlling the victim.

A young child's identity is shaped entirely by their caregivers and immediate environments. The Child Trends report identifies three primary risk factors in the home environment most strongly related to a child's later involvement in bullying:

1. Caregiver attachment,
2. Family and Parental characteristics, and
3. Child maltreatment.

It also identifies three other environmental influences on young children:

4. Early care and education settings,
5. Bias, and
6. Television exposure.

All of these factors are important to address to prevent school-age bullying behaviours.

Caregiver Attachment

The quality of the infant-parent attachment is a fundamental predictor of a child's trajectory later in life and is the foundation for all future interactions the child has with others. Securely attached infants feel cared for and protected, and this allows them to focus on exploring the environment and building relationships with others. Secure attachment build's self-confidence, helps children to control their emotions and enables them to experience an emotionally reciprocal relationship. Secure caregiver attachment is a primary protective factor against later violence. Insecurely attached children lack trust and have negative expectations of themselves and others. Insecurity causes difficulty in developing positive relationships with others, and aggression can become a way to increase their control with new people and situations.

Family and Parental Characteristics

Family and parental characteristics play a significant role in the development of bullying. According to the Child Trends report, "exposure to a variety of suboptimal parenting techniques, behaviours or traits may be a risk factor for later bullying involvement (e.g. inappropriate discipline, hostility, low empathy)."

Furthermore, the report, "shows that positive parent-child interactions (encompassing cognitive stimulation or emotional support) correlate to a lower likelihood of bullying."

In one study, family characteristics when a child was five, including low maternal warmth and witnessing domestic violence, were related to bullying at age seven. There is a strong link between home experiences for young children and later involvement in bullying. Conversely, research shows that positive parent-child interactions correlate with a lower likelihood of bullying. This includes being played with or read to and having meals with both parents.

Child Maltreatment

Research over decades has found that children who experience child maltreatment often suffer from a range of adverse problems in childhood, adolescence and adulthood. Infants and toddlers are disproportionately at risk for maltreatment. Research has found an association between physical abuse and aggressive behaviour in children and that "children who are directly victimized by caregivers may develop working models of relationships as dangerous and malevolent." Early and persistent maltreatment can lead to toxic stress and alter brain development, impacting social and emotional domains and more. Several studies have found that school-age children and youth who had experienced maltreatment were more likely to both engage in bullying behaviours and be victimized. Conversely, research has shown that the effects of child maltreatment are mitigated if a child has a positive attachment to a non-abusive caregiver, avoids deviant peer relationships and if teachers focus on positive interactions, address problem behaviours and provide support.

Child Care Environment

The child care or pre-school environment is also a major area to focus on when examining the development of later bullying behaviour, particularly because a large number of young children receive care outside of their home. Early educators can prevent bullying by providing a nurturing and welcoming environment for all. Children, instructing children in pro-social skills such as sharing and including others, and addressing mean or aggressive behaviour when it happens. However, the quality of early care and education programmes varies significantly. There are very few studies to date on child care experiences as a predictor of aggression in later childhood. Those studies that have been done focus on quantity (i.e. number of hours a child spends in child care) and more broadly examine externalizing behaviour problems. There is more research on problem behaviour generally in early childhood settings and the importance of social and emotional competence as a way to promote school and future success.

Other Environmental Factors

Two other areas of a child's environment have also been found to correlate with later bullying: bias and media exposure. Children as young as 3-years-old have developed gender stereotypes about "things that boys do" and "things that girls do", in which they apply to themselves and others in play. Research also suggests that young children develop "in group" preferences at an early age. The second area of environment is television exposure. Whether it is violent or not, significant television exposure has been linked to the development of bullying behaviours as well as being a victim of bullying. However, research also finds that quality television focused on building social and emotional skills, such as Mister Rogers' Neighbourhood and Sesame Street, do increase those important skills in young children.

The prevention of bullying and its consequences can be enhanced by focusing on behaviours and risk factors in early childhood. Recommendations include:

- Place a broader emphasis on positive social and emotional development in homes, early care settings and schools and use evidence-based practices whenever possible.
- Further expand and sustain EMTSS and VTPBiS in early child care settings and elementary schools.
- Given the number of studies documenting a significant relationship between insecure attachment and a likelihood of involvement in a bullying, continue to explore this link and consider the influence and importance of caregiver attachment when designing interventions.
- Increase evidence-based home visiting and other parent education so caregivers understand the importance of attachment and healthy social and emotional development from birth.
- To help prevent racial or gender stereotypes, parents and other caregivers can talk about race, cultures and gender with children, use books that breakdown racial and gender stereotyping, and talk about racial and gender stereotypes in the movies and television shows that children watch.
- Ensure early childhood classrooms provide a culture of inclusiveness and celebrate diversity. Limit the amount of television children watch. The American Academy of Paediatrics (AAP) recommends that children under 2-years-old do not watch *any* TV and that those older than 2-years old watch no more than one to two hours a day of quality programming.
- Ensure a continuum of child and family services and supports—beginning at birth—that focus on prevention, targeted services for at-risk families and early intervention and treatment, if necessary.
- Increase efforts to address social problems including poverty, substance abuse and adult mental health problems, which can negatively affect positive parenting.

References

Bullies in the Block Area: The Early Childhood Origins of "Mean" Behaviour. (2015). Retrieved November 9, 2015, from http://www.childtrends.org/wp-content/uploads/2015/08/2015-31BulliesBlockArea.pdf

Preventingbullying.promoteprevent.org. (n.d.). Retrieved November 9, 2015, from http://preventingbullying.promoteprevent.org/3-how-does-early-bullying-develop

Psychology Today. (n.d.). Retrieved November 9, 2015, from https://www.psychologytoday.com/basics/bullying

Reebye, P. (2005). Aggression During Early Years – Infancy and Preschool. Retrieved November 9, 2015, from Ainsworth, M. D. and J. Bowlby. (1991). An ethological approach to personality development. *American Psychologist*, 46: 333-341. Belacchi, C. and E. Farina. 2010.

Snow, Ph.D., K. (2014). Bullying in Early Childhood | National Association for the Education of Young Children | NAEYC. Retrieved November 9, 2015, http://www.naeyc.org/blogs/bullying-early-childhood

The Long Term Effects of Bullying. (n.d.). Retrieved November 9, 2015, from http://www.aaets.org/article204.html

20

Extreme Climate Variability and its Impact on Education Environment

Concerns in Assam

Luit Goswami

Background

Climate variability leading to erratic monsoon, frequent floods, drought-like situation and warmer winter are few common phenomenons witnessed by Assam for last few years.

Increase in intensity and frequency of flooding and flash floods are the common and regular phenomenon witnessed by Assam for years as results of extreme climatic variations yet drought-like situation also affected several districts of the state during 2005, 2006 and 2009.

Increased erosion of soil from upstream hills due to enhances and extreme rainfalls, land use and land cover patterns as well as bank line erosion due to frequent changes in course of rivers have been increasing the silt load of the rivers. The phenomenon has resulted in rising of river beds, and consequent flooding with less input of rainfall as well as causing damage to land and other infrastructures in large. Spreading of excessive silt and sand in the flood plains has been causing irreparable damages to the land and infrastructure in several districts of Assam like Dhemaji, Lakhimpur, Majuli, Sadiya Sub-Division of Tinsukia District, Morigaon, Nalbari, Dhuburi etc.

In this context, discussions and study although in a low scale is in progress across the thematic areas– "Sustainable agriculture and Livelihood security", "Water security", "Sustainable habitat",

Mitigating natural disaster and crisis management" and "Energy sufficiency and efficiency", but **impact of extreme climate variability on primary education environment of Assam** is yet to receive any importance for discussion and study.

As the concern has not received any importance hence little discussions and studies have been initiated to address the concerns. Moreover, the "National Action Plan for Climate Change", the first draft of "Recommendations for State of Assam's Strategy and Action Plan on Climate Change", "State rules under Right to Education Act, 2009" has not incorporated any strategy to deal with the concerns. It has also been seen that the survey/stock taking exercises undertaken by different agencies regarding implementation status of the RTE Act, 2009 totally ignores the climate concerns which is one of the major factors affecting adversely the primary education environment of Assam.

How Extreme Climate Variability Adversely Impacting Primary Education Environment of Assam

- Partial or full damage to the school buildings in large across the flood plains is an annual phenomenon in Assam affecting the education environment either partially or totally. In all the cases, the classroom education comes to a total halt for a period of 2-3 months and after 2-3 months most of the schools resume education in temporary/makeshift buildings continuing for a prolong period. The whole phenomenon adversely affects the regular attendance of the students as well as also leads to drop-out and perishes the most spoken education friendly environment.
- The phenomenon has increased over last few years with the increase in frequency and intensity of floods. Moreover, floods in new areas like flood 2007 in Bordoloni Block of Dhemaji District (the area had witnessed flood after 32 years) has ripped through 50 numbers of villages damaging near about 75 schools and in turn affecting the education of near about 10,000 children for a period of 3-6 months. Flood 2008 in Lakhimpur Block of Lakhimpur District (the area had experienced flood for the first time) had brought into halt the education system of near about 100 schools for a period of 2-3 months affecting the education of nearly 20,000 children.

- Increase in incidence of cloud-bursting across the Northern Himalayan belt leading to frequent flash flood in the foothill regions of Arunachal and Bhutan with unprecedented intensities have also been intensifying such incidences. Flood 2011, in Sissiborgaon Block of Dhemaji District severely damaged near about 50 schools affecting the education of near about 10,000 children for a period of 2-3 months. In almost all cases such incidences lead to drop-out of children.
- Increase in frequency of floods also increasing the incidences of inundation of the school buildings and campus, damage to road and bridges, affect inland water route (either due to high current or by sand deposition) leading to non-accessibility to the schools for a prolong period and impacting children's right to receive education.
- Moreover, increase in frequency and intensity of floods has also been increasing the numbers of severely affected populations and in turn the numbers of affected populations seeking shelter in relief camps increasing manifold every year. As across Assam the school buildings are mostly used as designated relief camps and thus education of the children is largely disrupted for prolong period on dates.
- Increase in incidences of "Changes of river courses" and "Bank line erosion" which are results of extreme precipitation, siltation and sand deposition in river beds largely damaging the educational and allied infrastructures across the state. The children inhabiting in the char areas of Assam are the worst sufferers in this pretext. Shifting of school buildings from one location to another or from one village to another after every wave of flood is a common phenomenon for last few years in char areas of Assam affecting the school-days largely. *Mr. Arupjyoti Das, Assistant Teacher, Bhakatar Shuti Lower Primary School in Barkhetri Education Block, Nalbari pointed out that out of the total 200 education days in the 2012 calendar year 77 days have been lost due to impact of flood. The area has witnessed 3 waves of major floods in the year 2012. During the first wave of flood, 21 days were lost due to inundation of the school building and inaccessibility to the school premises, during the second*

wave of flood 29 days were lost out of damage incurred to the school building due to change of river course. After the second wave of flood the school building was shifted to a nearby comparatively safer location but during the third wave of flood towards the end of September 2012, the school was again damaged by bank line erosion affecting 27 numbers of school days. In the given situation construction of permanent structures and in turn generating a education friendly environment as per the Right to Education Act is the biggest challenge across the char area of Assam.

- Changes in the ecosystem and loss of bio-diversity in all the 6 agro-climatic zones of Assam due to extreme climate variability have been leading to reduce agricultural outputs and increased food insecurity, adversely impacting the human settlements even making many human settlements uninhabitable. In the whole situation climate induced internal displacement is alarmingly rising across Assam. This means that the families are migrating with all their children, thus the children missing their education rights.
- Extreme weather variations faced by Assam since a decade are adversely impacting the production of Agriculture and allied sectors. As mentioned above wide variations in rainfall patterns leading to early flood, late flood, flash flood, drought like situation has become a common phenomenon in Assam and the farmers engaged in Agriculture and allied sectors are the worst sufferers. The whole situation is leading to sharp declination in average income of the farmer families which in turn compels the families to pull out their children from the formal education system and link them with income generation avenues in the unorganised sectors to increase household income thus completely alienating them from the education system.
- Two major effects of climate variability are extreme variation in rainfall pattern and intensity as well as drought-like situation which results in increasing "water scarcity" and "firewood". In societies across Assam, women and girls are traditionally responsible for collecting water and firewood, meaning that climate change is bringing increased burden on them, as they need to spend a greater part of each day collecting water and

firewood. In the whole situation, alienation of the girl-children from the formal education system and depriving the children from Right to education has been witnessed across Assam.

Flood 2016 in Assam and Observation

Background: Education plays a very important role in development of the society, it is a medium through which the society can be changed. Education is one of the major concerns in the state during the flood.

Situation analysis:

- Due to flood most of the schools were not accessible and there was less impact on education because most of the schools were having summer vacation during the period.
- Due to the recent flood the schools infrastructure has been damaged in Golaghat, Dhemaji, Morigaon and Kokrajhar district. Around 32 per cent of the villages it was reported that school infrastructure was damaged.
- With the schools being getting damaged by the flood the teaching learning material (TLM) was also damaged in most of the districts.
- Most of the schools building are used to shelter the displaced population. Out of 28 villages 39 per cent of schools were used as shelter for the displaced people. Although, the relief camps are been ceased before commencement of the school (after the summer vacation) but cleanliness drive to make the school children and education friendly in the post-relief camp period is not been undertaken.
- Many of the Schools are in risk due to flood and erosion.

Way forward:

- We should emphasize that impacts of climate change has more effects on women and girls' lives than men. The situation can be changed if human beings transform their ways of living to be more sustainable and friendly to the environment. Local and international community's need to find ways of reducing the impact of climate change such as reducing the emissions of green effect gases provide environment education to the members of their societies and take necessary precautions to prevent these impacts.

- Schools could be one of the strategic areas to introduce environment education. Education curriculum need to provide skills to students to understand causes of climate change, its effects on various social groups and how they can participate in improving their local environment. Let's act locally while think globally.
- Flood plain zoning (as per GoI,) 1976 notification should be taken with high priority.
- Climate resilient educational infrastructure should be promoted.

SECTION-V

Education and Empowerment

21

Educational Awareness in Karbi Anglong District: Problems and Issues

A Case Study of Lumbajong Development Block

Jyotismita Sharma and *Gagan Nepal*

Introduction

North-east India is considered as an educationally backward region of India. Ever since Independence, the educational facilities have been expanded all-over the country, however the pattern of growth of education is not same everywhere. It is different from one state to another state and from one district to the another district.

Karbi Anglong is one of the 35 districts of the State of Assam and is considered as the largest district of Assam. Geographically, it comprises of hills, plains covered with dense forest and is situated in the central part of Assam. It is an autonomous hill district constituted under the sixth-schedule of the Indian constitution (though a new district "West Karbi Anglong" has been formed with Hamren as the Headquarters, curving out from the old district of Karbi Anglong, but the new district has not started functioning fully till now). The district is subdivided into three sub-divisions namely Bokajan, Hamren and Diphu and 11 developement blocks such as the Lumbajong Development block, Samelangso, Langsomepi, Howraghat, Bokajan, Nilip, Rongmongve, Chingthong, Rongkhang, Amri, Socheng. The population of the district is predominantly tribal with Karbi being the major tribe. Other tribal populations includes the Bodo, Kuki, Mizo, Dimasa,

Hmar, Garo, Rengma, Naga, Tiwa, and Man (Tai speaking). Besides this, a number of non-tribal populations such as Assamese, Bengali, Bihari, Nepalese and other caste populations also live here. Agriculture is the main occupation of this region.

Education level in Karbi Anglong can be considered as not satisfactory or up to the mark compared to the other districts of the State of Assam. According to 2011 census, the literacy rate of Karbi Anglong was 73.52 per cent with female literacy (62%) and male literacy (76.14%). Government has taken many initiatives in order to provide education to the people of Karbi Anglong. At present, in Karbi Anglong, there are fourteen Degree Colleges and eleven Higher Secondaries or Junior Colleges besides large numbers of High schools, Middle schools, Primary and Pre-primary schools. But these numbers of schools cannot commensurate the change in the demand of the entire population. Primary education is under the control of the District Council. Diphu Government College, Diphu, is the only Government degree college in the district which imparts education not only for degree courses (Arts, Science and Commerce), but also for higher secondary courses. Besides, there is Assam University Diphu campus which offers Post-Graduate Degree and Doctorate degree (very recently) in Arts, Science and Commerce. Besides this there is Diphu Polytechnic Institute and Industrial Training Institute offering technical education. In nearly 75 per cent of the villages, a primary school is at 1 km distance. Again, in more than 60 per cent villages, the distance from the nearest secondary school is at 5 km or more. There are number of schools working in the Karbi Anglong district along with number of centres and institutes imparting education on different activities. However, the vast difference in the literacy rate between the male and female, urban and rural, limited scope for the higher education calls for improvement in the educational environment of the said area (*see* Fig. 21.1).

A Brief History of Education in Karbi Anglong

In the beginning, there was no formal education in the Karbi Anglong. The people were confined to their ancient form of education system called 'Jirkedam.' Jirkedam, is the traditional system of education in the Karbi society with an aim to generate culture transmission and personality development among the Karbi

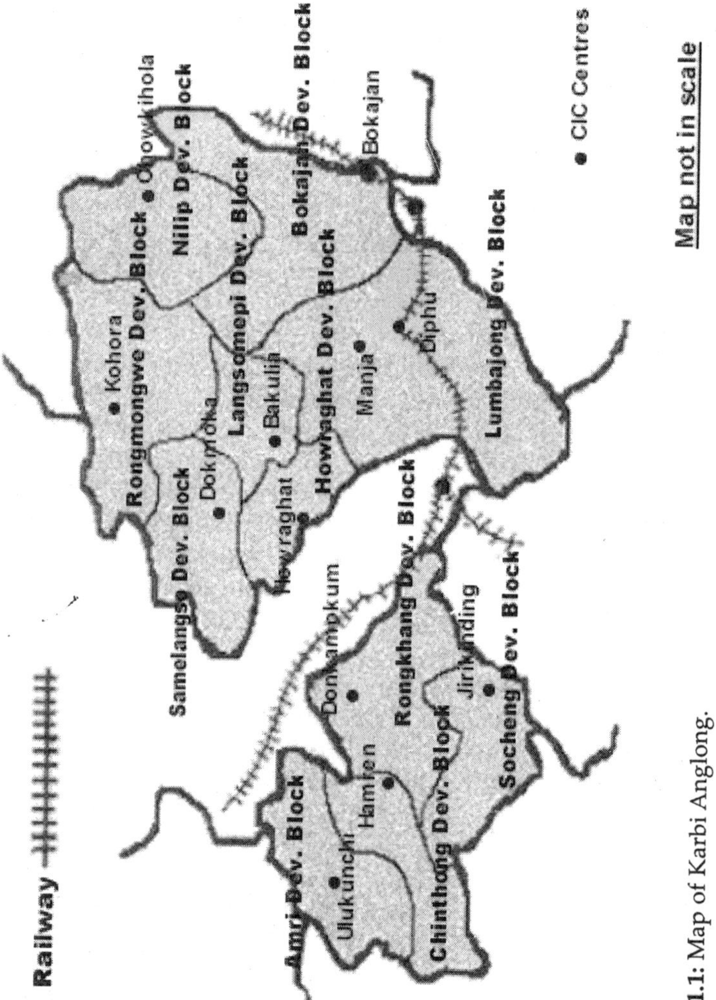

Fig. 21.1: Map of Karbi Anglong.
Source: www.karbianglong.nic.in

adolescents. Besides this, there were no reading and writing in Jirkadam.

Christian missionaries were the first people to introduce formal education in Karbi Anglong. They devoted their attention towards the spread of education besides the evangelistic works. However, the literacy rate was at scratch during those times. It was only after the Independence that an improvement in the development of education in Karbi Anglong was observed. Existing literature reveals that before independence, there was only one school opened in Tikapahar by the Christian Missionaries during eighteen fifties. This was the only school in Karbi Anglong at that time to meet the educational needs of the entire population of this region. Due to this, people were going to the nearby schools in other region of the state to get education. In 1891, the Christian Missionaries opened several schools, and did few translation works. They also started publishing books, writing dictionaries and began to develop the Karbi Language. But there were frequent outbreak of epidemics and poor climatic conditions which was a hindrance in the progress of the missionary works by the British. The schools were not receiving good response from the local peoples. There was a lack of educational awareness among the people. The Mikirs were thinking that the education is meant for only the Christian Missionaries. There was extreme social and economic backwardness among the population. Karbi Anglong was covered by dense forests with ferocious animals. Road and transport communication system was extremely poor. There were limited number of educational institutions in the district. People were living scattered from each other. Only people living nearby the primary schools were able to receive the education. There was no concept of higher education in those times as the missionaries were not paying any attention for the higher studies.

After independence, a change in the educational scenario of the Karbi Anglong was observed with the opening of significant number of primary schools, secondary schools.

In 1954, an Office of the Deputy Inspector of Schools was established which was a milestone in the development of the primary education.

Soon executive committee of the district council adopted some policies for primary education in the district and accordingly the council set a number of primary schools. Establishment of the venture schools were also encouraged during this period.

To improve the literacy rate, Karbi Anglong is now adopting Integrated Child Development Services (ICDS) and Anganwadi centres meant for the backward rural, urban, tribal areas of India. The district council has also adopted the Sarva Shiksha Abhiyan as well as mid-day-meal programmes to expand the literacy rate as well as increase educational awareness among the population. Jyoti Kendra is organized to look after the education of the children who are staying in slum areas, streets, railway platforms, Juvenile delinquency and children of the commercial sex workers. Kasturba Balika Vidyalaya Scheme (KBVS) is for the girls education. The government is also adopting RSMA (Rashtriya Shiksha Madhyamik Abhiyan) for the improvement of secondary education and at present there is the Rashtriya Shiksha Ussottor Abhiyan (RSUA) to increase higher education among the population.

Higher education is an area which still needs some improvement as there is very limited scope for the higher education in Karbi Anglong. Particularly, the quality of the courses is not sufficient to meet the educational needs of the present century. There is a great difference in the education-level of the district as compared to the other districts of the state. Vocational training is not provided in the schools and colleges of Karbi Anglong. Career guidance programme is not included in the educational curriculum. There is difference in the educational level between the urban and rural population in the district. The number of drop-out cases in case of female is higher than in the male in schools. Problem of insurgency is also contributing lot more damage to the education environment of the district. Poverty is also a major contributor in the backwardness of the status of education.

A Case Study of the Lumbajong Development Block

Karbi Anglong is the largest district of the State of Assam with three subdivisions and 11 development blocks. The present study is conducted in few villages the Lumbajong development block situated in the East Karbi Anglong subdivision. It is surrounded by Nagaland and Dima Hasao in the south, Nagaon in the west, Bakulia in the north and Bokajan in the east. The major places coming under this block includes Diphu and Manja. Lumbajong development block is considered as the largest block among the 11 blocks of Karbi Anglong with its headquarter at Manja and its sub-division at Diphu. According to 2011 census, the population of the Lumbajong development block was 55,870, with female population (29,818) and male population (26,052). The total number of literate people in the block is 16,729 which is about 3 per cent of the total literate people in the entire district. The female literacy rate is 31.7 per cent and the male literacy rate is about 68.3 per cent.

The district Karbi Anglong (25°33' N to 26°35' N latitude and 92°10' E to 93°50' E longitude) is the largest district of the state of Assam. According to the National Census 2011, the district had a population of 9,65,280 individuals (4,93,482 male; 4,71,798 female) with an average literacy rate of 73.52 per cent.

An exploratory fieldwork was conducted among the different villages (rural areas) of the Lumbajong development block area of Karbi Anglong District. A total sample of 200 (100 male and 100 female) have been covered in the course of the present study in the age group of 16-30 years. The subjects were selected using random sampling and/or stratified random sampling method. A pre-structured schedule is used to obtain the necessary data on the education status, socio-economic, and lifestyle variable including household income, occupations. The data is collected by interviewing the people through field visits.

The present study is conducted among different villages (rural areas) of the Lumbajong development block with an objective to understand the educational scenario of the district with a glance to its problems, issues and also tries to find out the remedy (if any) to improve the educational environment of the said area.

The data has been collected from 200 (100 male and 100 female) respondents (Fig. 21.2). Some figures have been given below for showing the field data which are as follows:

Tewnty five per cent respondents are illiterate while 75 per cent respondents are literate. It is seen that most of the respondents are literate. So, we can say that educational awareness in the district is satisfactory but cannot be called as successful completely (*see* Fig. 21.3).

It is already mentioned that 25 per cent respondents, that means 50 respondents are illiterate. So, now this graph shows the distribution of the educational status of rest (151) of the respondents.

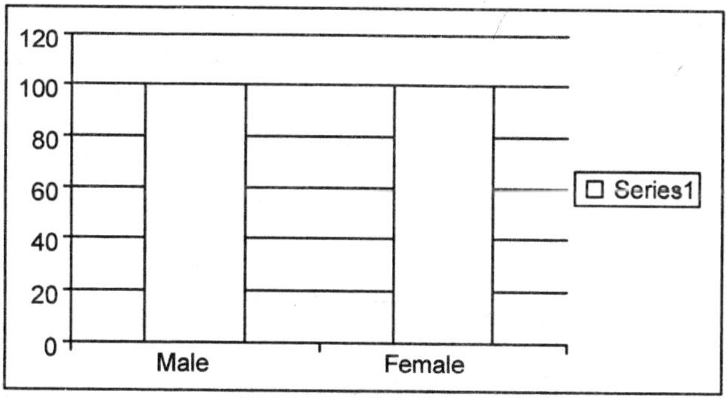

Fig. 21.2: Gender and its Representation.

Source: Based on data collected by author.

It states equal respondents from both male and female group.

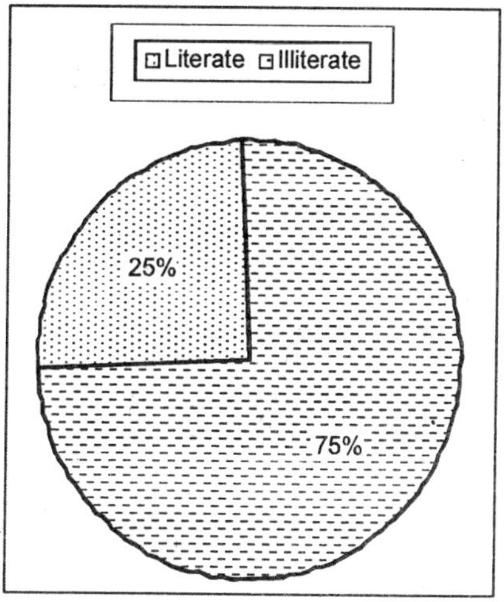

Fig. 21.3: Literacy Rate.

Source: Based on data collected by author.

Out of 151 literate respondents, 11 people had just completed the primary education, about 114 had completed the secondary level, 10 peoples had crossed the Higher Secondary level, 16 had completed the degree level (B.A.), and no people had done post-graduation. It is significant that highest 57 per cent people were educated up to secondary level and no people did post-graduation or other higher studies. This shows that the people of this region

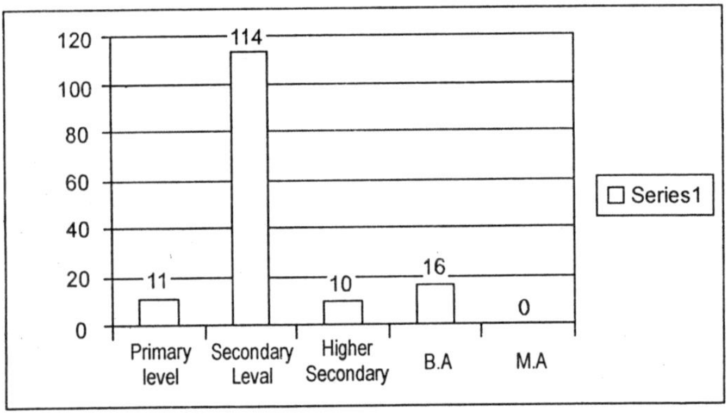

Fig. 21.4: Education Level of the People.

Source: Based on data collected by author.

are lagging behind in the field of higher education. This may be due to the lack of awareness towards gaining higher education (*see* Fig. 21.4).

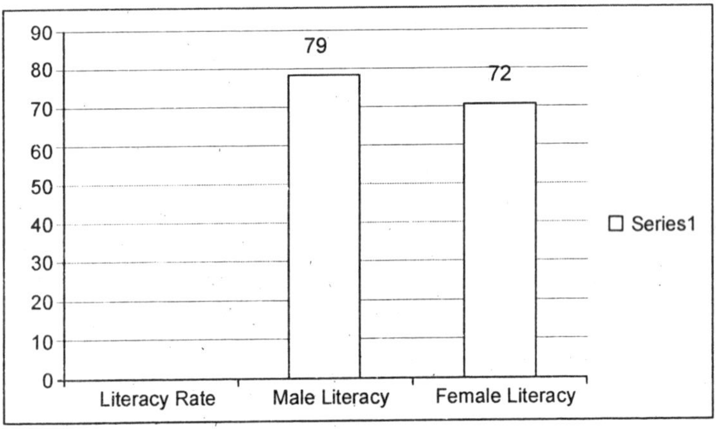

Fig. 21.5: Difference between Male Literacy and Female Literacy.

Source: Based on data collected by author.

Out of 200 samples (100 male, 100 female), 151 respondents were found literate and out of them 79 men were literate against 72 women (*see* Fig. 22.6).

Income level of majority of the people have income level below Rs.15,000.The lowest monthly income level is Rs. 2000 and the highest monthly income is about Rs. 35,000 (*see* Fig. 21.6).

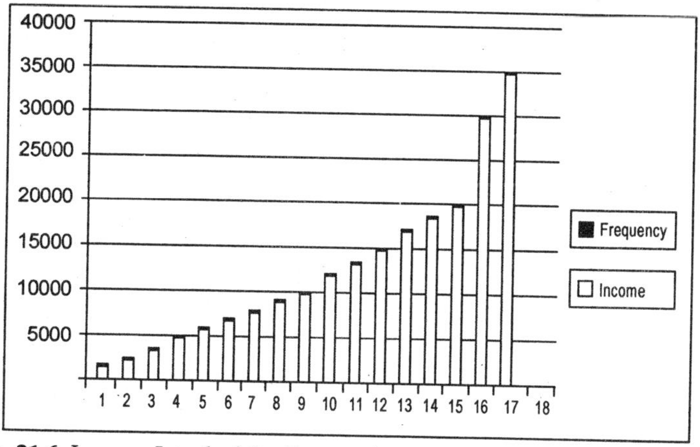

Fig. 21.6: Income Level of the Respondents.

Source: Based on data collected by author.

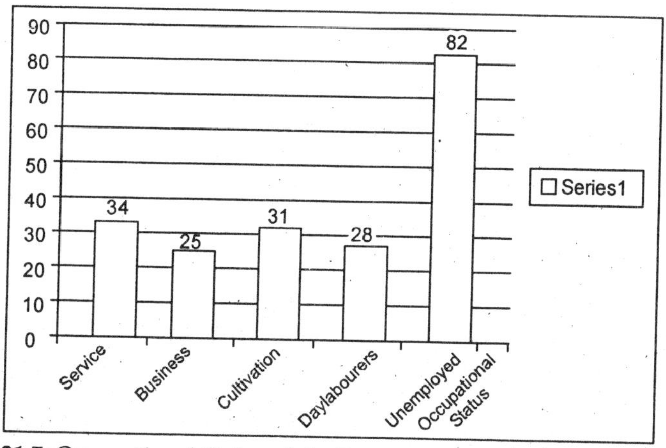

Fig. 21.7: Occupational Status of the Respondents.

Source: Based on data collected by author.

Out of the 200 respondents, 34 peoples are engaged in various governmental as well as private services. Twenty five of the people do small business, 31 of the people are involved in cultivation, 28 of the people are Day labourers and 82 people are unemployed. This shows poor economic condition of the respondents (*see* Fig. 21.7).

Ninety per cent of the people knows about ICDS, 50 per cent of the people are aware of the SSA, 2 per cent has heard about RMSA and 0 per cent knows about RUSA (Fig. 21.8)

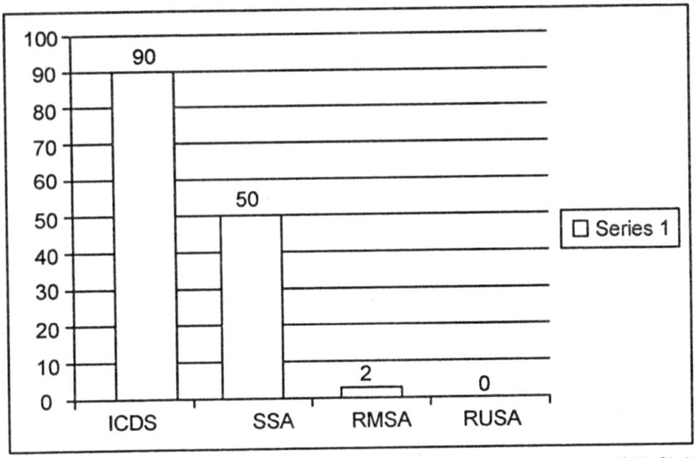

Fig. 21.8: Awareness of the People Towards the Governmental Policies.
Source: Based on data collected by author.

Critical Analysis

It is very difficult to be specific on the question about the causes of educational backwardness of Karbi Anglong District of Assam. The students have to leave schools because of their economic backwardness, frequent failure in the same class or lack of awareness for education. It is seen that many governmental policies are working in the district. The people are to be more conscious about the existing policies in the district such that they can be benefited from such plans and policies. The district does not have a competitive environment in educational field. Economically, people are not sound. Though a large number of populations in the district come from Karbi tribes, but there are no availability of Karbi medium schools in the district for the convenience of the Karbi people. The problem of transport and communication facilities in the district is also a cause in order to develop the district in education field. From informal talk with the people many things came to light. They think that people get education to get job and make lives happier. They do not understand the practical value of education in our day to day life. They condemn the government for not providing jobs to educated people. They think that being educated is meaningless unless government job is obtained. It was also important that people are interested in academic degrees and are ignorant to vocational education. Though there is a campus of a Central University set up in the district, but the aspirants of higher education are not benefited enough here as it has very limited numbers of departments.

Findings and Suggestions

We have found that people are not completely backward educationally in the district, but the level of education is not up to the mark compared to the rest of the country. There should be a competitive environment in the district so that the level of education goes up to the mark as developed as that is in the rest of India. The district is producing educated people but not quality human capitals that can compete in national level. The educational policies formulated by the governments are not transparent enough for the people though they know about the existence of those policies. Women of the district are still lagging behind in the field of education compared to men. The people are not conscious for higher education and vocational education in this region. Lack of the proper facilities and educational institutions may be the cause of this. This study finds that many people in the district are illiterate because of several causes. It may either be economic backwardness or lack of awareness about the education or frequent failure in the same class.

We suggest that the government policies must be formulated keeping the problems of common people in mind. The institutions for vocational education should also be set up in district. The educational institutions should be facilitated with the electricity, computers with internet and proper sanitation so that students are motivated as well as benefited. In many cases, it is seen that facilities are there but the facilities are either not properly utilised or not maintained properly. Government, every year, spends huge money in the educational sector, but that money is not properly utilised or eaten by the corrupt authorities of the educational institution. The women should be encouraged to have the educational facilities available there. Survey should be done by the government itself in intervals to examine the existing policies and to make them effective and implemented. It is realised that more research has to be done in this field to understand the educational environment and its response to governmental policies and the problem of the people.

Conclusion

The district Karbi Anglong has made much progress in the field of education since independence, but the progress cannot be considered as satisfactory. There are still a large number of illiterate people. There is lack of quality education due to which the people of Karbi Anglong cannot compete with the other districts or other states of the country. People are still unable to understand the value of education. Economic condition is also one reason for the vast backwardness. Enrolment, curriculum enrichment, availability of skill development courses, innovation, and also the importance of Massive Open Online Courses (MOOCs) in the education institutions along with best practices are some of the areas where stress has to be given to improve the educational scenario of the district. Apart from this, eradication of corruption in the educational field is also a much needed matter to be resolved at the earliest. Government plans and policies are not sufficient enough to solve these problems. The people should come forward and give their support to the government. Higher education is the area where people of this region are lagging behind. It is also seen that the most of the people are not aware of the government plans and policies for education existed in their area. Government and the people of this region should work hard to improve this situation.

Bibliography

Das, K., Dutta, S., 2003. "Developement of the primary education in Karbi Anglong district, Assam, India." *The Clarion* (2003), 2(1):141-146.

Das, K., 2006. "Developement of secondary education in the Sixth Scheduled Areas of Assam with special reference to Karbi Anglong District." *IJRAR*, 3(1). ESSN 2348-1269, PRINT ISSN 2349-5138.

Bazeley, B.R., 2006. *Development and Problems of Higher Education in Barak Valley and Karbi Anglong Areas of Assam*. Regency Publications, 20/36-G, Old 110008.

Roy, J.J., (2003). *Decentralization of Primary Education in the Autonomous District Council of Karbi Anglong–Assam*. National Institute of Educational Planning and Administration 17-B, Sri Aurobindo Marg, New Delhi -110016.

Appendix

List of Schools in the Lumbajong Development Block

1. A.B. Memorial L.P
2. Adarsh Hindi L.P.
3. Adarsha Hindi Memorial School
4. Amalapatty
5. Amlaiguri Egs
6. Amlokhi
7. Arlong Pharla L.P.
8. Arthemlangso Egs
9. Arthemlangso L.P. School
10. Artungso English
11. Asian Kids
12. Assam Rifles School, Diphu
13. Aturkimi Academy
14. Aturkimi English School
15. Bachok Rongphar L.P.
16. Badan Memorial High School
17. Barlangfer Memorial School
18. Bhelunala L.P.
19. Bhetagaon Egs
20. Binapani High School
21. Binapani L.p.
22. Binapani Memorial School
23. Borjan L.P.
24. Borjan Public Eng. School
25. Borlangfer
26. Borlangfer Model English
27. Borlangfer Tiniali L.P.
28. Borlangfer Tiniali Memorial School
29. Bura Phangcho Egs
30. Bura Terang Egs
31. Calvary Home Academy
32. Central School, Diphu
33. Chandra Sing Teron High School
34. Chandra Sing Teron L.P. (rec)
35. Chandra Teron Egs
36. Chandranath Kemprai Hindi Medium
37. Chekso Langso
38. Chengbong Rongpi L.P.
39. Cherat Bey Egs
40. Cherop Ingti L.P.
41. Chirikangnep English
42. Chirilangso L.P.
43. Chotalangpher L.P.
44. Christian Eng. High School
45. Chutianala L.P.
46. Convent High School (Pvt)
47. D.A.V. H.S. School
48. D.A.V. L.P.
49. Daldali Garo Basti English
50. Daldali Memorial School
51. Daldali Raijawdisa L.P. School
52. Daudikho Evergreen English School
53. Dawjingphang
54. Dayaram Diphusa Memorial School
55. Dengja Teron L.P. School
56. Dhansiri Bengali L.P. School
57. Dhansiri D/C

58. Dhansiri English L.P.
59. Dhansiri English Medium School
60. Dhansiri High School
61. Dhansiri Junior Basic L.P.
62. Dhansiri Linepar Eng. Egs
63. Dhansiri Memorial School
64. Dharamnala
65. Dhoniram Memorial Eng. L.P. School
66. Dhonsing Terang Egs (Salhang)
67. Dikreng Langso L.P.
68. Dilaji Mithiphang L.P.
69. Dilaji Mithiphang Memorial School
70. Dilangki Egs
71. Diliram Terang L.P.
72. Dillaimukh L.P.
73. Diphu Basic
74. Diphu Government Boys H.S. School
75. Diphu Government Girls High School
76. Diphu Town Primary
77. Diring Langso Egs
78. Disagedeba
79. Disagisim L.P.
80. Dok Terang Egs
81. Doldoli Government
82. Doldoli Rongphar Gaon L.P. Ven
83. Dolongbari Egs
84. Don Bosco H.S. School
85. Ekorani
86. Englongkiri L.P.
87. Erudite Academy
88. Everest English School
89. Gandhi Hindi L.P.
90. Gangjang English L.P. School
91. Gitajyoti L.P. School
92. Good Sepherd A.G. Eng. School
93. Ha-i-mu English L.P. School
94. Ha-i-mu English M.E. School
95. Hapjan
96. Hapjan Gidinpur
97. Harchi Ali L.P.
98. Hemari Killing Egs
99. Hemari Terang
100. Hemphu Engish School
101. Hemphu English L.P. School
102. Hojaipur L.P. School
103. Inglong Kiri Kramsa L.P.
104. Inglongkiri High School
105. Inglongpo Karbi Medium L.P. School
106. J.J.M. Nichols Roy Memorial English
107. Jakoi Nala
108. Jangphonglangso L.P.
109. Jari Teron English High School
110. Jari Teron Memorial Eng. L.P.
111. Jaru Nala Eng. School
112. Jawlian L.P. School
113. Jawlian Memorial School
114. Jensing Teron Egs
115. Jordanlangso Egs
116. Jorlep Teron
117. Jukripha L.P. School
118. K.S.T. Memorial Langcholiet
119. Kakoti Ronghang
120. Kalyan Bengali Medium School
121. Kania Ronghang Egs
122. Kania Terang

123. Kare Hansepi Memorial English School
124. Kathalguri L.P.
125. Kathebajong L.P.
126. Kehai Kro Egs
127. Kerelasing Egs
128. KGBV Lumbajong
129. Khangkhraidisa English L.P. Ve
130. Kharnaidisa Egs
131. Kherbari L.P.
132. Kheroni
133. Khonbamon L.P. School
134. Khorsing Terang Karbi Medium School
135. Khuti Colony Hindi Egs
136. Kiddies Corner English School
137. Kisan Hindi Medium School
138. Kishan Hindi L.P.
139. Klirdap Memorial School
140. Klirdap Sankardev Shishu Niketan
141. Komola Bagan Egs
142. Kothalguri Nepali Bosti Egs
143. Kramsa Hindi L.P.
144. Krist Jayanti School
145. Krokhu Adong L.P.
146. L.M. Memorial High School
147. Langcholiet Hindi L.P. School
148. Langcholiet Hindi Medium School
149. Langherang Me (venture).
150. Langhoi
151. Langkaijan L.P.
152. Langkhailu Egs
153. Langmili L.P.
154. Langsoliet Ass. Me
155. Langsoliet L.P.
156. Langsoliet PWD Egs
157. Langtibuk
158. Little Flower Egs
159. Little Flower Eng. School
160. Little Kids School
161. Little Star Eng. School
162. Long Terang Egs.
163. Longnit High School
164. Longnit Langroithom
165. Longnit Maz Gaon
166. Longri L.P.
167. Longrung Memorial School
168. Loringlangso L.P.
169. Loroplangso English L.P.
170. Lorulangso L.P.
171. Lorulangso Memorial School
172. Lower Dilaji
173. Lumbajong Memorial School
174. Lumbajong Ovechingthur Memorial
175. M.D.H. Arya Vidya Niketan School
176. Man Kro Egs
177. Manja Baptist Eng. School
178. Manja Garo Bosti Egs
179. Manja Hindi L.P.
180. Manja Hindi Medium School
181. Manja Tiniali L.P.
182. Manjanolai L.P.
183. Men Hanse Eng. L.P. (ven)
184. Mini English M.E. School
185. Mini English L.P. School
186. Misibailam English L.P. School
187. Modern English High School

188. Mohondijua Government Memorial School
189. Mohondijua High School
190. Mohondijua L.P.
191. Mongjang L.P.
192. Mongoldhon L.P.
193. Mouldam English L.P.
194. Mount Sea Wind Trinity Eng.
195. Mt. Calvary Eng. High School
196. Mt. Sinai English School
197. Nagachang L.P.
198. Nagaon Basti L.P.
199. Nahar Bari L.P. School
200. Navodaya Vidyalaya, Diphu
201. Nehru Memorial Hindi L.P.
202. New Dawn English School
203. New Disama L.P.
204. New Hope School
205. Nightingale English School
206. Nihang Timung English L.P. School
207. Nilalung Egs
208. Nilalung L.P.
209. No. 2 Lorulangso
210. No. 2 Taralangso L.P.
211. No. 3 Disama
212. No. 1 Bithiphang
213. No. 1 Bithiphang Egs
214. No. 1 Disama
215. No. 1 Phonglangso L.P.
216. No. 1 Taralangso L.P.
217. No. 2 Bithilangso L.P. School
218. No. 2 Disama
219. No. 2 Phonglangso L.P. School
220. North Point Eng. High School
221. North Point English School
222. Ove Chari English Me School
223. Oxford Model Eng. School
224. Panbari L.P.
225. Panbari Bapuram Rongphar Egs
226. Pandit Basti Egs
227. Pathor Gaon L.P.
228. Pepe Basti Egs
229. Phulbaram English L.P. School
230. Phulbaram L.P.
231. Pitaijal L.P.
232. Police Reserve
233. Presbyterian Mission High School
234. Presbyterian Mission School, Inglongpo
235. Prilangso L.P.
236. Prilangso L.P.
237. Rahalsing Diphusa Eng. Me (ven)
238. Raijandisa
239. Ram Inghi English
240. Rangsina Memorial School
241. Ratan Kro Memorial School
242. Rengbonghom
243. Rengbonghom H.S. School
244. Rong Ali Egs
245. Rongapahar
246. Rongapahar Siding English School
247. Rongbangso Egs
248. Rongbong Pathar Government School
249. Rongbong Timung Memorial Eng. School

250. Rongbong Tisso Egs
251. Rongchingrum Eng. L.P. School
252. Rongkangthir L.P.
253. Rongkimi
254. Rongkimi Egs
255. Rongkimi L.P.
256. Rongmarjong
257. Rongmili Medium
258. Rongmirdan Eng. Medium
259. Rongmirdan English L.P.
260. Rongmonjir L.P. School
261. Rongnihang (Assamese)
262. Rongnihang Eng. Medium
263. Rongnihang English
264. Rongplimplam L.P.
265. Rongplimplam Memorial School
266. Sacred Heart English High School
267. Sangtilangso (Silimphai) Egs
268. Santilangso Lumta Eng. L.P.
269. Sarada English
270. Sarlok Hanse English L.P.
271. Sarthe Kramsa (Serlongjon) Egs
272. Sedeng Terang English
273. Semson Sing Memorial L.P.
274. Serlongthu English L.P.
275. Shantipur Egs
276. Shiromani English L.P. School
277. Shiromoni English Medium School
278. Sibnagar L.P.
279. Sibnagar Rangapahar Milon Me
280. Sibunthiba L.P.
281. Sikari Bey L.P.
282. Sikari Hanse L.P.
283. Siloni
284. Sirim Langso
285. Sitlabari L.P.
286. Sitlabari Me School (Rec)
287. Son Sing Timung Egs
288. Sonai Rongchehon Memorial School
289. Sorsori Laidapdisa Egs
290. South Point English Academy
291. Springdale High School (Pvt.)
292. Sunrise Academy English High School
293. Tamul Bari
294. Tamulbari L.P. School
295. Tari Adong L.P.
296. Thadou Veng L.P.
297. Thaiphiungdisa L.P. School
298. Tharve Langso L.P.
299. Thedonglangso Egs
300. Thesoajur L.P.
301. Thesoajur Memorial School
302. Thong Nokbe Memorial School
303. Thong Timung L.P.
304. Tripuri Hindi L.P.
305. Tumenglangso L.P. School
306. Tungmenglangso Egs
307. Udeng Thang Rongphar Egs
308. Upper Borlangfer Memorial School
309. Upper Dikrong
310. Upper Dillaiji L.P.
311. Upper Dillaiji Me School

312. Upper Ekorani L.P.
313. Upper Hapjan L.P.
314. Upper Hapjan Me
315. Upper Jakoinala Egs
316. Upper Mohengdijua L.P.
317. Upper Rongnihang Model L.P. School
318. Vongjang L.P.
319. Wallingdisa L.P.
320. Wophong Timung L.P.
321. Wophong Tokbi L.P.

Names of Colleges

1. Diphu Government College
2. Renu Terangpi Junior College
3. Sing Kiri College

University

1. Assam University Diphu Campus, Near Lumding Road, K/A, Assam.

22

Education as a Human Right and for the Empowerment of Women in the North-East India with Special Reference to Assam

K. Nirupama Singha, Sumita Sinha and *K. Mema Singha*

Introduction

Education is considered as means of development of personality and awareness. Education can be used as an instrument in bringing about change in the status of women. Women are nearly the half of the total population size of a society. They are the indispensible part of a society and their education influence the coming generation. The development of future generation mainly depends upon the education of women section. The children learn their manners and behaviours at home and mostly mothers are responsible for cultivating good behaviour in their children. So, the education of women is realised to be the most essential part for the development of the society.

Education is one of the most important human rights, but the position of women's education in almost all the parts of India including the North-Eastern region is not at all satisfactory. Young girls may be brought up to believe that they are suited only to certain professions or in some cases to serve as wives and mothers. Despite of the improvement in the literacy rate after independence, there continues to be large gap between the literacy levels of men and women. Although the Right to education under Article 21 of the Indian Constitution has made it compulsory for the government to provide free education to everybody, the high rate of women's education is still a distant dream. Due to large percentage of uneducated women, they are not even aware of their basic human rights and can never fight for them. However, our cultural conditioning is the main source of atrocities against women (Haloi, 2015). The parents expect girls to look after the siblings while they are at work, working with the parents as seasonal labour during the cultivation period and managing the household work, the parents take more interest in boys education as against the girls as they feel that the girls are to be married off, increasing cost of education etc. But true womenhood is only understood and adhered to, when illuminated by education. It is education which makes a female competent enough to handle the issues of her life, to be self-sufficient, to become an able daughter who can have economic independence and support her family, to stand by her husband in difficult time and to rear up her children with the right education. Thus, the education of women is of great importance in our national and social life. It is the duty of the society and the government to provide adequate facilities for the education of women.

Status of Women in North-Eastern India

By status of women I mean the position of women in society in relation to men. There is a perception that the status of women is better in the states of the North-Eastern region of the country in comparison with the status of women in rest of India. The North-Eastern region of India or the North East (NE), as it is popularly known, comprises of eight states namely, Assam, Arunachal Pradesh, Manipur, Meghalaya, Mizoram, Nagaland, Sikkim and Tripura. With a population of 31.2 million in the year 2011, Assam is the most populated state in the north-eastern region, while the rest of the states are much smaller in terms of population size. In terms of geographical spread of areas, Arunachal Pradesh is the largest among the eight states.

The North-East region of India has been considered as a backward region in terms of growth in per capita income. But it is interesting to observe that apart from Arunachal Pradesh and Nagaland, the other six north-eastern states have sex-ratios that are considerably higher than all-India average. In North-East region, women enjoy greater mobility and visibility than women of other parts of the country. Practices such as dowry and bride burning are not very prevalent in the region. The position of women in North-East India in the post-independence era is considerable. The role and status of women have undergone notable changes even in the urban areas as well as in rural areas. The status of women in North-Eastern region in comparison with the rest of India is examined on the basis of different indicators, namely, Female Literacy, Female Work Place, Participation Rate, Drop-out Rates, Sex-Ratio, participation in decision-making/women empowerment etc. Recent studies reveal that the states with high women literacy rates are the States of North East (except Arunachal Pradesh). In North-Eastern States the gap in literacy rates between men and women is also low. Female work participation rates are higher in most of the North-Eastern states with hilly regions and those inhabited by tribal than other states of rest of India, except Assam, Manipur and Tripura, the female work participation rate is higher in North-East than all-India average. But it is shocking to note that the drop-out rates are very high in the States of North-East than many states of rest of India. Again, women's participation in public decision-making is gradually improving in North-East. The percentage of currently married women who usually participate in household decisions is more in the states of the North-East region than the national average. However, the percentage of women who are allowed to go alone to three places (market, health facility, and outside the community) is less in Assam, Meghalaya and Nagaland. Similarly, the percentage of women having a bank or savings account that they themselves use is less in Assam, Manipur, Mizoram and Nagaland than the national average (Das, 2013).

Status of Women in Assam

Assam is one of the major states in North-East India. It is the largest state in the region in terms of population and second to Arunachal Pradesh in geographical area. Assam is a multiethnic state with heterogeneous cultural backgrounds. The economy of this area depends mostly on cultivation. But it is a very serious matter that Assam is suffering from some serious economic and social problems like insufficient infrastructural facilities and economic backwardness, negligence of women education, superstitions etc. which are standing as hindrances on the way of development. To keep pace with global changing economic and social environment, Assam must has to solve all such problems.

Though the entire North-Eastern region including Assam is free from some of the social evils like dowry, *sati pratha,* female foeticide and infanticide because of the prevalence of tribal and indigenous culture, other forms of gender discrimination do exist as revealed in various gender gap studies. Generally, the women of Assam are very active in household as well as in economic activities. But in Assam, women's participation is significant only in agriculture, nursing and teaching. Women's contribution in other economic activities is very pitiable. Data collected by the North-East Network however suggests that violence against women, particularly domestic violence, is on the rise in the North-East. The rate of domestic violence in Assam is comparatively high than other states of North-East India (Das, 2012). Women are an integral part in every society. But status and education of women in Assam are still backward than men. The Indian Constitution has granted equal right and status to all irrespective of caste, creed and gender. But in practice women have been deprived of their Constitutional Rights in various ways. They are becoming victims of various social injustice and they are not being able to enjoy their due right and status in society.

The Status of Women Educational Rights in Assam

Human rights are those minimum rights which are compulsorily obtainable by every individual as he/she is a member of human family. The status of women mainly depends on their rights and privileges and the roles assigned to them. The Constitution of India also guarantees the equality of rights of men and women. Though women in India have been given more rights as compared to men, even then the condition of women in India is miserable.

Education is a fundamental human right of women and girls that education provides capability to make improved choices for themselves and their families. The right to education is marked priority on the agenda of the international community since right to education is not only a human right in itself, but also is quintessential for the exercise of all other human rights. Free and compulsory education to all children between the ages of 6 and 14 is a fundamental right of citizens under the 86th Amendment to the Constitution of India. But after so many years of the passing of the amendment there is no praiseworthy visible development in the field of education and literacy. Even most of the backward class parents from OBCs, Scheduled Caste, Scheduled Tribe and Other Minority Communities do not know about such right. In Assam, the number of school girl drop-outs is more than the number of girls completing education up to the age of fourteen.

Education for All (EFA) means not only having access to schooling but also having quality of education for all children. The government, through its various initiatives such as the Sarva Shiksha Abhiyan (2001), attempts to improve the education of women. One of the main objectives of the Sarva Shiksha Abhiyan was to bridge gender gaps in primary and secondary education by 2010. In the past two decades, women's participation in primary, middle and secondary level has increased considerably. The Government in India has introduced several other policies and schemes to increase the rate of women education and employment. The newest amongst it is *"Beti Bachao Beti Padhao"*. It is aimed at spreading awareness amongst the people in India towards protecting the daughters from social evils and to empower them through education.

However, the research studies indicate relative performance of women of Assam in educational attainment. It is mainly due to high drop-out rate among girls. Further enrolment in higher education is relatively low in Assam. But among the various North Indian States, the incidence of domestic violence is the least in Assam. This observation makes clear that position of women in Assam can be considered to be a mixed bag. In Assam though the increasing rate in female literacy is satisfactory, still it is not equal position with the male counterparts. In spite of the various projects for the upliftment of the plight of women in terms of education such as feminist critics, constitutional guarantees, and sincere efforts by the Central and State Governments through various schemes and programme the female education is still in the state of an enigma in Assam for several reasons (*see* Table 22.1).

Table 22.1 clearly shows that still the female literacy rate is wadding behind male literacy rate. The rate of school drop-outs is also found to be comparatively higher in case of women. This

Table 22.1: Literacy Rate in Assam 1951-2011

Years	*Person*	*Male*	*Female*
1951	18.53	28.01	7.58
1961	32.95	44.28	18.62
1971	33.94	43.72	22.76
1981	–	–	–
1991	52.89	61.87	43.03
2001	63.25	71.28	54.61
2011	73.18	78.81	67.27

Source: Census of India, 1951-2011.

higher rate of illiteracy of women is undoubtedly attributing for women dependence on men and to play a subordinate role. The lack of education is the root cause for women's exploitation and negligence. Still gender inequality is reinforced in education which is proved by the fact that the literacy rate for the women is only 67.27 per cent against 78.81 per cent of men as per 2011 Census. Again, the female literacy rate in the state is less as compared to the other states of the North-Eastern region as shown in Table 22.2:

Table 22.2: Female Literacy Rate in Assam

States	*Percentage*
Mizoram	89.40
Tripura	83.15
Nagaland	76.69
Sikkim	76.43
Meghalaya	73.78
Manipur	73.17
Assam	**67.27**
Arunachal Pradesh	59.57

Source: Census of India, 2011.

There can be various reasons for low literacy rate in the state, like lack of funds, inadequate facilities, inadequate manpower, sexual harassment, conflicting societal role expectations, government policies and lack of political will power to implement the entire educational programme. The growth of women's education in rural areas is very slow. This obviously means that still large womenfolk of Assam are illiterate, the weak, backward and exploited. In Assam, early marriage is one of the chief barriers which hinder the girl's further studies. The anxiety of parents towards the girl's future becomes hindrance in her development. It can be seen more in the rural areas where lack of proper knowledge and awareness exist (Dighe, 2016). Moreover, education is also not available to all equally. The middle class literate justified women's education so as to create suitable companions for educated men. The education for women should be such, which could teach them to become better wives, to live happily. Still in some places of Assam, people with strong patriarchal learning believe that since the role of male and female in society is biologically different, the nature of education imparted to them must also necessarily be different. It clearly reflects the narrow conservative outlook of their social circle.

But we cannot deny the fact that during the last two decades, there has been a significant rise in women's involvement in the field of education. Despite opposition of women education, a modest beginning had been made which saw the slow, but gradual emergence of an independent consciousness among the women.

Education for the Empowerment of Women

Women's empowerment implies the ability of the women to take all the important decisions independently, related to her, throughout her life span that will ensure her success in all aspects of life (Saryal, 2014). Empowerment is an active and multidimensional process which enables women to realize their full identity and powers in all spheres of life and allows them to reach their full potential to improve their political and social participation and to believe in their own capabilities. Among the various tools for the empowerment of women, education is the most effective, significant and surest one. Education is sometimes considered as a gateway towards empowerment. There is an inseparable relationship between education and empowerment. Education is a significant aspect for empowerment, particularly for women as it provides them the capability to make desired, fair and improved choices for themselves and also for their families. Empowered women can play a better role in the social revolution because they know their roles and duties towards the society which leads to development.

The State of Assam is developing on the certain parameters, but to understand the real development we need to focus on the empowerment of women. Now-a-days, we have noticed different Acts and Schemes of the Central Government as well as State Government to empower the women of India. But in Assam, women are found to be economically very poor, a few women are engaged in services and other activities. So, they need economic power to stand on their own legs on par with men. It is also observed that, as shown above, women are found to be less literate than men. Increasing education among women is of very importance in empowering them. Educating women can help in the overall development of the country. This can also lead to the generation of the feeling of self-confidence and self-reliance among women and will help them to understand the value of independent life. Educated women not only tend to promote education of their girl children, but also can provide better guidance to their children. They can also help in the reduction of infant mortality rate and growth of the population as infant mortality rate for female is high in Assam (Das, 2013). Thus, for the empowerment of women education is one of the most powerful means.

Another important point to be mentioned here while speaking about women empowerment in Assam is that there is a crucial need for educating women of rural areas and the backward sections of the society as more than half of the total population of Assam live in villages and other rural sections and they are unable to get benefits of various schemes of the government due to lack of education. Empowering women can contribute in promoting rural areas and in making economic progress of our state and thus women empowerment cannot be ignored while devising various policies for rural socio-economic development of the state. The goal of economic equality can be achieved through women's involvement in the process of empowerment.

In recent years, the empowerment of women has been recognized as the central issue in determining the status of women. The National Commission of Women was set up by an Act of Parliament in 1990 to safeguard the right and legal entitlements of women. The 73rd and 74th Constitutional Amendments (1992) to the Constitution of India have provided for reservation of seats in the local bodies of panchayats and Municipalities for women, laying a strong foundation for their participation in decision-making at the local level. In India, the Ministry of Human Resource Development (MHRD, 1985) and the National Commission for Women (NCW) have been working to safeguard the rights and legal entitlement of women. "The New Panchayati Raj" is the part of the effort to empower women at least at the village level (Hazarika, 2011). In order to fight against the socially constructed gender biases, women have to swim against the system that requires more strength. Such strength comes from the process of empowerment and empowerment will come from the education (Sonowal, 2013).

The Way Forward—Some Recommendations

For the empowerment of women in Assam we have to encourage the self-esteem of women and girls and should work for the gender balance in social, political, economic and cultural activities. Moreover, for women empowerment, it is mandatory that proper care should be taken for development of women education in rural and remote area of Assam. Guardian, teachers, NGO officials and government will have to take bold steps for empowerment of women. Although much work has been done to improve the state of education in Assam, we are still a long way off from attaining standards comparable to other developed places.

An attempt has to be made to remove the social, psychological and structural barriers, for participation of majority of women in education. Women reservation policy should strictly be maintained in all aspects like appointment in government and semi-government offices, admission in to the educational institutions, participating in the politics etc. The state must play a prominent role in preventing gender stereotyping and segregation in education. General awareness programmes should be taken among the women of village area to sensitizes them about the modern development of science and technology so that they could give up superstitious believes and attitudes.

It is a very important requirement for bringing about empowerment of women that both men and women of the society should change their attitude. The feeling that women are meant only for the household activities and to look after children needs should be replaced by a feeling of equal partnership of women and men.

Conclusion

Thus from the above discussion we can see that promoting education among women is of great importance not only for empowering them to accomplish their goals in par with men in different spheres of life, but also because education is their basic fundamental human right which cannot and should not be neglected. According to the Country Report of the Government of India, education of girls is the most powerful tool of change of position in society. Education also brings a reduction in inequalities and functions as a means of improving their status within the family. Women empowerment cannot be possible unless women come with and help to self-empower themselves. There is a need to formulate reducing feminized poverty, promoting education of women, and prevention and elimination of violence against women. In spite of the several problems and difficulties, it is found that modern education and facilities have influenced much in women empowerment. But still rural women in Assam are lagging behind in comparison to women living in urban areas. Education is the key factor for women empowerment and it is also significant to provide women with nurturing support and supervision so that they can achieve a peaceful life and secured future without depending upon others.

References

Baruah, S. L. (ed.) (1992): *Status of Women in Assam*, New Delhi: Omsons Publication.

Census Report of India, available at: <www.censusindia.gov.in>

Das, Dr. Ira (2013): "Status of women: North-Eastern Region of India *versus* India", *International Journal of Scientific and Research Publications*, 3(1), January. <www.ijsrp.org>

Das, Jogesh (2012): "Women's Human Rights in North- East India", *IOSR Journal of Humanities and Social Science* (*JHSS*), 3(4), Sep-Oct., 34-37. <www.iosrjournals.org>

Dighe, Pranjali (2016): "Empowerment of Women in the North-Eastern state: Assam", *International Journal of Research in Engineering, IT and Social Sciences*, 6(4), April. <www.indusedu.org/pdf/IJREISS>

Haloi, Nipan (2015): "Higher Education and Women Empowerment in the Context of Assam", *International Research Journal of*

Interdisciplinary and Multidisciplinary Studies (IRJIMS), I(XI), December, 56-60. <www.irjims.com>

Hazarika, Dhruba (2011): "Women Empowerment in India: A Brief Discussion", *International Journal of Educational Planning and Administration*, 1(3), 199-202. <www.ripublication.com/ijepa.htm>

Lyndem, Biloris and De, Utpal Kumar (eds.) (2004): *Education in North East India* (New Delhi: Concept Publishing Company).

Saryal, Sutapa (2014) "Women's Rights in India: Problems and Prospects", *International Research Journal of Social Sciences*, 3(7), July, 49-53. <www.isca.in>

Sonowal, Mukut Kumar. (2013): "Impact of Education in Women Empowerment: A Case Study of SC and ST Women of Sonitpur District, Assam", *IJCAES Special Issue on Basic, Applied and Social Sciences*, 3 January, 27-33.

23

Impact of Education on Hmar Women

Paul B. Chonzik

Human being can be broadly divided into two groups according to their biological factor of sex, namely, 'men' and 'women'. Just as there are differences in the biological made-up of the two, such as reproductive organs, body shape and secondary physical traits such as facial hair, muscular strength etc., so also the aims and objectives, desires and aspirations, duties and responsibilities, dress styles and behavioural patterns, of men and women are different. In the same way, roles and statuses of men and women are different in the different societies. Either men or women enjoy the higher status, and the other lower status.

Among the majority of societies around the world, the status of women is lower than that of men; and women are often treated as "weaker sex", and lower in status. American sociologist, Robert Bierstadt, said, "In all societies it is woman who has been subject and slave; man who has been ruler and master. Woman is a vessel, receptacle, utensil. She is conquered, subdued, vanquished, in sexual encounter as in life. Man takes, woman gives; man acts, woman waits."[1] Greek philosopher, Plato also is said to have thanked God for having been born free and not a slave and that he was man and not a woman.[2] Jewish prayer is reported to have it this way – "Blessed are You .... that You did not make me a non-Jew; Blessed are You .... that You did not make me a slave; Blessed are You .... that You did not make me a woman."[3] Apostle Paul also wrote, "For man did not come from woman, but woman from man; neither was man created for woman, but woman for man" (I Corinthians, 11:8-9).[4] This writing of Paul might have been inspired by the story of God's creation of man first, as found in Genesis of the Bible, in the person of Adam, and then out of whose ribs God created woman in the person of Eve (*see* Genesis 1-2).[5] Among the Hmar and cognate tribes also, the women were traditionally treated lower than men.

Traditional Status of Hmar Women

Hmar tribe is found and recognized as one of the Scheduled Tribes (ST) in the states of Manipur, Mizoram, Meghalaya and the two autonomous districts of Assam, namely Karbi Anglong and North Cachar Hills (now Dima Hasao). They belong to the larger *Chin-Kuki-Mizo*[*] group of tribes speaking a language which G.A. Grierson puts under the Chin group of Tibeto-Burman linguistic family.[6] They are mostly found in a rather compact area of southern Manipur, northern Mizoram, Cachar and North Cachar Hills of Assam, few pockets in Karbi Anglong Hills of Assam and some parts of Meghalaya, Tripura and trans-border Chin Hills of Myanmar and Chittagong Hill Tracts of Bangladesh. Their population as per Census of India 2001 is shown in Table 23.1.[+]

Table 23.1: Hmar population as per Census of India 2001

Manipur	42,933
Mizoram	18,155
Assam	14,460
Meghalaya	1,146
Total	**76,694**

Source: Census of India Special Tables for Scheduled Castes and Scheduled Tribes, 2001.

* The term *Chin-Kuki-Mizo* includes tribes closely related linguistically and culturally whom the British had variously identified them as *Chin, Kuki* and *Lushai* tribes and the various clans within them.

\+ Besides this, as per a joint memorandum submitted to the Chief Minister of Assam by various Hmar organizations based in Cachar in demand for recognition of Hmar as Scheduled Tribe in the Barak Valley in 2004, there were also Hmar tribe in the following districts of Assam: Cachar – 36,648, Hailakandi – 12,880 and Karimganj – 13,877, totaling 63,405. The credibility of this figure is in readers' discretion. The Hmar population in Myanmar and Bangladesh are also not available to the present author.

The Hmar tribe follows a patriarchal system of societal set-up. The father in the family is the head, and all lineages are reckoned from the male line. Since the father is the head in the family, he represents the family in any negotiations with others; in any decision-making procedures – family, village/town level etc. Even if the father is no more, not the mother, but the eldest son, or brother of the deceased father will take the place of the father. Only when there is no son, no male member/s in the father's side, is the wife consulted in any matter concerning the family. The Hmars are traditionally a tribe which used to have joint family and as such the father remains the head even among his son's family when the later made a family of his own. Therefore, women in Hmar society practically do not have a say in the family as well as in the societal level. The position of Hmar woman is something like this – from her birth to her death, both in spirit and flesh, first under the father's authority and also under her brother's subordination, after marriage, under the husband and also her husband's father. Such being the case, no wonder, there are many sayings among the Hmars ridiculing the position of women among in a society. Some of these are:[7]

(a) The wisdom of woman does extend beyond the (other) bank (of a river)! [In Hmar: *Nuhmei varin varāl a kai nawh!*].
(b) A woman (wife) and old (broken) fences (for *mithun*[#]) may be replaced any time! [In Hmar: *Nuhmei le se-dai chu thleng hlak an nāwm!*]
(c) Let women and dogs bark as they like (in vain)! [In Hmar, *Nuhmei le ui chu inbauh mei mei raw hai se!*]
(d) Women and crabs have no religion! [In Hmar: *Nuhmei le ai-in sakhuo an nei nawh!*]

\# *Mithun,* called *Siel* or '*se*' (when used in combination) as in adjectives, *se-pui* = she-*mithun* or *se-chal* = he *mithun;* also *se-ki* = the horn of *mithun,* where '*se*' = *mithun,* and *ki* = horn; therefore '*se-ki*' = the *ki* (horn) of *siel* (*mithun*). The Hmar forefathers used to keep many *mithuns,* and one's wealth is often measured in terms of how many *mithuns* (*siel*) one keeps. The Hmar forefathers used to make fences of split bamboos to keep their own *mithuns* (*siel*) under their control and watchful eyes. In the same way, '*se-dai*' stands for fence (*dai*) of '*siel*' or '*se*' (used in adjective combination).

Position of Hmar Women in Everyday Life

Even though the Hmar women may be in such a subordinate position in the society, they play important roles in the day-to-day life of the traditional Hmar society. Some examples may be given. A Hmar woman does almost every household work in the family such as drawing water (called *tui-chawi* in Hmar) in the morning from whatever source that be (usually one or two small rivers/ spring in a hilly village, often quite far from the village), pounding paddy with a pestle (large wooden pestle called *fahrel* in Hmar) on a wooden mortar (called *sum* in Hmar) to un-husk the rice. The art of un-husking the rice in this manner is called *bu-suk* (to pound rice).[+] A Hmar woman is also expected to sift or winnow the un-husked rice to remove the husks with the help of a plaited bamboo tray, called *leidār*[##] in Hmar. This act of separating the rice and the husks and collecting the cleaned rice is called *bū-sep* (*bu*=rice; *sêp* = sift). Every Hmar girl is expected to be good in this art. A Hmar girl, and not the boy in the family, is also expected to cook food for the family, and also prepare tea for the family and visitor/s (if any) in the morning. If the family members have anything to wash, the responsibility falls on the womenfolk in the family. Any women in the family who could not or do not perform such tasks only receives open blame from the community. Because of this, any girl child in the family is taught to learn such tasks from a very young age; and was taught everything what a 'subordinated' girl in the Hmar society is expected to do.

A Hmar young girl in a family is expected to rise up early before everyone else. Even if a young man or young man visit a girl in her house (popular practice among the Hmar society called *lêng* in Hmar) till late at night, the girl is expected to speak to him/ them and treat him/them nicely (even if the boy or anyone of them is not her lover/boyfriend); if she did not treat them nicely, she is liable to be condemned openly by the young man or young man, which could have a bad and long term consequences on the girl. It

---

\+ *Bu* = rice; *suk* = to pound, therefore, *bu-suk* = to un-husk the rice by pounding it on the wooden mortar with a pestle.

Leidār of the Hmars is a kind of sieve for separating rice from the husks, but it has no holes in it; rather, the Hmar women sift the husks, separating the husks and chaff from the rice by shaking the *leidār* in certain manner so that the rice and the husks and chaff separated.

is largely because of this that the Hmar young women, even if they had to work very hard in the day time, mostly jhuming works, had to stay awake in the night till late at night. Even then, she is still expected to be the first to rise in the morning; if not, she would be the target of open rebuke from the family and more seriously so from the community![8]

The Hmars traditionally are jhuming community depending on slash and burn method of cultivation for their livelihood. In such jhuming activities, the girls share a big chunk of the works. Even if the more tougher tasks of clearing the jungle (called *ram vāt* in Hmar; *ram*= jungle, *vāt* = to clear) and burning up the dried up bamboo and trees that had been cut down (called *chap* in Hmar), felling down big trees and pruning (cutting off) the big branches of big trees which they could not cut down, in the field; the women folk do the major chunk of the rest of the works such as clearing up the burnt and un-burnt bamboos and branches of the trees, sowing seeds of rice and other vegetables, weeding, and harvesting of paddy and other vegetables. They did more in these works than the men folk did. Over and above these, the women folk carries with their back-carrier baskets (called *paikawng*) such items as daos, hoes, tiffin-bundle[±] and any other necessary materials to the *jhum* land; and on the way back, not only these, but fire-wood, and the vegetables whichever is harvested. Harvesting of paddy is also a busy time for the women folk in the jhuming society. Usually, it is the women folk who cut the sheaves and put them on the *paikawng* to a pre-arranged threshing place, usually a raised plaited split bamboo-platform on which the paddies were threshed, so as the grains will fall on a cleaned up ground below it. The threshed rice paddies are collected in baskets which are taken to a temporary granary. Part of the paddies are carried home on the same day, by both men and womenfolk, while the rest may be taken home in due time. In all these, even though the men folk do some of the work, the major chunk works are done by the womenfolk, especially because most of the men go for hunting in the jungle.

Even though the womenfolk in the Hmar community played such an important role in the society, their status remained in a subordinate position *vis-à-vis* the men folk. This is particularly true

± *Tiffin* in those days were usually wrapped in a plantain leaves.

of inheritance of family property, marriage and divorce etc. Position of Hmar women in respect of inheritance, marriage and divorce are discussed briefly as follows:

1. Inheritance ('*Rohluo dān*' in Hmar): The Hmars traditionally follow a patriarchal system. Therefore, all inheritances go to the male members. Among many of the Hmar clans, except the Faihriem and Hmar Lushai clans, primogeniture is a rule and the eldest son inherits the family property. In case of the Faihriem and Hmar Lushai clans, the youngest male issue inherits the family property. In either case, the daughters, by traditional custom, never inherit the family properties. According to the Hmar traditional custom, 'Property' or '*Ro*' refers to money, house or land, farming land, utensils in the house, other items in the house of the ancestral home such as wooden/iron/steel properties, textile items, machines, farming land, and position of the father in the society etc.[9] The father of a family, as head of the family, distributes the ancestral property to his male issues (sons); the daughters/female issues do not have a share in the ancestral property. This could probably be because the daughter/female issue in the family is to marry and become part of the husband's household. It is, therefore, quite understandable that the father and brothers of a wife-to-be sister used to gift different items to their beloved daughter/sister to take to the husband's home when she get married. However, no one can object when a father gives a share of his properties to his daughter, even if it is against the general rule.

2. Bride Price: According to the Hmar customary law, the boy (or boy's family) needs to pay bride price, without which a couple can never become "man and wife" or considered 'married'. Even if a man has woman in his possession, and had taken a women to his or his parent's home and lived together with, yet, until he pays the most important of the various components of the bride prices called, "*pa inhawn*" that goes to the father of the bride, the woman concerned cannot be considered (customarily) as his 'wife'.[10] If by chance the woman dies, the boy (husband) cannot conduct her funeral as his wife; instead the girl's family will conduct the funeral. If the 'husband' had to treat her as her wife, he had to pay the "*pa inhawn*" on the day of the death of his 'wife' so as to claim the dead as his 'wife'. This custom is effective till today.[11]

3. Items bride take with to husband's home (called *sawm* in Hmar): There are certain things a bride is by custom to carry with (to the groom's household called *sawm* in Hmar)[$] on marriage. Such items include a coarse cotton blanket called variously as *puonri/puonchil/puonphasa* in Hmar), axe (*hreipui* in Hmar), bamboo-slit fully plaited basket (called *dawrawn* in Hmar), bamboo-slit open plaited basket (called *kawngvār* in Hmar), small iron hoe with a wooden or bamboo handle (called *tuthlaw* in Hmar), wooden box called *thingrem* in Hmar), thin aluminium pot (called *belvār* in Hmar), Hmar cotton gin (called *hmui* in Hmar) and weaving gear (*puonkawl*).

The fact that the bride prices and one of them, the *pa-inhawn*, is necessary to be paid to enable a man to call a woman he married as his 'wife' have often resulted in some men treating their wives as someone whom he had 'bought'. This may have greatly diminished the position of women in Hmar society. However, the fact is that Hmar women cannot be bought and sold as a commodity. Instead, the bride price only signifies the agreement between the bride's family and groom's family to bring the two together as man and wife. Also, as indicated earlier, the items that a bride need to take with her to the groom's household (*sawm*) are not mandatory, but are more of the practice that may make the bride to have a feeling of having contributed to the groom's family and be more at home there.

4. Separation and Divorce: There are certain manners in which the husband and wife may be separated or divorced according to Hmar customary laws. In these conditions, the position of women is very deplorable. In tune with the saying, "A woman (wife) and old/broken fence (for *mithun**) can be replaced any time!, the

---

$ The item a girl take to husband's home on marriage is not the same as '*dowry*' (practiced among some other communities in India) in the sense that these are **not** mandatory, but are taken willingly which had been contributed by the family or near ones. If a wife-to-be had prepared or accumulated items on her own to take to her new (husband's) home, no one can stop her.

* *Mithun* (called *Siel* or '*se*' in combination in adjectives, as in *se-pui* = she-*mithun* or *se-chal* = he *mithun*; also *se-ki* = the horn of *mithun*, where *se* = *mithun* and *ki* = horn). The Hmar forefathers used to keep domesticated *mithuns*, and one's wealth is often measured in terms of how many *mithuns* (*siel*) one keeps; and the Hmar forefathers used to make fences of split bamboos to keep their own *mithuns* (*siel*) under their control and watchful eyes.

custom allows the husband to simply say, "I disown (divorce) you" and throw out his wife. However, without very good reason or reasons, divorce hardly happens, because if it happens without very reasonable cause, the husband will receive public condemnation. There are different reasons when divorce may happen such as adultery (*uirè*), to divorce (*māk*) by husband, to divorce by wife by giving back the bride price (*sum-insuo*), to divorce by mutual consent and not giving back the bride price paid by the husband (*pêksa chang*).

(a) Adultery (*uirè*): A married woman having sexual affair with another man other than her husband is an adulterer. If her husband could not forgive her, then he can divorce her and make her leave his house only with the clothes she was then wearing; she cannot claim all the other items she had taken with herd (*swam*) during the wedding.

(b) Divorce by Man (*māk*): Among the Hmars, if a husband has good reason, he may divorce his wife. In such condition, as per Hmar traditional custom, he has to give one *mithun* to the wife's family, which may however be commutated with Rs. 40 by those who do not have *mithun* in their possession. This has recently been raised to Rs. 500,[12] [which of course is still very low]. The woman also is to get all the items she had taken with her during the wedding (*sawm*); these shall be delivered to her by the husband's family or their near ones.

(c) Divorce by Wife (*sum insuo*): This is how a wife may divorce her husband. If a wife, because of certain reasons, felt that she does not love her husband anymore and would feel that she should leave him, she can just leave her by giving back all the bride price that had been given by the husband's family. This is called *sum insuo* (literally meaning to release money or bride price).[13] Thus, there are certain fairness towards the women in Hmar customary laws.

(d) Divorce by Mutual Agreement (*pêksa chang*): If both husband and wife, because of certain reasons, feel that to remain "husband and wife" is no more possible, then they can separate or divorce as per mutual agreement, and there is no need to give back the bride price paid by the husband and the practice is called *pêksa chang* which literally means "to keep what's been paid". If they already had children, the husband will keep the children. Even if the children were still too small and the mother had to keep them and nurse them, still the children will be reckoned after the father's family/clan name. In fact, in any form of divorce, the children shall go with the father, and if for any reason/s, the mother had to look after the children, the children shall take the father's family/clan name.

Progress in Hmar Women's Position

The above discussion clearly reflects the low status of Hmar women. However, with the passage of time, their lot improved greatly, and education had to play a lot in the improvement of their status in the society. The public also, gradually coming out of traditionalism to modernity, recognized the great contribution the women, especially the educated women, could make in the society, and, naturally, the way the society look on to them also witnessed a sea change. Swami Vivekananda had clearly understood the importance of women and said, "That country and that nation which did not respect women have never become great nor will ever in future."[14] Possibly, the Hmar society also had been taught that lesson as shall be seen.

Brief History of Education among the Hmar People

In early part of 1910, Mr. Watkin R. Roberts a young Welsh chemist, who was then helping Dr. Peter Freshers in his clinic in Aizawl, visited Senvon, the biggest Hmar village in southern Manipur and introduced Christianity among them.[++] Soon the gospel spread among the Hmar and other tribes of southern Manipur through the enthusiastic evangelizing mission of the native converts. One of the tools of evangelism was starting schools where not only religious lessons, but also secular lessons were taught. Thus, after Watkin Roberts had gone back to Aizawl, he sent three native converts to Senvon to open a school there in May, 1910.[15] In 1911, four more schools were started in the outlying villages where

++ Date of Watkin R. Robert's arrival at Senvon is a disputed issue. However, the majority of the Hmars agreed that he arrived at Senvon and spread Christianity among the Hmar tribes living there, on February 5, 1910. (See Lal Dena, 2013, *In Search of Identity: Hmars of North-East India,*New Delhi: Akanksha Publishing House, pp. 47-51.

Christianity had spread, and by 1920, there were already thirty schools.[16] At the beginning the parents of the Hmar families did not want to send their daughters to school, mainly because they needed their services, for the girls did almost every household works at home, besides the jhumming works where the girls' share of work is very big. "Who would work if the girls were sent to school?" was the usual remarks of the parents.[17] Nevertheless, as time passed, largely under the pressure from the missionaries, education of the girls cannot be stopped altogether, and soon, many Hmar girls began to get education. In short, a girl with education became more broadminded, and dressed more properly and become more useful in different walks of life. This led to parents changing their mindset on sending their girl children to school, so that more and more Hmar girls were sent to schools. Among them, mention may be made of Miss Lalring[18] who became the first among Hmar speaking women to get graduation (Bachelor of Arts) degree in the year, 1965, who got married the next year (1966) to Mr. Hrilrokhum Thiek, who happened to be the first among Hmar speaking men to have passed B.Sc.[19] More Hmar women then went to schools and continued to higher education and were absorbed into Governmental and Non-governmental offices and schools.

Table 23.2 shows sex-wise literacy figure of the Hmar tribe according to the Census of India, 2001.

Table 23.2 shows that among the Hmars, there are more males than the females in all the levels of education, especially the gap between male and female literacy rate widens in higher educational levels. This is partly due to the fact that the Hmar parents were reluctant to send their daughters to educational institutions in the early years when education was introduced. Another big reason is that even after things have changed and many Hmar parents sent their daughters to schools; in higher levels, largely because the parents, and also their husbands (after marriage) discourage their wives to go for higher studies and would rather put them in charge of the household works and looking after the family. Hence, the gap between male and female in higher level education from Higher Secondary onwards is bigger and bigger. For the male counterpart, even after marriage, they continue pursuing higher studies and reached up to M.A., M.Phil. and Ph.D. The women folk hardly countered this, mainly because among Hmar

Table 24.2: Sex-wise Literacy Rate of Hmars, 2001

States	Total Population	Literates			Matric			HS			Graduate		
	Total	M	F	Total	M	F	Total	M	F	Total	M	F	Total
Manipur	42,933	15,560	13,708	29,268	1,689	1,217	2,906	678	500	1,178	910	431	1,341
Mizoram	18,155	7,086	6,437	13,523	341	210	551	127	48	175	155	46	330
Assam*	14,460	5,659	4,757	10,416	1,095	766	1,861	252	149	401	232	78	310
Meghalaya	1,146	446	403	849	86	61	147	45	48	93	56	36	92
Total	**76,694**	**28,751**	**25,305**	**54,056**	**3,211**	**2,254**	**5,465**	**1,102**	**745**	**1,847**	**1,353**	**591**	**2,073**

Source: Census of India, 2001.

* North Cachar Hills, Karbi Anglong Districts.

community, the father is considered to be the main bread-earner of the family.

Eventually, more of the younger generation Hmar women do not like to be confined within the limits of tradition. Instead, they want to be exposed to modern world. Educated women, through their readings, were becoming aware of the gender equality brought about by the ethos of democracy. In the meantime, there are widening opportunities for women becoming economically independent. Today, Hmar women with professional degree feel that they are wasting their talent if they just sit at home. Again, because of family planning programmes, the Hmar families do not have too many children to look after and find that they can continue with the jobs even after child bearing without much strain. The preference of urban families for small family makes it possible for modern women to take up jobs. Today, there are a number of Hmar women who are gainfully employed in medicine, teaching, engineering, designing, management, air-hostess, police etc. As of the year 2017, more than a dozen Hmar women are teaching in Colleges and Universities around the world, about a dozen are physicians (doctors), a few I.A.S. and allied services in Indian Central services, besides many in mission and church services. In such a situation, the position of women cannot be the same any more.

Hmar Women Association

The position of women among Hmar community is again brought up to higher status with the founding of **Hmar Women Association** in 1988. This organization was mainly formed to alleviate the position of Hmar women and to safeguard the rights of the women within the Hmar society. Amongst others, the aims and objectives of the organization include—[20]

(a) To work for the welfare and progress of Hmar women.
(b) To safeguard the rights of Hmar women in the society.
(c) To take steps to promote Hmar women in the field of education.
(d) To help Hmar women in their endeavour to earning.

This organization had done a commendable work in

improving the status of Hmar women in the society. Not only did the organization strife to improve the lot of the Hmar women, but the leaders did a lot of societal work such as trying to stop forced prostitution, drug abuse etc. among the Hmar women, and received support from the male counterparts in their moves and had contributed a lot towards improving Hmar society as a whole and the Hmar women in particular.

Conclusion

Among the Hmar society, women's role as producers and rearer of children and of labour power is more and more considered and their economic contribution is more and more appreciated. Therefore, the biasness against women is diminishing fast. However, customary practices, emotional pressure, social sanctions, appear to prevail in certain matters. For instance, the *Hmar Hnam Dān*, published by Hmar Youth Association General Headquarters, Churachandpur, Manipur, which is expected to be followed by all Hmar communities, still follows the male inheritance laws, and other traditional terms the Hmar had followed. However, the Hmar families have started giving part of family property to their daughters, to which no one can object. In short, the status of Hmar women have improved a lot thanks to education. Time will tell when men and women in Hmar society will enjoy equal status.

Notes

1. Quoted in C.N. Shankar Rao, 2013, *Sociology: Principles of Sociology with and Introduction to Social Thought*, Revised Edition, p. 281.
2. This quotation has been ascribed variously to Thales, Socrates, or Plato. See www.myjewsishlearning.com/article/who-has-not-made-me-a-woman/(accessed on May 22, 2017)
3. See http://www.jewishanswers.org/ask-the-rabbi-3716/jewish-prayer-and-freuds-views-on-women/(accessed on May 22, 2017)
4. *Holy Bible*, New International Version, Zondervan, Grand Rapids, Michigan, 1984, p. 812.
5. *Holy Bible, Ibid.*, pp. 1-2.
6. G.A. Grierson, 2005, *Linguistic Survey of India*, Vol. III, Part-III, (1904), Low Price Publication, Distributed by D.K. Publishers Distributors (P) Ltd., New Delhi, (Reprint), pp. 256-261.

7. Also see Lal Dena, 2013, *In Search of Identity: Hmars of North-East India,* Akanksha Publishing House, New Delhi, p. 36. [brackets mine]
8. The position/status of woman in Hmar society in the present paper is accounted from the personal experience of the present author which hardly received attention of scholars and writers earlier.
9. Hmar Youth Association, 2001. *Hmar Hnam Dān (Hmar Customary Laws)*, published by Hmar Youth Association, General Headquarters, Manipur.
10. *Ibid.*
11. *Ibid.*
12. *Ibid.*
13. *Ibid.*
14. Quoted in C.N. Shankar Rao, *op. cit.*, p. 813.
15. S.N. Ngurte and Dr. Rosiem Pudaite, 2015 , *History of Hmar Literature,* Hmar Literature Society, Churachandpur, Manipur, p. 162.
16. Darliensung, 2013. *The Hmars,* Akanksha Publishing House, New Delhi, p. 87.
17. Lal Dena, *op. cit.*, p. 38.
18. Information collected through Telephonic conversation with Mrs. Lalring Ṭhiek (Name of Miss Lalring after marriage) on 25.05.2017 at 08:35.
19. *Manmasi Year Book,* Vol. II, 2006-2007, edited by Timothy Z. Zote, Churachandpur, Manipur, 2007, p. 270.
20. See *Constitution* of Hmar Women Association, 1988.

24

Women Educational Situation among Muslim Community of Assam (India)

Himangi Kalita and *Nitish Mondal*

Introduction

Education is considered to be one of the significant social indicators having bearing on the achievement and the growth of an individual or community. This is perceived to be highly suitable for providing employment and, thereby, improving the quality of life (Misra *et al.*, 2007). Therefore, it is a crucial social factor that initiates the process of social, economic and cultural development of a country as also of a religious group. The National Commission for Minorities in India has identified Muslims, Christians, Sikhs, Buddhists and Parsees which constitute 18.80 per cent of the total population of the country as religious minorities, while Hindus are the majority group. Muslims constitute India's largest religious minority group (14.20%, nearly 184 million individuals) (Census, 2011) as well as the third largest Muslim population in the world after Indonesia and Pakistan. The population distribution showed that they represent a majority of the population in Lakshadweep and Jammu & Kashmir. The largest concentrations of all Muslims in India, nearly half of the populations are living in the States of Uttar Pradesh, West Bengal, Bihar and Assam. Moreover, the high concentrations of Muslims are also found in States of Kerala, Maharashtra, Jharkhand, Karnataka, and Telangana. Assam recorded to be the highest increase in the share of Muslims, from

30.90 per cent of the state's population to 34.20 per cent (Census, 2011). Muslims are poorer and less often employed in the formal sector, which is generally better remunerated than informal-sector employment (Sachar Committee, 2006; Census, 2011).

Educationally, Muslims constitute one of the most backward communities in the country causing concern. More than half of the Muslims were illiterate in the Muslim majority state of Jammu & Kashmir. Similarly, in the States of Haryana, Uttar Pradesh, Bihar, Nagaland, Meghalaya and Assam also, the Muslim literacy rates were found to be below 50 per cent (Government of India, 2006). The growth of the total Muslim population in India according to the census data is depicted in Fig. 24.1 Gender inequality in education is highly existent in general and minority women in particular and Muslim women's access to higher education and their educational attainments are generally lower than those of Hindu caste women. Data shows that the educational status of Muslim women is worse than that of men among the marginalised groups and women of other Indian communities. Thus, the situation of the Muslim females was much more precarious as only half of the Muslim females were literate. The truth, however, is that like women from other communities, Muslim women too are differentiated across class, caste, community, and geographical location. According to 2011 census data in Assam, only 45.8 per cent of Muslim women are literate, which is lower than all other religious communities. When compared to women from other faiths in India, the majority of Muslim women are among the most disadvantaged, least literate, most economically impoverished and politically marginalised sections of Indian society.

The major objectives of the present study are as follows:

1. To observe the educational status of women in general and Muslim women in particular.
2. Comparing the educational status of the Muslims with the other religious communities of India.
3. To find out the reason of such educational status of Muslim women and its relation to their socio-economic development.

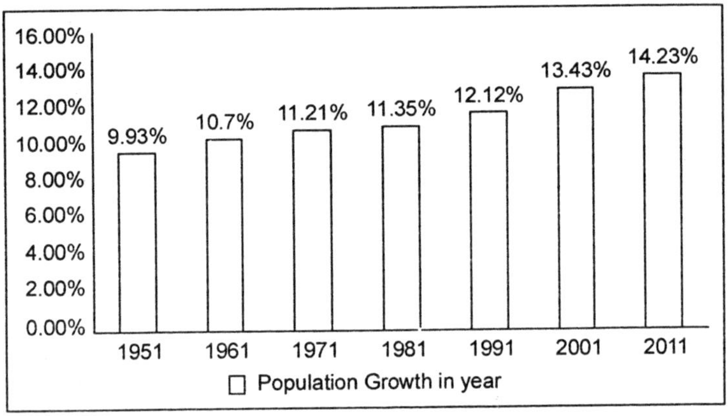

Fig. 24.1: Growth of Total Muslim Population in India

Methodology

The present chapter is based on secondary sources which are collected from various research journals, articles, census report, Government reports and internet etc. The online databases (e.g., Google Scholar and PUBMED) and search engines (e.g., Google) were used to search the relevant resource material for the present study. The keywords "Muslim, Education status, Women, Literacy, Women status, India" was also been used to retrieve various e-resources.

Results and Discussion

The comparison of the literacy rate at the all India level except the Muslims, all other religious groups found to have higher literacy rates than the Hindus who are a majority group. Jains have the highest literacy rate of 86.4 per cent, followed by Christians (74.3%), Buddhists (71.8%), Sikhs (67.4%), Hindus (63.6%) and Muslims (57.3%) (Census, 2011) (Table 24.1).

The descriptive study method has been adopted for the present study with a special emphasis was given in the state of Assam. The total population of the state is 3,12,05,576 individuals, out of which 34.2 per cent (males 51.2%; females 48.8%) are Muslim population (Census, 2011) (Table 24.2). A positive decadal growth of 0.80 per cent has been observed between 2001 and 2011

Table 24.1: Distribution of Population by Religious Groups and their Sex-Ratios

Religious groups	*Census 2001*		*Census 2011*	
	National		*National*	*Assam*
	Total population (%)	*Sex-ratio*	*Total population (%)*	*Total population (%)*
Hindu	80.50	931	79.8	61.5
Muslim	13.40	936	14.2	34.2
Christian	2.30	1009	2.3	3.80
Sikhs	1.90	893	1.72	0.07
Buddhist	0.80	953	0.69	0.18
Jains	0.40	940	0.37	0.08
Other religions	0.60	992	0.66	0.09
India	**100**	**993**	**100**	**100**

Source: Census of India, 2011.

Table 24.2: District-wise Total Muslim Population in Assam, India

Districts	*Total population*	*Muslim population*	*%*
Baksa	950,075	135,750	14.29
Barpeta	1,693,622	1,198,036	70.74
Bongaigaon	738,804	371,033	50.22
Cachar	1,736,617	654,816	37.71
Chirang	482,162	109,248	22.66
Darrang	928,500	597,392	64.34
Dhemaji	686,133	13,475	1.96
Dhubri	1,949,258	1,553,023	79.67
Dibrugarh	1,326,335	64,526	4.86
Dima Hasao	214,102	4,358	2.04
Goalpara	1,008,183	579,929	57.52
Golaghat	1,066,888	90,312	8.46
Hailakandi	659,296	397,653	60.31
Jorhat	1,092,256	54,684	5.01
Kamrup	1,517,542	601,784	39.66
Kamrup Metropolitan	1,253,938	151,071	12.05
Karbi Anglong	256,313	20,290	2.12
Karimganj	1,228,686	692,489	56.36
Kokrajhar	887,142	252,271	28.44
Lakhipur	1,042,137	193,476	18.57
Marigaon	957,423	503,257	52.56
Nagaon	2,823,768	1,563,203	55.36
Nalbari	771,639	277,488	35.96
Sivsagar	1,151,050	95,553	8.30
Sonitpur	1,924,110	350,536	18.22
Tinsukia	1,327,929	48,373	3.64
Udalguri	831,668	105,319	12.66
Assam (Total)	**31,205,576**	**10,679,345**	**34.22**

Source: Census of India, 2011.

(Table 24.1). The district-wise population distribution of Muslim population in Assam is also depicted in Table 24.2. The highest concentration of Muslim population was observed in the district of Dhubri (79.67%), Barpeta (70.74%) and Darag (64.34%) of Assam. The lowest concentration were seen the district of Dhemaji (1.96%), Dima-Hasao (2.04%) and Karbi Anglong (2.12%) (Table 24.2).

Education is perceived to be highly suitable for providing employment and, thereby, improving the quality of life, the level of human well-being and access to basic social services (Misra, 2007), but the educational status of the Muslim community in general and Muslim women in particular is found to be very poor, vulnerable and lead them one of the most educationally backward community. The age-specific distribution of child population in the age-group of 0-6 years and their sex-ratio are presented in Table 24.3. The highest prevalence of children in the age-group of 0-6 years was observed to be higher among the Muslim in both Census 2001 (18.70%) and 2011 (16.40%), which indicates the existence of higher rate of fertility among Muslim women, but the lower prevalence was observed among the Jain in both Census 2001 and 2011. The distributions of children aged 0-6 years were observed to be higher in Assam (19.4%) among the religious groups. As many as 25.0 per cent of Muslim children in the 6-14 year age group have either never attended school or have dropped out.

Table 24.3: Child population in the Age Group 0-6 years and their Sex-Ratios

Religious groups	*Census 2001*		*Census 2011*	
	National		*National*	*Assam*
	0-6 year's population (%)	*Sex-ratio*	*0-6 year's population (%)*	*0-6 year's population (%)*
Hindu	15.6	925	13.2	12.3
Muslim	18.7	950	16.4	19.4
Christian	13.5	964	12.1	12.1
Sikhs	12.8	786	10.5	8.6
Buddhist	14.4	942	11.6	11.5
Jains	10.6	870	8.9	10.0
Other	18.0	976	16.0	13.1
India	**100**	**927**	**13.6**	**14.9**

Source: Census of India, 2011.

Drop-out rates among Muslims are higher in the levels of primary, middle and higher secondary as compared to all the socio-religious categories. Only one out of the 25 per cent undergraduate students and one out of the 50 per cent post-graduate students is a Muslim in premier colleges. The share of Muslims in all courses is found to be low, particularly at the post-graduate-level and marginal in the science stream (Sachar Committee, 2006). There is a negative attitude towards girls' education among Muslims. Due to hurdles from family they lose the zeal to achieve something through education and thus they themselves do not have an academic interest. If at all they are fortunate enough to go to a good school, they are often discouraged to go for higher education, especially overseas.

The most important reason is that there is difficulty in finding educated groom if the girl becomes highly educated. For this reason, the Muslim girls and women lag behind their male counterparts and women of all other communities. They have the lowest work participation rate and most of them engage in the self-employment activities. According to Census 2011 in India, the literacy rate among Muslim female (44.2%) was far below the National average of female literacy (56%). In Assam also Muslim female literacy rate (45.8%) is one of the lowest among other religious community and the state average (56.4%). In a study in Lakhimpur district of Assam revealed that more than half of Muslim women (67.5%) were below the 10th standard education and only 5.83 per cent of women were above the 10th standard education of the district (Dutta, 2015). The poor attainment of education resulted in the married women depending on their husbands for undertaking any decisions concerning the family and also affected their awareness of certain factors affecting their lives such as family planning, Right to Information Act, domestic violence laws etc. (Dutta, 2015).

The distribution of literacy rates among the religious groups at the national and Assam is depicted in Table 25.4. According to the National Census data, the distribution of literacy rate was observed to be significantly lower among the Muslim. The sex-specific distribution of literacy rate was observed to be significantly lower among Muslim women than men. It is evident from the table that the female literacy rate of Jain community is the highest 85.1 per cent among the different communities of Assam followed by

Table 24.4: Literacy Rate of Religious Communities of India and Assam

(*in* %)

Religious groups	Census 2001			Census 2011					
	National			National			Assam		
	Literacy rate	Male literacy	Female literacy	Literacy rate	Male literacy	Female literacy	Literacy rate	Male literacy	Female literacy
Hindu	65.1	76.2	53.2	63.6	57.4	42.6	68.1	73.4	62.5
Muslim	59.1	67.6	50.1	57.3	55.8	44.2	49.9	53.8	45.8
Christian	80.3	84.4	76.2	74.3	51.0	49.0	56.9	62.2	51.5
Sikhs	69.4	75.2	63.1	67.5	55.5	44.5	84.3	87.8	79.9
Buddhist	72.7	83.1	61.7	71.8	55.2	44.8	68.4	74.4	62.2
Jains	94.1	97.4	90.6	86.4	52.0	48.0	86.5	87.8	85.1
Others	47.0	60.8	33.2	50.3	58.7	41.3	68.9	73.6	64.0
India	**64.8**	**75.3**	**53.7**	**63.0**	**56.9**	**55.9**	**61.5**	**66.3**	**56.4**

Source: Census of India, 2011.

Sikh 79.9 per cent, Hindu 62.5 per cent. While as the females belong to the Muslim community have the lowest literacy rate 45.8 per cent, followed by Christian 51.5 per cent, Buddhist 62.2 per cent, respectively (Table 24.4). It can be depicted from the above data that Muslim women in Assam are found to be educationally more vulnerable as compared to the other religious communities. The educational gap was observed to be 40 per cent between the lowest (Muslim) and the highest (Jains).

Several factors are responsible for Muslim women's low literacy rate in Assam. Some of the most common reasons of low educational status of Muslim women can be stated as high fertility, poverty, lack of women teachers and absence of separate schools for girls, opposition to secular education for girls, early marriage and conservative attitudes. The data showed that the Muslims in India have a much higher fertility rates as compared to that of other religious communities in the country. The growth of Muslims in India has risen from about 10 per cent in 1951 to 14.23 per cent by 2011 (Fig. 24.1). The overall growth of the population is also attributable to the fact that majority of Muslim populations are concentrated in the states that are lagging behind in social and educational reforms and services. The *Purdah* system, dowry system, early marriage, age-old superstitions and beliefs, orthodoxy are still a strong part of Muslim women in Indian society in general and Assam in particular. Lack of an adequate number of schools and infrastructural facilities in the Muslim dominated areas was a major cause of educational backwardness of this community (Government of India, 2006). Moreover, the traditional Islamic injunction restricting girls to go in attainment of education in public places or institutions—especially higher co-educational institutions—still seem to guide the minds of most of the Muslim parents (Ruhela, 1998). The drop-out rates of both boys and girls in Assam remained higher than all-India average from 2001 to 2011 census.

The distribution of work participation rate by religious communities of India and Assam is depicted in Table 25.5. The overall rate of work participation was observed to be markedly lower in both 2001 (31.3%) and 2011 (31.6%) among the Muslim population. The sex-specific distribution was observed to be lower among Jain's women followed by Muslim. In Assam, the overall work participation rate was also observed to be lower among Muslim as compared the major religious groups (Table 25.5). Furthermore, the committee report has also stated that Muslim women have minimal participation in Government micro-finance programmes such as Self-Help Groups (SHGs), Watershed Programmes and Panchayati Raj (Sachar, 2006). The educational backwardness of women makes them the largest group hindering the process of social change. The low literacy among the Muslims was largely the result of their poor socio-economic condition and

Table 24.5: Work Participation Rate by Religious Communities of India and Assam (*in* %)

Religious groups	*Census 2001*			*Census 2011*					
	National			*National*			*Assam*		
	Total	*Male*	*Female*	*Total*	*Male*	*Female*	*Total*	*Male*	*Female*
Hindu	40.4	52.4	27.5	41.0	53.9	27.3	41.5	55.6	26.7
Muslim	31.3	47.5	14.1	32.6	49.5	14.8	32.2	50.2	13.3
Christian	39.7	50.7	28.7	41.9	52.9	31.2	43.8	51.4	36.1
Sikhs	37.7	53.3	20.2	36.3	55.4	15.2	44.9	65.5	17.5
Buddhist	40.6	49.2	31.7	43.1	53.4	32.5	43.0	55.8	29.7
Jains	32.9	55.2	9.2	35.5	57.7	12.3	35.5	60.5	8.33
Others	48.4	52.5	44.2	48.5	53.2	43.8	44.0	51.4	36.5
India	**64.8**	**51.7**	**25.6**	**39.8**	**53.3**	**25.5**	**38.4**	**53.6**	**22.5**

Source: Census of India 2011.

vice versa. Moreover, illiteracy and ignorance also cause their poor health care behaviour, unhygienic sanitation, knowledge about nutritious food. A poor-level of education is also affected their awareness of certain factors affecting their lives, such as family planning, Right to Information Act, domestic violence laws etc. It was seen that lack of education or poor educational status resulted in the married women, depending on their husbands for undertaking any decisions concerning the family. There is a need for special efforts to bring the educationally backward minorities on par with the rest of the society and to make them participate fully in the national development activities.

Conclusion

The education has been recognized as an essential social agent to bring change and development in community or society. Therefore, it is the instrument which can bring equality and improves the status of women in the family and society. The Muslims, the largest minority community in the country are seriously lagging behind in terms of most of the human development indicators and education. The perception of deprivation is widespread among Muslims and women are among them least educated sections of Indian society. Therefore, the emphasis with regard to women's education should be to equip her multiple role as citizen and contributor to family income, builders of new societies. To improve the educational status of women in India is important to improve the Muslim women thereby the empowerment and position in the society. The Government should make special committees and commissions on women from time to time and take special steps for the improvement of education and situation among Muslim women. There is a need of a comprehensive and inclusive national programme of action for advancement of education of Muslim women especially residing in both rural-urban regions in India.

References

Dutta, Swapna (2015): "Socio-economic status of Muslim women in Lakhimpur district of Assam", *Advance Research Journal of Social Science*, 6(1): 56-60.

Registrar General of India (2001): "*Census of India, 2001*". New Delhi: Office of the Registrar General and Census Commissioner.

Registrar General of India (2011): "*Census of India 2011*". New Delhi: Office of the Registrar General and Census Commissioner.

Ruhela, S.P. (1998): "Religion, Social Class and Educational Opportunity: Case Studies of Eight Muslim Girls", in S. P. Ruhela (ed.) *Empowerment of the Indian Muslim Women*, New Delhi: MD Publications, pp. 1-22.

Government of India (2006): "Social, Economic and Educational Backwardness of Muslims in India: A Report. Report of the Prime Minister's High Level Committee", Government of India, New Delhi 63-88.

Misra, J.R., *et al.*, (2007): Report of the National Commission for Religious and Linguistic Minorities. Delhi: Government of India. Retrieved on June 20, 2013 from http://www.minorityaffairs.gov.in/ncrlm

Sachar Committee Report. Prime Minister's High Level Committee, (Government of India) (2006) "Social, Economic and Educational Status of the Muslim Community in India". New Delhi: Cabinet Secretariat, Government of India.

25

Child Labour's Experience of Education

A Study of Darjeeling District

Nimkit Lepcha and *Maheema Rai*

Introduction

All over the world children continue to work, putting at stake their education, their health, their normal development to adulthood, and even their lives. Millions of them work under hazardous conditions which present dangers to their health, safety and welfare. They toil in mines and quarries, are exposed to agro-chemicals in agriculture, squat in crippling positions to weave rugs and carpets, and scavenge in rubbish tips. Too many are enslaved in bonded labour, isolated in domestic service, and traumatised and abused in the commercial sex trade. Child Labour is a complex social and political issue with a long evolving history. Poverty is a very important factor, but the other factors are education, rigid social and cultural roles, economic greed, family size, geography and global economy, all contribute to the emergence of Child Labour.

In 2001, out of a 12.6 million child workers, about 1,20,000 children in India were in hazardous jobs. UNICEF estimates that India with its large population has the highest number of Child Labourers in the world who are under 14 years of age. Different factors contribute to the Child Labour in India like social, cultural, economic etc. The work in hazards and risks that affect adult workers can affect Child Labourers even more strongly. Children often suffer psychological damages as well for working and living in an environment where they are denigrated, harassed or experience violence and abuse. Child Labour in India is bad and the condition is getting worse day-by-day.

Hence, in order to understand the determinants of the rise of Child Labour, this study seeks to examine different factors that help the growth of Child Labour in India and Darjeeling. This study is based on fieldwork survey in Darjeeling district highlighting how the Child Labour endangers human society and how it affects individual and the society at large. So, the issues associated with child labour have been investigated to understand the relevance of education and also to examine the obstacles in achieving education for the child labourers in Darjeeling district. The policies and programmes of the government in terms of child labour's education will also be critically examined. It would also bring out the role of the government, culture and society for rise of Child Labour in India and particularly in Darjeeling. Moreover, it would analyse the works of the Government and the Non-Governmental Organizations' efforts in eradicating Child Labour in Darjeeling.

Child Labour in Global Scenario

In different parts of the world, at different stages of history, a labouring child has been a part of economic life. Children have worked in bulk in factories from the time of the industrial revolution in Europe and from mid-19th century in America. The work of children is a global issue. The manifestation varies widely in impact depending on the condition of poverty, economy, history and position in the global social and economic system. Child Labour has become challenge to children's rights and well-being. Working children are denied their right to survival and development, education, leisure and pay and adequate standard of living etc. Poverty is the major precipitating factor, but education, rigid social and cultural roles, economic greed, family size, geography and global economics all contributes (Bachman, 2000). In an economically, socially, culturally diversified world, children constitute one third of the population. In these diverse conditions many children are even struggling for the basic needs of survival, *e.g.* food and shelter (*see* Fig. 25.1).

Children are considered future citizens and it is expected that every society creates a favourable environment and provides adequate opportunities for their overall development. Due to such

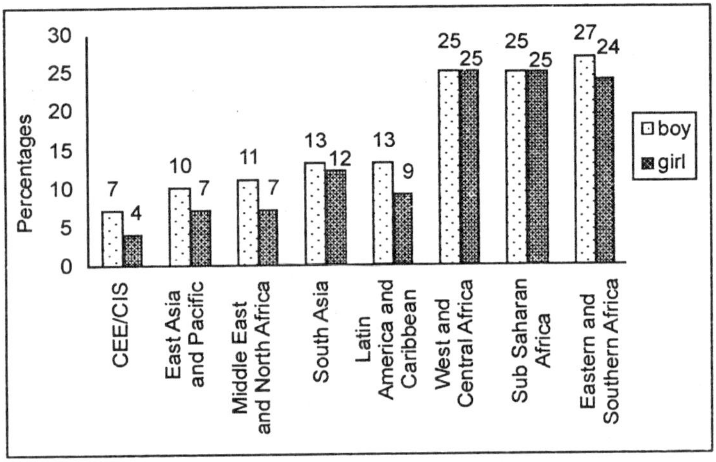

Fig. 25.1: Percentage of Children Aged 5 to 14 Years Engaged in Child Labour by Sex.

Source: UNICEF Global Databases, 2014, 2005-2012.

widespread poverty and to escape from malnutrition, over 150 million children between the ages of ten to fourteen years are working in the world (UNICEF, 2014: 5). It is estimated that there are around 215 million child labour around the world where 50 millions are out of school, where half of them are working under hazardous industries. In sub-Saharan Africa, the region with the largest out-of-school population, 10 million children are working (Brown, 2011:9). Child labour and educational deprivation produces a self-reinforcing cycle of disadvantage.

South Asian region is also one of those areas, which provide congenial environment for the practice of Child Labour. Malnutrition, health problems, gender discrimination, illiteracy and ignorance are common features of this region. Here approximately 53 per cent people live below the poverty line and 41 per cent people are illiterate (UNICEF, 2014: 98).

Legal Conventions for Child Labour and Education: There are three main Conventions which seek to protect children from child labour and ensure their access to education and other fundamental rights:

- *ILO Convention on Minimum Age for Employment, 1973 (No. 138)* sets standards for the minimum age of employment. The convention requires countries to establish a minimum age for employment not less than the age of finishing compulsory education, and which in any case, should not be less than 15 years. However, a country, whose economy and educational facilities are insufficiently developed, may initially specify a minimum age of 14 years.

- *UN Convention on the Rights of the Child, 1989 (CRC)* specifies in Article 32 that children have the right to be protected from performing any work that is likely to be hazardous or to interfere with the child's education, or to be harmful to the child's health or physical, mental, spiritual, moral or social development.
- *ILO Convention on Worst Forms of Child Labour, 1999 (No. 182)* applies to all persons under the age of 18 and calls for the prohibition and elimination of the worst forms of child labour as a matter of urgency. Children in the worst forms of child labour must be removed or rehabilitated and have access to free basic education or vocational training. There has been many ratification done in terms of these convention in order to increase the education among the child labourers are concerned.

Child Labour in India

Participation of children in work is not a new phenomenon. It has existed in different forms in every society throughout human history. Child Labour existed in the form of child slaves in ancient India and the cruel practice of possessing children was prevalent. Children in India have been associated with work from time immemorial. The work that they were asked to undertake used to provide them an opportunity for direct fulfilment of their natural abilities and for creating potentialities and was thus conducive to their healthy growth and development (Bhashkar, 1997: 107). (*see* Table 25.1).

India accounts for the second highest number where Child Labour in the world is concerned. Africa accounts for the highest number of children employed and exploited. Though, India is signatory of various international conventions and agreements, there is a growing number of Child Labours in India. In India, there is a grave relation between child labour and illiteracy. The NSS report on literacy and levels of education in India show that

Table 25.1: Child Labour in India from Census of 1951 to 2011

Census	No. of Child Labour (millions)
1951	13.39
1961	14.47
1971	10.7
1981	13.0
1991	11.3
2001	12.6
2011	11.7

Source: V.V. Giri National Labour Institute and Census of India, 1971-2011.

in families with higher monthly per capita expenditure, literacy rates are also higher (NSS, 2001).

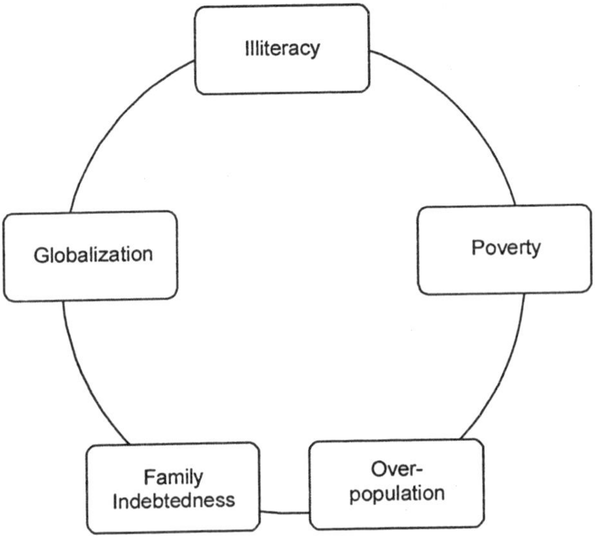

Fig. 25.2: Causes of Child Labour in India.

Poverty dumps a crowd of problems onto a child. In order to survive, a poor child in India will probably be forced to sacrifice education and training; without skills the child will, as an adult, remain at the bottom of the economic heap. The increasing gap between the rich and poor, privatization of basic services and the neo-liberal economic policies are causes that major sections of the population out of employment and without basic needs. This adversely affects children more than any other group. Entry of multi-national corporations into industry without proper mechanisms to hold them accountable has lead to the use of Child Labour. While poverty, illness or disability of the breadwinners and other crises within the household often lead to Child Labour may be so deeply ingrained in local customs and habits that the parents and the children do not realize that it is illegal or against the interests of the children (ILO, 2010).

Legal system to impart education among Child Labour in India: The Constitution of India (26 January, 1950), through various articles enshrined in the Fundamental Right and the Directive Principles of State Policy, lays down that:

- No child below the age of 14 years shall be employed to work in any factory or mine or engaged in any other hazardous employment (Article 24).
- The state shall provide free and compulsory education to all children of the age six to 14 years [Article 21(A)].
- Children shall be given opportunities and facilities to develop in a healthy manner and in conditions of freedom and dignity (Article 39-f).
- The state shall endeavour to provide within a period of 10 years from the commencement of the constitution for free and compulsory education for all children until they complete the age of 14 years (Article 45).

Government Policies and Programmes: Apart from this, Government of India as formulated many policies and schemes for addressing Child Labour like National Child Labour Policy (NCLP). This was started in pursuance of India's development goals and strategies; a National Child Labour Policy was adopted in 1987 following the Child Labour (Prohibition and Regulation) Act, 1986. The Schemes is sanctioned in 270 districts of India (*see* Table 25.2).

The strategy for the NCLP includes the establishment of special schools to provide non-formal education and pre-vocational skills training, promoting additional income and employment generation opportunities, raising public awareness and conducting surveys and evaluations of Child Labour. Around 100 NCLPs were launched across the country to rehabilitate children working in

Table 25.2: Year-wise Budget Allocation and Expenditure incurred under the NCPLS During Last Five Year

Year	Budget Allocation in Crores	Expenditure in Crores
2010-11	92.80	92.71
2011-12	143.00	142.66
2012-13	130.18	128.01
2013-14	111.00	110.73
2014-15 as on 31-12-2014	175.00	49.90

Source: Annual Report 2014-15, Ministry of Labour and Management (Government of India).

hazardous industries such as glass and bangles, brassware, locks, carpets, matches, fireworks and gems. Children in the age group of 5-9 years were enrolled directly under the Sarva Shiksha Abhiyan or the Education for All Movement commenced under the Tenth Five Year Plan. Further, those in the age group of 9-14 were admitted to special schools under the NCLP schemes. Besides this components of healthcare and vocational training are also augmented.

Important Schemes for Well-Being of Children: There are number of schemes formulated by Government of India for the well-being of children and which are also helpful for eliminating Child Labour to some extent, some of the schemes are as follows:

- Integrated Child Development Service Scheme.
- Integrated Child Protection Scheme.
- National Awards for Child Welfare.
- Rajiv Gandhi Manav Seva Awards for Service to Children.
- Balika Samriddhi Yojana.
- Nutrition Programme for Adolescent Girls.
- Early Childhood Education for 3-6 age group children.
- Welfare of working children in need of Care and Protection.
- Childline services.
- Rajiv Gandhi National Creche Scheme for children of working mothers.
- UJJAWAL: A Comprehensive Scheme for Prevention of Trafficking and Rescue.
- Rehabilitation and Re-integration of Victims of Trafficking and Commercial Sexual Exploitation.
- National Rural Health Mission.

- Rajiv Gandhi Scheme for empowerment of Adolescent Girls—SABLA.
- Dhana Lakshmi—Conditional Cash Transfer for Girl Child with insurance cover.
- National Commission for Protection of Child Rights (Mandlik, Dhananjay, 2015: 169).

Apart from Governmental policies and programmes there are number of Non-governmental Organizations (NGOs) like Bachpan Bachao Aandolan, CARE India, Child Rights and You, Global March against Child Labour, RIDE India etc. have been working to eradicate Child Labour and promoting education for them in India. Pratham is the India's largest Non-Governmental Organisation with the mission "every child in school and learning well". Founded in 1994, Pratham has aimed to reduce Child Labour and offer schooling to children irrespective of their gender, religion and social background. Bachpan Bachao Aandolan (BBA), is a people's movement of over 75,000 individual members and approximately 750 civil society groups who have been working on the issue of child rights, especially trafficking, Child Labour etc. in order to achieve its vision of child friendly society and education for all, BBA initiated a model of child friendly village (Bal Mitra Gram hereinafter BMG) in 2001. A BMG works to eradicate Child Labour by withdrawing children from work and putting every child in school. Till date more than 350 BMDs have been successfully formed by BBA across India enrolling around 50,000 children in schools (BBA Report, 2014: 5).

There have been multiple methods and way in dealing child labour problems, but the greatest progress has been in recognising the link between eliminating child labour and guaranteeing "Education for All". China, Brazil, Sri Lanka are the burning examples to show that in addition to poverty reduction, mass education has been critical in tackling child labour. UNICEF's research proves that children who grow-up without the basic education find it harder to sustain themselves and their families. India has the second largest network of school system in the world. Yet, of the three lots enrolled in school in class one, two tend to leave school before reaching class three. The fact that only one out of three children is a girl partly explains why nearly two out of three women are able to read and write in India (Roa, 2015:60).

Again the situation is still worst in rural areas. Evidences show that due to lack of awareness and education of parents also many students are sent to work because there illiteracy. Thus, it is fact that the lack of appreciation by parents of the role of the education in improving the life and the living condition, has contributed the prevalence of child labour.

Child Labour and Education in Darjeeling District

Darjeeling is on the verge of being the most vulnerable districts in terms of Child Labour in the West Bengal. According to the Labour Investigation Committee the children below 15 constituted 21.1 per cent of labour force in Darjeeling. The Child Labourers are not only engrossed in daily works like manual workers, household worker etc., but they are also involved in illegal works which pose a great threat to the state as well to them. It was estimated that around 3,942 children are engaged in illegal jobs across Darjeeling district because of the socio-economic condition of the family. There are many cases of girls being trafficked in the name of jobs and they were forced to work in the fields like forced labour, sexual exploitation, child soldiers, in the drugs trade, and in begging. Drugs trafficking and taking drugs is not a new phenomena in Darjeeling.

The condition of the Child Labour in Darjeeling do not cope with the Government of India had dreamed for. The Child Labour in Darjeeling as mostly work due to the low income of the family or lack of proper basic necessity in the household that makes them to opt for the work. So, the lack of economic cost of the household had forced the children to give-up their hope and dreams in the hills of Darjeeling. The Darjeeling district is divided into sub-division Darjeeling, Kalimpong and Kurseong. There are many children who are working as labourers in these four areas. The real reason behind the employment of children is that they are cheaper and more acquiescent than adults. Sometimes, child involved in labour has no access to their earnings and enjoys no privacy, no freedom, no opportunity to go to school and no social interaction with peers or parents. The child labourers are brought from these areas Nepal, Dooars, Khorabari, Makaibari, Jai Goan, Malbazar, Gorubathan, Bijanbari, Bhutan, Assam, Bihar, Sikkim etc. In the Darjeeling Hill areas, the respondents are brought from the rural areas of Darjeeling district. Each and every Child Labour faces different kind of work due to their gender. Child Labourer's work may be divided into four parts namely domestic work, industrial work, business and others.

Table 25.3: Works of the Child Labourers

Work	*No. of respondents*	*Percentage*
Domestic	20	40
Industrial	5	10
Business	25	50
Others	0	0
Total	**50**	**100**

Education among child labourers in Darjeeling District: The most important thing among the Child Labour is illiteracy. Not only the literacy of the children is important but literacy of the employer of the child is important. As most of the incidents occur among the Child Labour like the physical violence has a direct relation to literacy. As the Constitution of India and Human Rights has initiated many laws to protect the children from the direct as well as indirect violence.

Table 25.4: Educational Qualifications of the Child Labourers

Class	*No. of respondents*	*Percentage*
Pre-primary	10	20
Primary	17	34
Read and write	11	22
No formal schooling	12	24
Total	**50**	**100**

Table 26.4 gives the information that most of the respondents are not literate as most of them did not have formal education around 24 per cent of them has not been able to get any kind of education. And around 20 per cent and 4 per cent of them have got some kind of schooling in their life. Though most of them did not have formal education but they can read and write. The reasons may be that most of the children want to study and some of them are getting education irrespective of their work.

Table 25.5: Education Facilities

Education Facilities	*No. of Respondents*	*Percentage*
School	17	34
Self-study	3	6
Home tutor	1	2
No facilities	29	58
Total	**50**	**100**

Table 25.5 indicates that around 34 per cent of the respondents have the facilities of going to school and round 6 per cent and. 2 per cent have the option of self-study and home tutor. The facts given above reveal that the respondents in the study have the privilege of getting education. Not only that they are not restricted from getting education. Most of the respondents if not going to school have the option of self-study or with the home tutors. But most of the respondents have the notion of not studying as they say that they get tired after work so they do not have time to study. It is not that they do not have any option or they are restricted from getting education most of them do not apply for it. But they have time schedule to go to school as most of them go to school for few days not the whole week.

Table 25.6: School Attended by Respondents

Days in a Week	*No. of Respondents*	*Percentage*
Three days	5	10
Five days	43	86
Four days	2	4
No school	0	0
Total	**50**	**100**

Around 86 per cent of the respondents attend school all the days in a week and around 10 per cent of them three days and, 4 per cent in four days. Most of the respondents are allowed to go to schools as the data shows nil respondents in not going to school which means they are allowed to go to school. But according to the law, the Child Labourers and all the children below 14 years of age have the facilities of free education which they are not getting totally.

The works of the NGOs: The problem of children working and not going to school is a critical problem. According to the census 2001, West Bengal had 6.77 per cent Child Labour in the country. Where the incidents of Child Labour is highest in Malda where the children were migrated inside and outside West Bengal and India or taken into different places. As in Darjeeling the most important incidence is that there is outflow as well as inflow of children and women for labour. In Darjeeling most of the NGOs are supported by the internal as well as external source for the cause of the child like Caritas India supports a programme to two NGOs in Darjeeling District one Baal Suraksha Abhiyan which is located in Kalimpong and the other one MARG located in Darjeeling town. This institution has the major goal to see Darjeeling District as a "Child Labour Free" District. In the Bal Suraksha Abhiyan which is run by the Convent's nun takes care of the children who are been rescued and given shelter to the homeless children. Both Girls and Boys from the age of 6-14 are kept in the rehabilitation centre. Children staying in the centre are those who have been rescued from hotels, domestic sectors, tea stalls, garages etc. and who are unable to be reunited with their family. While older children, i.e. who have crossed the age of 14 are put, up in different school hostels and paying guests. This BSA has enrolled children in 25 schools around Kalimpong so that the each and every child will be independent.

Table 25.7: List of the Schools where the Children are Studying

Kumudini Homes, St. Michel's School	Nepali Girl's High School
St. Philomena Girl's Higher Secondary School	St. Joseph's School, St. Xavier's School
Gandhi Ashram, St. Joseph Convent, J.K.M.S.	Salvation Army for Deaf and Dumb
S.U.M.I. Jubilee High School.	Edith Wilkin Street Children Foundation
Cluny Community College	Holy Angel's Bethany, St. Joseph's College
St. Anges Boy's School	St. George Higher Secondary School
Salvation Army For The Blind	Chandramaya High School
Central Tibetan School	Albela Boys School
7th Mile Basic School	St. Joseph's Primary School

Findings from the Field

- Most of the Child Labour came from the suburbs of rural areas of Darjeeling, Dooars, Khorabari, border of India and Bhutan, Nepal and Assam.

- Though saving many children still around 50 per cent to 60 per cent more children are yet to be saved.
- The socio-economic condition of the family is the main reason of the existence of Child Labour and even due to child trafficking.
- The child who are working lack basic education which means the failure of the Government policy of free education.
- The other reason for the lack of education is also the lack of concentration and no interest in school among the children has created maximum number of drop-outs.
- Due to the lack of education most of the child as well as the people are not aware of child rights and its penalties.
- No uniform civil societies are present in the study area or it can be said that no works of the existing NGOs.
- Government policies as well as the people participation is lacking in terms of Child Labour.

Conclusion

Child labour is about the exploitation of the most vulnerable, disadvantaged and marginalised in society. The links between child labour and education are clear children with no access to education have little alternative but to enter the labour market, where they are often forced to work in dangerous and exploitative conditions. Hence, expanding access to free and compulsory education is crucial to reducing child labour, as is the provision of quality education. Only quality education can ensure that children are enrolled and stay in school. As Darjeeling district has large number for children who are working as Child Labours in such a vulnerable condition which is due to various socio-economic factors. Poverty, illiteracy, not proper facilities in government primary schools ignorance of people is the root cause for the prevalence of Child Labour. Though there are excessive laws dealing with problem of Child Labour, but due to their proper implementation by the law enforcement agencies Child Labour practice is far from eradication.

References

Bachman, S.L. (2000). A New Economics of Child Labour. *Journal of International Affairs*, Vol. 53, No. 2.

Bachpan Bachao Andolan. (2011). *Right to Education Impact 2010-2011*. New Delhi: Retrieved from www.bba.org.in. accessed on 1/12/2106.

Bachpan Bachao Andolan. (2015). *Status of Rehabilitation of Rescued Bonded Labourers. Analysis of Data with Bachpan Bachao Andolan (2010-2014)*. New Delhi: Retrieved from www.bba.org.in. accessed on 1/12/2106

Brown, Gordon. (2011). *Child Labour and Educational disadvantage, Breaking the link, building opportunities*. London: Gordon and Sarah Brown Limited.

Global March Against Child Labour (2015). Annual Report January-December 2014. New Delhi: Retrieved from: www.globalmarch.org accessed on 01/01/2016

ILO (2010).The Worst Form of Child Labour: Education and Violent Conflict (2001 and 2010). Geneva: International Labour Organization.

ILO (2010). The Worst Forms of Child Labour, Education and Violent Conflicts. *United Nations Educational, Scientific and Cultural Organization*, No. 46.

Mandlik, D. and Parag, Kalkar,. (2015). Child Labour in India: A curse on humanity. *American International Journal of Research in Humanities, Arts and Social Sciences*. 9(2), 165-169.

Ministry of Labour. (2010). Government of India. Retrieved from: www.labour.nic.in accessed 19/09/2014.

Ministry of Women and Child Development. (2012-2013). *Annual Report*. New Delhi: Government of India.

Ministry of Women and Child Development. (2013-2014). *Annual Report*. New Delhi: Government of India.

Ministry of Women and Child Development. (2014-2015). *Annual Report*. New Delhi. Government of India.

Ministry of Labour and Employment Labour Bureau. (2013). Child Labour in India. *Indian Labour Journal*, 54(11), 1099-1163.

Nation Commission for Protection of Child Right (2012-2013) *Status of Children from 14 to 18 years*. New Delhi: Government of India.

Nation Commission for Protection of Child Right (2011-2012) *Child Labour always in front of you but why constantly hidden from your views?* New Delhi: Government of India.

Roa, Ramana (2015). Child Labour and Education in India. *International Journal of Academic Research*, 2(5),57-62.

UNICEF (2015). Child Labour. New York: United Nations Children's Fund (UNICEF). Retrieved from; data.unicef.org/childprotection/childlabour.html

UNICEF (2012). *How sensitive are estimates of working children and Child Labour to definitions?: A comparative analysis. Statistics and Monitoring Section/Division of Policy and Strategy.* New York: United Nations Children's Fund (UNICEF).

UNICEF (2013). *How sensitive are estimates of working children and Child Labour to definitions?: A comparative analysis. Statistics and Monitoring Section and Division of Policy and Strategy.* New York: United Nations Children's Fund (UNICEF).

26

Empowering Marginalised Communities through Existing Education System

A Case Study

Girin Chetia

Assam, being the rendezvous of Mongolaid, Caucasoid, and Austric clans, bears typical marginality, which has crippled the state socially, economically, educationally and culturally beyond measure. Likewise, the status of literacy is shockingly alarming. The graph of literacy in respect of SCs, STs, OBCs and other minority groups of Assam is evident from the ups and downs depending upon their ethnicity, entity, and social trait. Sadiya located in the extreme remotest corner to the east of Assam, inhabits such marginalised and downtrodden communities of the society that, over the decades, they have been forced to fall prey to the clutch of the so-called silence culture. The title of my chapter is exclusively based on the complaints and statements narrated to us by the ill-fated people of Sadiya. The case studies reflected here in respect of past and present educational system will speak for itself.

Different remarks on education—

- Some educationists are very much used to complain that education is bias, towards, the creamy layer of the society, which controls the state.
- There is no book for empowering marginalized groups, because majority of them are not lettered and books are of no use to them.

- Day-to-day experiences is the sole lesions for them to educate themselves. The only option open to them is learning by doing.
- The North-East Affected Area Development Society (NEADS) with confusions, limited knowledge and experiences camped at Ambikapur, Sadiya as partner organization of Action Aid, India in 2007.

Background of the area: Sadiya situated in the extreme Eastern corner of India, is bounded by Arunachal Pradesh to the East, Dhemaji district to the West, Arunachal Pradesh to the North and Dhola–Dibang river to the South. Sadiya is 500 kms away from the State capital, 70 kms from Tinsukia and approximately 250 kms away from NEADS head office, Dhekiakhowa. It is the remotest and at the same time underdeveloped Sub-Division of Assam. Development initiatives are far from reach here. Delinquent Government officers, and officials are grounded by way of transferring them to Sadiya ironically called *kaliapani* of Assam. It is often times alleged that some employees draw their salary from Sadiya offices, but stay in the main land, i.e. other side of the Brahmaputra. This is one of the major factors as to why Sadiya is not in the wheel. Pub (East) Ambikapur is humorously called a mini *kaliapani* within a big *kaliapani*. It is in the foothills of Arunachal Prodesh is and lacks infrastructure like communication, health, schools infrastructure etc. In Pub Ambikapur there are 9 villages inhabited by 7000 population and they are resettling there of their own. Most of them are being flood affected and landless are hailing from different parts of upper Assam districts. Till 2009, there was not a single Government lower primary school in the area. There were 8 community run venture schools with no proper school building and furniture etc. Community people felt the need of educating their children and consequently started schools with their own effort. Normally, they build school building with local materials, pay teacher's honorarium in kind, i.e. 5 to 10 quintals of paddy per annum. But because of low harvest, sometimes the community fails to pay the teachers regularly and as a result schooling comes to a halt. The community being unorganised, has fail to exert pressure on the Government to meet their unmet needs. This is not the only instance, but the story is same for other development perspective. It is not a denying fact paying the teachers and maintaining school buildings has always been a nightmare of the community lending to such unavoidable circumstances, two out of nine community run schools had to be wound up in 2007 and others were also not functioning well.

Joint Interventional Strategies of Community and NEADS

We know that "**Culture of Marginalised community is Culture of Silence**". By nature the community do not raise question against injustice, because since time immemorial, they learn from their experiences, their voice is not listened by the fortunate class, so they keep mum. NEADS has been trying to break the silence of the community by engaging themselves in the endeavour. Tools used for this purpose were arrangement of a common place to sit together (later on this became a community facility centre), facilitation of community story telling programme in every evening. Holding group discussion on community issues and staging community cultural programme was a part of the evening programme. Participation of community members was not compulsory. Any person interested in the subject felt free to come and join, but after few months number of participants started gaining momentum. As time rolled out we took the advantage to add some new agenda which were proposed by some individuals for discussion. NEADS volunteers left no stone unturned to facilitate the process without imposing any agenda from their end. The community took forwards their agenda. In the beginning most of the resolutions were for community involvement on the common issues. Action like building community common place to sit together, organising community meetings on specific issues etc. were put to operation. Through this process community came out of the culture of silence and started articulating their grievances.

Impacts of Evening Storytelling Programme Gaining Momentum

The community members, who were sitting hours together without speaking a single word, could speak boldly, shared their problems with each other. They started feeling that they have known better about their village lifestyle and have a role to play for the betterment of the society. Interestingly within three years, community has been able to identify four common issues pertaining to child education, land settlement, gender discrimination and poverty. Being encouraged by their understanding and deep feeling they decided to work in association but not in isolation.

Communities were facilitated to prepare issue specific action plan. After having series of issue-wise brain storming and group discussion sessions at the common facility centre, the following issue specific action were earmarked by the communities.

On child education—

- The communities of Ambikapur decided to restart or run their schools for their children like the evening story-telling programme, where everyone is enjoying to learn by involving some selected members and finally planned two community educational programs namely–(1) "Gurukul Jatiya Vidyalaya" community school; (2) Joyful Learning Centres for Children (JLCC) in addition to existing venture schools. JLCCs are non-formal classes for students to attend on Saturday and Sunday and run by the selected youth from the community, NEADS's volunteers act as facilitator. Here students were taught some extra-curricular activities like singing, dancing, debating, delivering extempore speech and lectures etc. to promote schools as joyful centre, in the initial stage children were allowed to do whatever they like. The very purpose of this programme was to make them enjoy during class time and start sharing among themselves regarding the village environment, village issues, child right etc. and finally enlighten children to realize as equal citizen of our country and perform their duty as responsible citizen. Programmes came into operation from 2009.

  "Gurukul Jatiya Vidyalaya", Pub Ambikapur, a community initiative towards self-education,

  Promoted by, North-East Affected area development Society (NEADS), a grassroots level NGO.

  Gurukul Jatiya Vidyalaya: Instead of having bitter experiences of failure in community run venture schools in Ambikapur area, they hopefully rejuvenated the "Gurukul Jatiya Vidyalaya" (community run private school) in 2010. This time after a series of discussions,

NEADS and community decided to start a new community managed private school in a central place of Pub—Ambikapur covering 9 villages on First January, 2010, the School started with 53 students on the roll (39 boys and 22 girls). The school is going on well. At present this school has enrolled 65 students. There are 7 classrooms with 5 teachers. Other facilities in the school include one library, playground with Play items, Musical instruments, Joyful Learning Centre, demonstration Organic Kitchen Garden and provision of residences for student etc.

Impact of JLCC

Student enjoyed the schools, enrolment is 100 per cent, quality of education is hiring. Through CCA (Child Competitive Assessment), it is found that results of school having JLCC are far better than other schools. Community confidence is build-up. Now, community members like to engage themselves with schools. School activities have geared them up to learn as to how to resolve community issues. They have started realising that community can do many things with consorted effort. Within 8 years the communities have been able to draw many facilities from the Government. Five community run venture schools received Government grant and each school has appropriate infrastructures.

Next to education, the community started engaging them in sustainable land based livelihood programme, 1100 families have initiated organic culture in their land. The community is now serious about soil health too. They are promoting community grain bank in the name and style of "Kangali Bharal" to help each other at the time of crisis. In that bank community contributes paddy to form the capital, 18 Kangali Bharal are functioning now in full swing and as a matter of fact the poorest of the poor are greatly relieved from hardship.

The third initiative of the community is women empowerment. In the community get together development debates and discussions, issues of gender based discrimination usually take place without farther intervention. The community has decided to organise women to deal with the issues of gender discrimination. One independent women organisation has came to being and the name of the women organisation goes as "Sammilita Nari Adhikar

Suraksha Manch" (SNASM). Manch is very active in dealing with gender specific violence. They are also energetic in raising voice on socio-economic issues and also promoted a "One Stop Crisis Centre" to support violence victims. Advocacy with the local administration to open women cell in each Panchayat to facilitate women in getting appropriate share from the Government development programmes is in practice. The Nari Manch has 3000 members at Sadiya now. The branches of Manch are organising "Beti Jindabad" Campaign and Fortnightly VAW Campaign regularly.

From the last year onward Community is fighting for their land right. They have formed one "Land Right Protection Committee". As in the Sadiya Sub-Division, almost all the families are possessing land for decades together without proper land settlement document. It is creating problem in getting Government facilities like grant in add, Job, PRC, bank loan, compensation etc. So, the community decided to fight for land right by organising themselves under the banner of "Land Right Protection Committee".

If minutely observed the activities initiated by the community of Ambikapur, Sadia, we could realize that the conventional education system is not helping them to resolve their problems. They are learning from their own experiences and by engaging themselves in task. New thought process generating in the community facilitation centre. Both the community run institutes, i.e. "Evening storytelling community centre" and "JLCC" has been building awareness among the children as well as the elders. They are learning by doing. As we were closely associating with the community learning process, we found that sometimes the community takes inappropriate decision, but we do not interfere willingly because such incidence is likely to pave the way to correct decision-making.

SUPPORTING CASE HISTORY

Children's Participation in Rally Brought Teacher to School

Parth Pratim Gogoi (10) says, "I am studying in class 5 in Bosagaon Lower Primary School. My father Hemonta Gogoi (27) is a farmer and my mother Mamu Gogoi (24) is a home maker. I have a younger brother Akash Gogoi (7) studying in class 1. My school has classes

1 to 5. There are 59 students. It is just half a kilometer away from my home. School starts at 9 a.m. and ends at 1.30 p.m. Our school has only one teacher who was not regular and as a result there would be many days when there were no classes".

He continues "ActionAid-NEADS organised a programme on Right to Education. I and a few of my friends attended the meeting along with other children and parents. They told us how important education is to every child and that it is our right. After this the elders of the village filed a complaint about the teacher in the Deputy Inspector (DI) of School's Office. But there was no response. Then they decided to organise a mass rally in which many children including me took part. The participation of school children drew the attention of the DI and immediate action was taken. Now, we have a new teacher who is regular and we enjoy our classes".

Children Demanding Rights at Xadiya

Context of the Issue

Xadiya is one of the remotest Subdivision of Assam under Tinsukia district. Eight years back there was not a single Government School in most of the villages of NEADS core LRP (Local Rights Programme) area. Out of 20 project villages, 13 villages did not have a Government LP school and even in villages where there were venture schools, there was no proper infrastructure. Also the Government schools that were there in the villages were not functioning properly. Schools had no infrastructure and irregular attendance of teachers was one of the major problems in the schools. Parents were also not very concerned as most of them are illiterate.

Now, after 8 (eight) years of intervention by ActionAid and NEADS through the "Child Sponsorship Programme" situation have changed in these villages. NEADS organised lots of community sensitization programmes and organised the children under Joyful Learning Centre and child parliament etc.

Some of the visible effects of these interventions can be seen in the villages: many venture schools have been adopted as Government Schools, school buildings were constructed and TET (Teacher Eligibility Test) qualified teachers have been appointed to the schools. But still quality education is not very high. NEADS has conducted child assessment test to see the quality of education in 23 villages among 500 students (including LRP and non-LRP areas) but results were not satisfactory. The main problem seems to be that the involvement of the people still seems to be very low in many areas; as a result the schools work in the same old fashion where the teachers are not held accountable. As a result, the problem of low teacher attendance and low quality of education is still prevalent.

NEADS has discussed the issue with the community and SMC (School Management Committee) etc. The community submitted many applications for improvement, but results were not positive. The same issue was discussed with the children in the JLCC and Child parliament. Ultimately, the children decided to deal with the situation themselves. Accordingly, the school children with their mothers went to the District Education office to put-up their demand for regular attendance of teacher. When that effort had gone in vain the children organised a rally demanding the same. This drew the attention of the department and a new teacher was appointed who is attending schools regularly.

27

Indigenous Interactive Learning Centre (IILC) Manipur

A Case Study

Lanu Waneithang Aimol and *Tongpao Hoakip*

Introduction

ActionAid through its LRP Reach-M has been involved in various development initiatives in the Chandel district of Manipur for last one decade. The emphasis has been on preserving and traditional farming and other indigenous occupations. It has also been involved in rights issues—making the community aware of their various rights as well as helping them in asserting the rights when necessary.

About Reach-M

Rural education and action for change, Manipur (Reach-M) is major civil society organisation of Manipur which has been successfully working in the Chandel District since its inception twenty five years back. It has great organisational strength as it has developed expertise of working in a multi-ethnic society. Reach-M has been involved in conflict resolution and bringing peace and harmony in the state especially during the Kuki-Naga conflict in early 1990s. Since then Reach-M has formed people's organizational networks to work through grassroots level and village organisations. Through series of workshops, trainings and numerable meetings SHGs were established way back in 90's. In the process started giving importance to women and other silent voices in the decision-making.

It has also been successful in establishing 14 childcare centres in the district. Though education is one of the major focus area of the organisation since its beginning, it never shied away from the other major issues that were important in their operational area.

This way they have got involved in last twenty five years in diverse issues affecting agriculture, land resources, environment and forest, rights related to them, indigenous food, crafts, tribal customs and oral civic codes etc. once involved in them and as they are organisational strength increased it also got involved in mass literacy, Legal awareness and Aid, health and family well-fare, Disaster Risk Reduction and empowerment of various disadvantaged groups.

Thus, Reach-M, over the years, has developed strong social advocacy network which has been touching the different vital issues of the contemporary society including the delivery of education. Many of the functionaries as well as partners have exposure to innovative education models and solid experience of working in the education sector resulting in good understanding of pedagogical issues. They have their own schools where they tried many innovative experiments. Strength of any organisation is evaluated in terms of vision, tradition and relationships. Schools or the groups/agencies running them, having a clear and long term vision, seem to be effective to a great extent in establishing and maintaining desirable teaching learning practices. Similarly, schools/institutions having long traditions, often are successful, if not anything else, then, in drawing good students and teachers to them and try to follow certain norms and routines which they inherit as tradition and leading to good practices.

The Initiative of IILCs

Manipur is one of the few states in the country where the presence of government in education sector especially at primary level is very negligible. Though there is a education department and a number of schools and teachers in the state most of the primary schools are almost dysfunctional today. Almost every parent is forced to send their children to private schools. Education has become a commodity (not a right) which they try to buy for their children with whatever resources they have and whichever schools available. As a result, not only the government schooling system has become casualty, but also both the right to education and the RTE Act has become quite meaningless in the state. As the education has fully gone into the hands of private sector, many aspects of education get seriously neglected. While the poor has to go to whatever schools they can afford, even the so-called 'good' private schools are somewhat delinked from indigenous traditions values and knowledge. Thus, many major aims of education remain unaddressed.

Above scenario creates a major challenge for NGOs like Reach-M which is involved in the education sector. While involvement in the government sector may not lead to any significant impact in terms of learning of the children, the private schools running solely with profit motive cannot be expected to do justice to the children's rights of education.

So agencies like ActionAid and civil society organisation like Reach-M, which are involved in right to education campaign, found themselves in the odd situation of either working with the private schools or doing nothing. Challenged with this they felt there are many issues related to right to education—especially of child rights—which are not and cannot be addressed by the private sector. That is where the need for some kind of learning centres were felt and eventually conceptualised.

In this context, Reach-M with its diverse experience of working both in the community and in the schooling sector visualised to start some "Learning Centres" themselves as a pilot project. These learning centers were planned as vibrant centres where students interact with learning resources, community members as well as amongst themselves. They are called "Indigenous Interactive Learning Centers" (IILC).

Understanding the Indigenous

In its transformation from an agrarian society through industrial society to modern knowledge society, the world today has become kind of a global village. In the age of access to rapid and all pervading gadgets of communication people are fast becoming citizens of a almost uniform lifestyle, in the process somewhat loosing they are unique identities and age-old traditions. Though, it has benefited all in many ways and it has become kind of irreversible yet it is emerging as a threat to all indigenous knowledge and culture. The biggest danger of becoming, or, trying blindly to become, a global citizen is that one not only loses one's language tradition and culture but also loses respect for once own indigenous knowledge customs and culture. This is how cultural hegemony of dominant groups can lead to virtual death of minority ethnic cultures. The irony is that those who try to become part of the dominant culture by either imitating people from such cultures or being educated in a mode designed for that dominant culture, fails to become 'fully' a member of that dominant culture either. So many end of being neither here nor there becoming kind of misfit either for the "global village" or for the village they left behind.

Those involved in the development, especially education of the marginalised communities are aware of this paradoxical situation. While development for that matter education emphasizes the need for the individual to be prepared for surviving in his or her surrounding environment, in fast changing world the individuals require inputs for both surviving in the immediate environment as well as the wider world. ActionAid beliefs learning involves both to be interactive and indigenous to prepare children for the both.

Phase 2

What Happens in IILCs

IILCs are simply about learning. Though we all know learning keeps happening all the time, yet there are both formal and informal aspects to it. The IILCs are envisaged to catch both these dimensions of learning.

As Learning by definition is experiential, interactive, inclusive and indigenous, an effective school or learning centre tries to provide the children meaningful learning experiences including indigenous knowledge through interactive process. These centres (IILCs) are visualised as semi-formal learning centres where children of the age group between 7 to 14 years will be provided diverse learning opportunities.

What is meaningful learning experience...

We all learn from our experience, whether it be small or big, direct or indirect. A child learns what is sweet or bitter in taste by experiencing it just he or she learns what is painful or dangerous. Most of it the child experiences it from his or her immediate environment. While lots of these learning are informal and spontaneous, it is equally important how much further exposure we try to give ourselves. Meaningful learning occurs when we reflect upon whatever experience we get from our environment and try to bring some meaning out of it. That is why it is important that learning should be both interactive and indigenous.

Interactive Learning

As indicated above, meaningful learning is result of reflection upon experience that we go through. This can be achieved better through interactions. The learner has to interact either with the nature or with his or her friends and the teachers. The learner learns best when he or she observes what is available or happens in his or surrounding and compares it with others. Interactive learning includes asking questions and debating with others. For this it is very important to use one's linguistic skills, i.e. listen, speak, discuss and debate.

Indigenous Learning

Apparently indigenous learning is quite opposite of the interactive learning. Yes, here also observation plays a major role. But here both observation and reflection is natural and happens mostly in a silent manner. Usually, no body teaches it formally or talks about it. Nor are the children encouraged to ask questions in this learning. Even if somebody asks, not many, including the parents may not be able to answer the question. Such knowledge is mostly passed on from one generation to another traditionally. For example, every community has certain food habits—they eat certain things and does not eat certain others. Even something, certain things are eaten only in certain times. They do not teach it formally to the children. However, children acquire it as a habit. Many from the community may not be able to explain why they follow such habits. But it might have been there since ages. If reflected carefully it may appear that such habits have very strong reasons may be linked with their environment or socio-cultural evolution. This we call as indigenous knowledge. Indigenous knowledge is not only restricted to food habits but it can extend to the fields of agriculture, health and hygiene, social values, safe habitations, disaster preparedness etc. It may even cover areas like inter-community relations, and environment-friendly livelihood.

Why Indigenous Learning

Education or learning ultimately prepares us— or supposed to prepare— for life. It includes both strategies for survival as well as livelihood. In today's globalised world and knowledge society, anyone or any trend can go anywhere. So, the learner has to be prepared for surviving anywhere in the world. That is why in today's education interactive learning is more emphasized which is supposed to be preparing us for this kind of a society.

However, now-a-days, it is also felt that it is much more important for an individual to survive or do well in his or her immediate environment. Often individuals educated in the formal system finds it difficult to adapt to his or her own environment or culture if one has to come back. It has led to many social upheavals in the current times. As discussed above, indigenous knowledge has many desirable elements, which help both the individuals and society to lead an enriched life.

Phase 3

Know Your Community

It is essentially a tribal community where each centre ideally has children from single tribe from a homogeneous village as its student. As with most of the tribal communities, the people have an existence close to their environment (whether it be hills valleys or forest). At the same time, the people here cannot remain far away from the modern ways of life. Especially, the younger generation's aspirations—expectations are very much influenced by the modern day needs and opportunities. This creates a paradoxical situation as far as the educational needs of such areas are concerned. While the education needs to be rooted in local environment and indigenous knowledge, the skills and values for adapting modern/urban lifestyle is equally relevant.

Know your child (child right, curious, creative, imaginative, like to learn by doing, learn through role play, short attention span)

Contrary to popular belief, a child is also a complete human being. Even very young children (including news born babies) have an independent mind having faculties of perceptions, observation and thinking. Lots of researches have confirmed, in fact, it is much sharper in case of children than in adults. Unlike what many believe and try to make others believe, a child is not an empty vessel. She/he is curious from the very beginning about his/her surroundings. This makes them full of questions—sometimes irritating the adults. Actually, it is there inherent eagerness to learn which makes them curious about everything around and ask questions. Because of this quality they like to learn by doing things—at times going to the extent opening or breaking they find!

Children are also very imaginative and creative. They still have the imagination and creativity that most of us adults have lost.

Just as they are very observant and like to learn by doing, they appear to be very imitative. Actually, children like to role play. We all have examples of children trying to act like their parents or other adults.

However, it is also observed that the children have shorter attentions span. Whether it is games, activities, any work or learning, they cannot concentrate for very long. So, those involved in the education of child has to keep this in mind.

Child Rights

As the child is very much a human being he or she is as much entitled to the human rights. In fact, they are more entitled to them as they are not strong enough to get their rights or even articulate them. So, adults have to be very conscious of the rights of the children. Most importantly those rights of children related to learning or education are very crucial. In other words, children right to education or learn is the most important of the child rights.

Of these rights, the most important right is the child right to be curious. The parents, teachers or the school must honour his or her curiosity and try to satisfy it. This leads to the other important right to learn through observation and to learn by doing. Obviously, these rights include the freedom to learn through imagination and creativity. The school should not do anything to impinge upon these rights. So, the child has a right to have a learning environment which is interactive, enjoyable, free from fear and other bindings full of games, songs, drama, role play etc.

What is Learning?

Learning is one of the most personal activities. We learn when we admit that we do not know something and want to know it. In fact this is what we call curiosity.

That's the reason why learning takes place mostly in informal settings. There is a certain age up to which we are ready to learn from somebody or somewhere more easily. School is the place where learning takes place formally and systematically. And classroom is the place where a group of learners/individuals are engaged in the act of learning together. Ideally and usually, the learners in the same classrooms despite their individual differences have much common learning needs.

Schooling prepares the pupils for a particular kind of life that they or their parents want for them. The whole edifice of formal schooling is hence based on the aims of education. It is quite accepted that education/schooling is mostly about acquiring of certain skills and knowledge and formation of certain concepts and values. Over the ages it has been accepted that the school is the place where children learn about important facts of life, society and the world. It is also the place where they acquire various skills from the basic ones like speaking, reading, writing, counting, adding etc. much more complicated ones such as writing articles, solving differential equations or analyzing the chemical composition of salts. However, while earlier the focus was on acquiring more and more information—even through rote learning— in current times, the focus has shifted towards developments of concepts and mastery of skills.

In formal learning the focus is on all-round development of the individual, enabling him or her to both survive in his or her immediate environment and the society and make their livelihood. With essential aim the formal education/schooling tries to provide the learner necessary learning experience this may include certain skills, understanding, information and values or morality.

Skill

Skill is basically ability to do something. That way we need all sorts of the skills all the time. While some skills are essential for us both to survive and earn a living, there are others skills involved in formal education as well as those required for advance thinking?

For example primary math includes skills of counting, adding, multiplication etc. language is basically the skills to speak read and write, science involves the skills of observing, comparing, hypothesizing and experimenting. (Acquiring, mastering of skills)

Understanding

Mastering a skill pre-supposes understanding it. This is also known as acquiring the basic concept inherent in the skill. In a way it is a mental skill. Before doing or trying to do anything we try to understand or mentally construct the phenomenon. For example, before acquiring the skill of counting the child has to grasp the number concept. The same is true of basic survival skills as well as higher order mental skill. A concept or the understanding of it involves grasping of the common element of more than one apparently dissimilar example.

Information

Till now generally people mistake information for education. In fact in most of the schools today what is provided is information in the name of education. Though skills and understanding are the most essential parts of education, the significance of information cannot however be ignored. It is common knowledge that we need much information to survive in the today's world. It may include the names of objects or people to qualities and characteristics various phenomena. However, the problem with information is that it can be unlimited while human beings have limited time to acquire and ability to memorize. That is why it is more important to possess the skills of acquiring storing and using the information when needed.

Values and Morality

Twenty years back values and moral education was not so much emphasized in class room teaching as the focus was much more on imparting information and developing skills and concepts. Currently, however, it is felt that values and moral education can play a vital role in education. The society or education devoid of values suffers from many handicaps. It has emerged that the children not aware of the traditional values of their communities or tribes, despite having 'full' education find it difficult socially.

It is said thousands of years for a civilization to form a value and a life time to possess it. Values are caught rather than taught.

Not only skill but also value, responsibility.

(*Contd. ...*)

(Contd. ...)

> What is value? Differ according to the environment. Need according to the situation demand. Learning from the primitive cultures, traditions. Indigenous things come naturally.
>
> How do we define value?
>
> Price is different thing, Respect, relationship, earlier culture, responsibility. Mutual respects.
>
> Incorporate values in the learning centers, using oral history.

How Children Learn? (Environment/Books/Tradition)

As stated above we all learn all the time both formally informally. Though a major chunk of learning is through books and inside the school, we learn a lot informally and outside the school too. In fact most of the learning is constructive—a fact acknowledge by "National Curricular Framework 2005" (NCERT). Actually, a child learns mostly by constructing his or her knowledge. The role of a teacher or a textbook is that of a facilitator or trigger only. The child can learn from his or her environment through observations and experiments. They also learn by interacting with his friends, family, community as well as the teachers. So, tradition plays a major role in shaping the child's learning.

Though learning takes place all the time and everywhere, there are certain learning strategizes which are considered to be more effective. They definitely influence the pace of learning. Based upon them certain teaching learning methods such as experiential learning, activity based learning, joyful learning, interactive learning etc. are developed.

(a) *Experiential learning:* In a way any learning is experiential learning. We learn what we experience. However, by experiential learning we mean getting or going through a particular experience to acquire a skill. Some even call this experience as activity. This experience is followed by some guided reflections on the experience.

(b) *Activity based learning:* Activity based learning is quite same as experiential learning. The method followed the same. Activities are also one form of experience. While the experience in experiential learning can be broader, in activity-based learning it is through specific activities or games. As such here application plays a crucial role.

(c) *Joyful learning:* One can say joyful learning is another name for activity based learning. Here the emphasis is upon the joyful/enjoyable nature of activities employed in the learning process. It is more appropriate for younger children. However, the principle is equally applicable to all ages and all spheres of learning. It is said that the joy of learning which is more important than the mere joyful learning. For example, the tales, rhymes, riddles, songs dances role play drama etc. are the means of joyful learning.

(d) *Interactive learning:* It is felt one learns much faster through interactions than from teachers and books. By interacting with our peers, teachers and the surroundings one constructs learning which is very effective. So, every effective learning setting has to be interactive.

Phase 4

Making and Doing Activities

Activities are essential for teaching learning whether we use interactive or experiential or activity based methods. In all of them activities are the tools which the teachers have to use. However, as every new teacher realizes it is not easy initially. Both selecting, making and doing activities is not so easy, which requires much practice. In fact making and doing activities are also skills (for Teachers) which are mastered only through practice.

The Making of Activities

How can a Teacher Master the Skill of Making of Activity?

This is a very important skill for teachers. Because for activity based teaching a teacher will require many activities to be conducted for the children for different subjects and classes. And more importantly all these activities have to be good learning activities. This is important as all activities may not or are not good learning activities. A good learning activity is age appropriate, participatory, joyful and leading to thinking hence learning. This is why any teacher needs a big activity bank to draw upon.

However, experienced teachers know how to make good learning activities themselves. Before discussing how can we make activities let us try to understand types of the activities?

Types of Activities

Style/ mode	*Whole group*	*Small group*	*Individual*
Oral or Verbal	✓ +	✓ +	?
Written	?	✓ +	✓ +
Material based	?	✓ +	✓ +

✓ Possible mark, + Desirable mark, ? Difficult or not so effective

From the above matrix, we can observe that learning activities mainly are of nine categories. Of them six are possible as well as very effective for learning.

(a) Oral Whole Group Work

Many learning activities can be done in oral form and with the whole group of student. Poems action song, story-telling, role play, Drama etc. are some of the examples. This is very useful with younger children and especially for developing language skills listening and speaking (both for mother tongue and second language).

(b) Oral Small Group Work

Oral small group work is more useful for intensive learning. This is also useful as practice activities. Riddles, question answer, role play story-telling, debates and discussion are some examples. One advantage of this type of activities is that the teacher need not be involved continuously and the children can remain engaged sometimes on their own.

(c) Written Small Group Work

These activities include both reading, writing and drawing in groups. These activities can keep children engaged even for longer periods. And here the children can learn from each other as well as check each others.

(d) Written Individual Work

Written individual work is much more intensive. Such activities are also designed for extension or practice of idea. It can last much longer and can even as home work. This is very important for developing writing skills.

(e) Material Based Small Group Work

Material based work is very essential for development of concepts especially of mathematics and science of primary level. Doing it in small groups makes it interesting, interactive and challenging.

(f) Material Based Individual Work

As in written individual work material based individual work are also designed for extending and consolidating one's concepts and skills. These activities too can keep the learner engaged for much longer period and can be given as home work and projects.

Now, the question is how can the above typology of activities help us in making activities?

Learners need activities from all the above six categories in balanced form. So, the teacher has to maintain the balance both within the daily and long term routine. While in the beginning oral whole group activities are needed more, in later part other types have also to be provided. Interestingly, activities from one category can be changed into that of another category very easily just by adapting them.

For example, an oral whole group activity can easily be modified into a small group written activity. Further, the activities can be modified for different subjects and age groups.

Let us discuss the steps for making activities:

(a) Decide the level or expectation of the children
(b) Activity for what subject
(c) Activity for how much time
(d) Selecting the type of activity for the purpose

Class Room Management
(Maintenance, New Accommodation, Space Management and Time Management)

Classroom management basically involves doing appropriate activities while managing both available time and space in the class room.

Doing activities as we discussed about is not so easy. It has many parts where both the teacher and the student/learners are involved.

Teacher	*Student/learner*
Select the appropriate activity	
Gives instructions	Tries to understand
Clarifies if not understood	Understand the instructions
	Begins the activity
Monitors	Continues the activity
Helps where needed	Completes the activity
Sums up the learning	Internalizes the learning

Each part of the activity requires certain amount of time for it being effective. For example, in oral whole activity, selecting the activity and giving instructions may require two three minutes while the students too may require another two three minutes to comprehend the instructions. The student may require five to ten minutes to actually do the activity. And the teacher can take another five ten minutes to sum up.

In case of the small group or individual written/material based activities it may take almost double the time for each of these parts.

Time Management

So, the facilitator or the teacher has to carefully calculate the time required for doing the activities he or she selects. And while doing the activity has to monitor the time required for each part. He should take special care for keeping time for giving instructions, summing up and practice if required.

Space Management

Activity requires space. While the oral whole group activities more space may be required the teacher has to organise the available space for small group and material based activities. Some activities are better done outside. Similarly, some activities can be done better in open space or on the floor; others can be done with desks and benches. So, the teacher has to keep all that in mind.

Class Room Planning (Decorations, Equipments, Objectives, Level of Students, Materials)

Any work to be effective requires planning and preparations in advance. It is equally true in case of teaching especially in case of experiential learning. It is the presence of planning which can make classroom transactions effective and teaching much easy. On the other hand, its absence makes teaching tough and clumsy. From above discussions, it has become clear that teaching learning process is experiential and interactive. While the learner learns from the experience and interaction the facilitator or teacher has to plan and trigger such experience or interaction leading to meaningful learning.

Now, the Question is What is Involved in Classroom Planning?

As in other areas of life, in teaching too planning involves setting the target or objectives and dividing them into slots of time.

Tips for planning...

- Look at the curriculum or the textbook lessons to be taught during the year. Then divide the lessons into two or three parts of the year.
- Look at the lessons of the first part of the year and allot particular months or weeks to teach them.
- Weekly plan: This is more detailed. It includes objectives of the lesson, Time required (in hours) and the appropriate activities.
- Daily plan: This is much more detailed. This also requires specific objectives, specific activities, instructions, material required and preparation needed.

Daily plan: From the above it is very clear that the daily plan is most crucial for the teacher. Especially in the activity based teaching the teacher has to provide a balance of oral, written material based, whole group, small group and individual activities during the whole day. In this experienced teachers follow certain patterns. They start the day or the class with whole group oral activities. Then, they move to small group activities and finally in to individual activities. Again in the post-lunch session, either they start with whole group activities or give material based activities. It is ideal to sum up with whole activities.

Evaluations

Evaluation is very important for teaching learning especially for classroom planning. One can set objectives and select appropriate activities only depending upon the learning levels of the children. It is obvious all the children in a class are not of the same level as they may come from different backgrounds. So, same objectives or activities cannot be equally appropriate or effective for teaching them all. That is why the teacher has to assess or evaluate the learning levels of the children before planning for the whole class. While this assessments has to be done in the very beginning, it has to be done later also time-to-time.

While such evaluations can be done formally and the teacher can use various tools for that, the teacher can also do it informally all the time.

Mainstreaming

Mainstreaming is the major challenge for any learning centre or institute. The children learning in these centres may learn many diverse things here. But eventually when they pass out, they either have to get admission into other institutions for higher learning or prepared for the job market. So, while teaching in these centres we always have to keep this in mind.

Phase 5

Some Suggested Games and Activities for ILCs

Here, some suggested games are described to be practised in the IILCs. The games are very general but that should have practised in the IILCs with the motto of the establishing of the centres. The exercises can be linked or guided by the indigenous thoughts and ideas, materials and behaviours of the people and the society. Even, the basic objectives of the IILCs can be sought out through these games/exercises.

Fruits-Vegetables-Flower

Children stand in a circle. The teacher/facilitator pretend to be vegetables vendor carrying in a basket. He/she go in front of the children asking "do you need fruits, vegetables or flowers?" then he may stop in front of a child. Then the child will have to give a name of a fruit, vegetable or a flower according to exactly what the teacher wanted. If the child can name promptly and correctly, the teacher will move to the next children. But if the children cannot, then he will have to take the basket and will now have to sale the fruits, vegetables and flowers. This activity is very useful for environmental sciences. Children are not only made aware of names of objects but also learn about classifying nature's objects.

This is a good activity for listening and speaking especially for younger children. Though it is ideally done as an oral activity in the whole group, it can easily be modified for other classes, subjects and contexts.

Pen activity

Children sit in a circle. The facilitator/teacher takes a pen in the hand and utters a sentence about it. Then he asks the children to make more sentences about the pen one after another. The only condition is that no one can repeat what somebody may have used before. If the children find the activity interesting and challenging this can be done in two three rounds. The facilitator, then, can also ask the children to compile the sentences and try to write an essay (in group or individual).

In this method, essays on various other topics can be composed by the student.

Stick Activity

The facilitator takes a stick and tries to play a role by using the stick, for example, using as a cricket bat or gun, and asks what he is doing. The children try to guess. Next, the children are also supposed to role play using the stick in similar manner, one by one.

Housie

The children are asked to draw a table of nine boxes (or more) as the sample shown below:

1	88	68
65	56	90
34	54	77

Then the children are asked to fill-up these boxes with any numbers between 1 and 99 that comes to their mind. Next, the facilitator gives a series of instructions. Here are some samples –

- ✓ *Cut/cross all the boxes having single digit numbers*
- ✓ *Cut/cross all the boxes having even numbers*
- ✓ *Cut/cross all the boxes having numbers smaller than fifty*

This way whoever gets all the boxes crossed wins. To complete the activity the facilitator can say—

- ✓ Cut/cross the boxes having odd numbers

The activity can be made simpler or more complicated depending upon the level of the children. It can be used for even language or sciences.

Pass Activity

The children sit in a circle. Then they are supposed to count the numbers. The one starting saying 'one', the next one saying 'two' and so on. This can continue in rounds and rounds up to hundred or more. However, when the number 'four' or one of the multiples of 'four' comes, the children cannot say the number but has to say 'pass'. If the child makes mistake, the activity starts again from him/her. Later on the same activity can be done for other numbers as like three, five, six, seven etc. It is an good activity for knowing multiplication.

Guess the Objects/Classification

The facilitator keeps some objects (around 20, 25) on the floor in between the class room. Children are divided into two groups facing each other with the objects in between them. The one group decides one object out of them and writes the name secretly and gives it to the teacher. The other group has to guess the objects. For this they can ask up to 10 questions to which the other group can answer only in yes or no. If the first group can find out the name within 10 questions, they win. If they cannot, then the other wins.

This game helps in learning about classification of objects.

Guess the Number

This activity is similar to the earlier activity. Only here one thinks of a number while the other has to guess the number by asking questions.

Collecting Objects, Classification and Patterns

Children are asked to go out and each of them is expected to bring any five objects from outside. They can be leaves, stones, match boxes, nails, flowers, or anything. After they come back they are asked to sit in groups of four or five. They show to each other what they have brought. Next, they collect all that they have together and try to put them in different categories like living, non-living; small, big or on the basis of colour. They can also make various patterns with the leaves or the stones.

Word Making, Sentence Making and Story Making

The facilitator gives a name — for example 'Manipur'. The children are asked to make as many words as possible from the letters in this word *e.g.* M,A,N,I,P,U,R. The only condition is the word has to be meaningful. The word can be two letter, three letter or more. They can repeat the letters two. After five minutes or so the children can be asked to complete the activity in groups. The challenge can be which group can make hundred words earlier. Next, they can be asked to make some sentences or stories using these words.

Emotions, Role Play and Drama, Dumb Charades

The children are asked to act out emotions like anger, sadness, happiness, envy, fear etc. Next, children are given certain situations where such emotions emerged. They do it in groups where they all play different roles. Later, it can be developed as full drama.

Dumb Charades

Children are divided into small groups. While one group member thinks of objects or event the other shows it to the whole group without speaking only using gesture. The other children have to guess the object or the event.

Fire in the Mountain, run run run

Children stand in a circle. The facilitator stands in the middle and sings fire in the mountain, run run run.... The children keep running in the circle in one direction. The facilitator suddenly stops and utters a number, for example- 7. The children have to stop and form groups of seven. Those who cannot, are out and has to do the next round of activity. This is good activity for the younger children for developing number concepts as well for knowing number names.

Giving and following Instructions, Maps

The facilitator gives a set of instructions while the children have to perform something following those instructions. Next, they have to give such instructions to other groups of children.

The children are expected to draw map of the class room or the school compound following instructions given by the teacher or others.

Dawa *or Claim*

This activity can have many versions—simple or complex. One simplest version being the teacher or a child makes a claim right or wrong such as there are elephants having three feet. The other child not only has to say it is wrong but has to make the right claim.

What is Round? What is Long?

The facilitator sings what is round and what is long and point out any one child. That child has to name two objects one round and one long. Next, teacher point out to the next child and he too has to name two new objects one round and long. This continues so on.

What is White? What is Black?

This activity is similar to the above.

Jam sessions/Extempore Speech

Just a minute (JAM) session is as the name suggests activities where every child has to do or say something for a minute. The moment it is over, the next child has to continue. The extempore speech is similar. Here topics are given for children to talk about.

Indigenous Games and Learning Activities

1. Tang- si- Tang (Aimol indigenous game)
   Children are divided into two groups. The groups make one king and one each member of the group will attend the king. Then, one member of the first group goes to the king and names one of the members of the other group. One of the members of the second group will go to the king. If the later person was the one named by the former, he will be shot by the king and is disqualified. The game goes on until one of the group is completely disqualified.
2. Javelin throw.

Though all the above games and learning activities can be adapted for indigenous learning, here are some suggestions for making use of some local games and activities which would help in transferring indigenous knowledge:

(a) The facilitator asks the children what are the games they have played or they know? Out of these if some games turns out to be indigenous or little known games the facilitator asks the children to show or explain how it is played. Later as assignment, the children can be asked to find out about some more indigenous or local games from their parent or the villagers.

(b) The facilitator discusses about the indigenous games – how it is played or how it helps in development of certain skills.

(c) The facilitator asks the children make list of various fruits, vegetables, flowers, fish, animals etc. which are unique to their locality. Next, the children can be asked to talk about or write about them so that a non-local person knows what they are, where they are found, how they are used etc.

(d) The facilitator asks the children to discuss about their food habits—what they usually eat, what they eat in morning, what during day time etc. Next, there can be discussion how food habits are related to seasons and climate, has there any change in last two or three generations, if so, why.

(e) The facilitator discusses about local means of livelihood such as agriculture, floriculture, hunting, fishing etc.

(f) The children can also be given projects of finding out about above from the community. In case, not many people not being involved in above occupations now, old people knowing about these can be invited and requested to skills and knowledge.

(g) Various persons from the community knowing about indigenous crafts, customs and traditions are invited to talk to the children.

(h) Children are asked to sing and dance. Are any of them traditional folk song and dances, when are they performed? Festival?

(i) Children are asked to tell stories. Next they are asked whether they know any folk tales. If so to share them, if not teacher shares some folk tale with them or invites somebody who knows folk tales.

(j) Facilitator discusses about various customs, traditions etc. about the tribes that the children come from. He also encourages them to find out more.

Phase 6: Curriculum

Indigenous Learning Points

1. Folk Song
2. Folk Tales
3. Cultural Dance
4. Customs and Practices
5. Herbal Medicines
6. Musical Instrumentation
7. Weaving
8. Indigenous Cultivation
9. Family Genealogy
10. Village Governance
11. Handicraft
12. Skills of hunting

13. Indigenous Cooking
14. Indigenous games
15. Tools
16. Flora and Fauna
17. Languages
18. Making manure
19. Indigenous pesticide and insecticide

Learning Points from Activity

1. Classification
2. Language development
3. Quality/quantity of the object
4. Observation and concentration
5. Making sentences/paragraph/essay/story
6. Reasoning and thinking
7. Analyses/guess/creativity
8. Prime no/odd no/multiplication/classification/number/identification
9. Multiplication/mental alertness
10. Investigation/reasoning/questioning
11. Classification of objects/identification/living or non-living
12. Compose
13. Imitation/smartness/creativity
14. Questing/creativity.
15. Number/alertness
16. Innovative/instruction/concept of space scaling/direction
17. Debate/verification
18. Noun/classification
19. Personality development/language development/presence of mind
20. Speaking/documenting/interacting/time management/climate condition/fishing/hunting/agriculture/eatable or non-eatable/classification/occupation/festival and occasion/types of people/knowing community/customary practices and law/culture.

IILC CURRICULUM

Mathematic	*Environmental Science*	*Language*	*Social Science*
Reasoning Analyses Guess Prime number Odd number Multiplication Classification Number Identification Mental alertness Reasoning Time management Addition Multiplication Shapes and sizes	Classification Quantity/Quality Observation Thinking Creativity Identification Investigation Questioning Object identification Living and non-living Concept of scaling Direction Debate	Language development Making sentence and paragraph and essay Thinking Creativity Mental alertness Questioning Imitation Innovative Instruction Debate Noun Speaking Explaining	Creativity Smartness Concept of scaling Direction Personality development Climate condition Occupation Eatable and non-eatable Festival and occupation Types of people Culture

ANNUAL

1st Quarter	*2nd Quarter*	*3rd Quarter*	*4th Quarter*
Mathematic	*Mathematic*	*Mathematic*	*Mathematic*
1. Reasoning 2. Number 3. Identification	1. Odd and prime no. 2. Shape and size 3. Classification	1. Questioning 2. Time management 3. Addition	1. Division 2. Simply 3. Analyses
Environmental science	*Environmental science*	*Environmental science*	*Environmental science*
1. Living/non-living 2. Thinking 3. Identification 4. Classification 5. Quality\Quantity	1. Observation 2. Questioning 3. Debate 4. Object identification	1. Concept of scale and space 2. Direction 3. Creativity	1. Investigation 2. Debate 3. Observation
Language	*Language*	*Language*	*Language*
1. Language devpt. 2. Noun 3. Speaking/explaining 4. Limitation 5. Creativity	1. Speaking 2. Thinking 3. Making sentence	1. Questioning 2. Instruction 3. Innovative	1. Speaking 2. Essay 3. Story making
Social Science	*Social Science*	*Social Science*	*Social Science*
1. Personality devpt 2. Knowing community 3. Types of people 4. Eatable or non-eatable	1. Concept and direction 2. Climate condition 3. Smartness	1. Culture practices 2. Agriculture 3. Hunting 4. Fishing	1. Festival 2. Occasion 3. Revision

Achievement

IILC influences the local government schools. The schools have availed free textbook and provide MDM.

Since IILC came into being in the village, the village is hardly witnessed a lot of changes little by little but progressively.

1. IILC influences the local government schools. The schools have availed free textbook and provide MDM.
2. Personality of children have been developed. Participation of children has increased ever since before.
3. More freedom of expression is seen among children. They have spoken out their thought without hesitation. They could even debate/argue their superiors against the ideas indifferences. They could not be easily deceived.
4. We can are observe changes in children in moral characters. Reduced using abusive words and started complimenting each other. Happy to say "thank you" and admitted to say 'sorry'.
5. Time management is maintained. Children are on their own routine.
6. Enhanced children creativity.
7. The children came to know that they also have a rich culture, customs, tradition and literature/language. They have started learning.
8. Children have started wearing traditional dresses more seriously on occasions and church services.
9. Replacing addressing words like 'uncle' by their own dialect.
10. IILC puts the village into action.
11. *Sanitation:* Dustbin is known but use of it in the village is minimal. IILC in collaboration with local club initiated installing public dustbins in the village.
12. *Environments:* As far as the threatening of environment is concerned, IILC's campaign on World Environment Day planted saplings in and around the village.
13. *Indigenous:* It is talking about indigenous and concerned of it. Observation of International Day of World Indigenous People in the villages are the first ever in the district which have given more consciousness on indigenous.

14. *Campaign on Beti Jindabad:* After the observation of International Girl Child Day and follow-up programmes of *Beti Jindabad,* the village has witnessed some equal sharing or opportunities through opening of saving account for girl children under SSY Scheme. Girls children have also been sent to reputed/expensive schools and participation of girl children is increased.
15. *Father's Day:* Mother's Day is observed every year in the village as to honour mothers however Father's Day is ignored. IILC in association with Sunday school organised Father's Day. Cards were distributed and organised, essay competition to sensitise the role and responsibilities, care and concerned of a father for a family.
16. *Children Day:* IILC initiated Children Day observation to give more awareness on child rights.
17. IILC has promoted more indigenous way of gardening.
18. IILC has promoted peace through games.
19. IILC has set up five centres within three years of initiation.
20. Some students have been selected and got the opportunity to show it their talents at inter-school sports events.

Challenges

- Even though IILC had many positive impacts in the village, many quarters of the village could not be convinced the ideology of IILC. They are still in darkness by accusing and giving wrong light that IILC is just for the organisation selfish gain. On the other hand, they are still on to say that useless for learning indigenous when men have been to the moon. However IILC challenges to prove the truth concept of IILC through its activities.
- IILC motivates its children freedom of learning and expression. They are trained reasoning and analysis. They are encouraged to give their opinion/expression. Now, IILC has been blamed that it makes the student stubborn. There is also a controversial interpretation of a bible verse: "Children obey your parent in the lord". And in another version it is said that— "It is a Christian duty to obey your parents." IILC interprets that we should only obey our parents whether their instructions are worth for being a

Christian. We ought not to obey our parents if their instructions are for their selfish end which may result adversely in society or church. And some elders of the church rejected our interpretation. But IILC challenges to produce a future visionary, leaders and speakers.

- IILC has reopened the forgotten closed chapter of tribal history which is condemned outdated and useless by its own people. It realises the missing or mistaken part of the present society which we regard the most advanced and modernised way of livelihood. IILC challenges the needs to preserve and promote timely for the future generations.
- IILC challenges to make the village free zone of plastic and create eco-friendly environment.
- It is planning to establish 33 centres for each indigenous tribe in the state.
- It is planning to turn each centre into Community Research Centre.
- Influencing concerned education department for inclusion of more indigenous learning and culture.

Index